THE
GOSPEL OF
MATTHEW

WILLIAM MacDONALD

Emmaus Bible Study
PO Box 735
Lynn Haven, FL 32444

LUKE 24:27

Developed as a study course by Emmaus Correspondence School, founded in 1942.

The Gospel of Matthew
William Macdonald
Published by:
Emmaus Correspondence School
(A division of ECS Ministries)
PO Box 1028
Dubuque, IA 52004-1028
phone: (563) 585-2070
email: ecsorders@ecsministries.org
website: www.ecsministries.org
First Printed 2010 (AK '10), 2 Units
ISBN 978-1-59387-125-3
Code: MATT

Printed in the United States of America

STUDENT INSTRUCTIONS

Lessons You Will Study

Course Components

This course has two parts: this study course and the exam booklet.

How To Study

This study has twelve chapters, and each chapter has its own exam. Begin by asking God to help you understand the material. Read the chapter through at least twice, once to get a general idea of its contents and then again, slowly, looking up any Bible references given.

Begin studying immediately, or if you are in a group, as soon as the group begins. We suggest that you keep a regular schedule by trying to complete at least one chapter per week.

Exams

In the exam booklet there is one exam for each chapter (exam 1 covers chapter 1 of the course). Do not answer the questions by what you think or have always believed. The questions are designed to find out if you understand the material given in the course.

After you have completed each chapter, review the related exam and see how well you know the answers. If you find that you are having difficulty answering the questions, review the material until you think you can answer the questions. It is important that you read the Bible passages referenced as some questions may be based on the Bible text.

How Your Exams Are Graded

Your instructor will mark any incorrectly answered questions. You will be referred back to the place in the course where the correct answer is to be found. After finishing this course with a passing average, you will be awarded a certificate.

If you enrolled in a class, submit your exam papers to the leader or secretary of the class who will send them for the entire group to the Correspondence School.

See the back of the exam booklet for more information on returning the exams for grading.

INTRODUCTION

In his gospel, Matthew shows that Jesus is the long-expected Messiah of Israel, the only one with a right to the throne of David.

The book does not claim to be a complete biography of Christ's life on earth. It begins with His genealogy and early years, then jumps to the beginning of His public ministry when He was about thirty. Guided by the Holy Spirit, Matthew selects those aspects of the Savior's life and ministry which proclaim Him as God's Anointed One—for that is what the title "Messiah" means.

The book moves toward a climax—the trial, death, burial, resurrection, and ascension of the Lord Jesus. And in that climax, of course, is laid the foundation for man's salvation. That is why the book is called a "gospel"—not so much because it explains the way by which sinful man may receive eternal salvation, but rather because it describes the sacrificial work of Christ by which our salvation was made possible.

We do not know when Matthew wrote this book, whether it was AD 40 or 70 or at some time in between. And even if we did, this information would not add to our enjoyment of it or benefit from it. We have purposely avoided the so-called "critical problems"—that is, the questions concerning the sources and history of the text. Our purpose is to concentrate on the exposition of the text as it is found in our Bibles.

This course and commentary seeks to stimulate independent study and meditation. Most of all, it is aimed at creating in the reader's heart an intense longing for the return of the King.

1

MATTHEW 1–2

The Royal Genealogy (1:1-17)

Those who read the New Testament for the first time may wonder why it begins with something as seemingly dull as a family tree. They might easily conclude that this catalog of names is really not very significant and choose to skip over it to where the "action" begins.

The truth is, the genealogy is essential. It lays the foundation for everything that follows. Unless it can be shown that Jesus was a legal descendant of David through the royal line, it is hopeless to try to prove that He was—and is—the Messiah-King of Israel. Matthew begins where he *must* begin—with documentary evidence that Jesus inherited the legal right to be King of the Jews through His stepfather, Joseph.

It is good to remember that this genealogy traces the *legal* descent of Jesus as King of Israel and that the genealogy in Luke's gospel traces His *lineal* descent as Son of David.

> The genealogy
> lays the foundation
> for everything
> that follows.

Matthew's genealogy follows the *royal* line from David through his son Solomon, who succeeded him as king; Luke's genealogy follows the *blood* line from David through another of his sons, Nathan. This genealogy descends from Abraham and David down to Joseph, of whom Jesus was the *adopted* Son; the genealogy in Luke 3 is generally believed to trace the ancestry of Mary, of whom Jesus was the *real* Son.

A thousand years before Jesus' birth, God had made an unconditional agreement with David. He promised him a kingdom that would last forever, and that his actual descendants would sit upon the throne forever (2 Sam. 7:12-13). The covenant is fulfilled in Jesus Christ: because He lives forever,

His kingdom will last forever, and He will reign forever as great David's Greater Son.

Matthew begins with the formula: "The book of the genealogy of Jesus Christ, the Son of David, the Son of Abraham." A similar expression is found in Genesis 5:1: "This is the book of the genealogy of Adam." There it is used in connection with the first Adam; here it introduces the genealogy of the last Adam. The first Adam was head of the first creation, that is, the physical creation. Christ is Head of the new creation, the spiritual creation. Since there will never be another creation for man, Christ is the last Adam.

The grand subject of this book is Jesus Christ. The name "Jesus" presents Him as Jehovah-Savior. The name "Christ" presents Him as the long-awaited Messiah of Israel (*Christ* being the New Testament term for "Messiah"). The title "Son of David" has two connotations: it is closely associated with the role of Messiah and also of King. The title "Son of Abraham" presents our Lord as the One who is the ultimate fulfillment of the glorious promises made to the father of the Hebrew people.

—— ✐ ——

The grand subject of this book is Jesus Christ.

—— ✐ ——

The genealogy itself is divided into three historical sections: from Abraham to Jesse; from David to Josiah; and from Jeconiah to Joseph. The first section leads up to David; the second covers the kingdom from the height of its prosperity to its downfall; the third preserves the record of royal descent during the dark years following Judah's deportation to Babylon (586 BC).

There are many interesting features in this remarkable register. First of all, four women are mentioned: Tamar (v. 3); Rahab (v. 5); Ruth (v. 5); and the wife of Uriah (i.e. Bathsheba [v. 6]). Aside from the fact that women were rarely mentioned in eastern genealogical tables, it is noteworthy that three of these women were public sinners (Tamar, Rahab, and Bathsheba) and two of them were members of doomed Gentile nations (Rahab and Ruth). Perhaps we have here a subtle suggestion that Christ's coming would bring salvation to sinners and grace to Gentiles, and that in Him, barriers of race and sex would be torn down.

Also of interest is the mention of a king named Jeconiah (vv. 11-12). In Jeremiah 22:30, we find that God pronounced a curse upon this man. Coniah (Jer. 22:28) is another form of the name Jeconiah. "Thus says the Lord, 'Write this man down as childless, a man who shall not prosper in his days; for none of his descendants shall prosper, sitting on the throne of David, and ruling anymore in Judah.'" If Jesus had been the *real* son of Joseph, he would have come under this curse. Yet He had to be a legal son of Joseph in order to inherit the rights to the Davidic throne. The problem was solved by the miracle of virgin birth: Jesus was the legal heir to the throne through Joseph, and He was the real Son of David through Mary. The curse upon Jeconiah did not fall upon Mary or her Child.

Notice another interesting touch in verse 16. It reads: "And Jacob begot Joseph the husband of Mary, of whom was born Jesus who is called Christ." A person reading this casually might assume that the word "whom" refers back to Joseph and Mary, and that therefore Jesus was born of Joseph and Mary. But the Spirit of God has guarded against such a conclusion: the word "whom" in the Greek is in the feminine gender. Jesus was born of Mary, but not of Joseph.

But while the genealogy has its interesting features, it has its difficulties too. We will mention three of them.

1. The genealogy is divided into three sections of fourteen generations each (v. 17). However, for some unknown reason, certain names are missing from the list. We know, for instance, that Ahaziah, Joash, and Amaziah reigned as kings between Joram and Uzziah (v. 8). These omissions are not however uncommon in biblical genealogies; they do not always present a complete line.

2. The genealogies in Matthew and Luke seem to overlap by the mention of two names, Shealtiel and Zerubbabel (compare Matthew 1:12-13 with Luke 3:27). It seems strange that the ancestry of both Joseph and Mary should merge in these two men, then separate again. The difficulty is increased when we notice that Matthew and Luke list Zerubbabel as the son of Shealtiel, whereas in 1 Chronicles 3:19 he is listed as the son of Pedaiah.

3. The third difficulty is that Matthew counts twenty-seven generations from David to the Lord Jesus while Luke gives forty-two. Even allowing that the evangelists are describing different family trees, it still seems odd that there should be such a wide difference in the number of generations.

What attitude should we take toward these difficulties and seeming discrepancies? First, we should adopt as our foundational premise is the truth that the Bible is the inspired Word of God and that therefore it cannot contain errors or contradictions. Second, because it is the Word of God, it is infinite; we can never expect to understand all there is in it, even though the fundamental truths are clear. So when we come to difficulties, we should conclude that the problem is in our lack of knowledge rather than in the Book's fallibility. Bible problems should challenge us to study and search for the answers.

Past experience should warn men against confident assertions that the Bible contains errors. Careful research by historians and painstaking excavations by archaeologists have repeatedly confirmed the biblical narrative—to the confusion of its critics. What seem to us like difficulties and contradictions all have reasonable explanations, and these explanations are filled with spiritual significance and profit. We should seek the meanings like silver, and search for them as for hidden treasures (Prov. 2:4).

The Miracle Birth (1:18-25)

The birth of Jesus Christ was different from any of the births mentioned in the genealogy. There we found the repeated formula, "so-and-so was the father of so-and-so." But now we have the record of a birth without the involvement of a human father.

The facts connected with the miraculous conception are stated with dignity and simplicity. Mary had been promised in marriage to Joseph, but the wedding had not yet taken place. In Bible times betrothal was a form of engagement, but it was more binding than engagement is today; it could be broken only by divorce. A man who was betrothed to a woman was legally her husband (Gen. 29:21; Deut. 22:23). Although they did not live together as husband and wife till they actually got married, breach of faithfulness on the part of the betrothed was treated as adultery and punished with death.

> The birth of Jesus Christ was different from any of the births mentioned in the genealogy.

During the time of her betrothal, Mary became pregnant by a miracle of the Holy Spirit (Luke 1:35). A cloud of suspicion, shame, and scandal soon hung ominously over her. In all of human history there had never been a genuine virgin birth. When people saw an unwed woman who was pregnant, they had only one possible explanation.

Even Joseph did not yet know the true explanation of Mary's condition. He might have been highly indignant at his fiancée for her apparent unfaithfulness to him and because he would almost inevitably be accused of being the child's father. But love and mercy triumphed over any feelings of bitterness and vindictiveness he might have had. Rather than expose her to the publicity and disgrace that would normally accompany a divorce action, Joseph decided to break the betrothal quietly.

─────── ✿ ───────

Mary's pregnancy was a miracle of the Holy Spirit.

─────── ✿ ───────

While this gentle and deliberate man was mapping his strategy to protect Mary, an angel of the Lord appeared to him in a dream. The greeting, "Joseph, son of David," was doubtless designed to stir up the consciousness of his royal pedigree and to prepare him for the unusual advent of Israel's Messiah-King. He should have no misgivings about marrying Mary. Any suspicions he might have concerning her moral purity were groundless. Her pregnancy was a miracle of the Holy Spirit.

The angel then revealed the unborn child's sex, name, and mission. Mary would bear a son. He was to be named Jesus, which means "Jehovah is salvation," or "Jehovah, the Savior." True to His name, He would save His people from their sins. This wonderful Child of destiny was Jehovah Himself, visiting this planet to save men from the penalty of sins, from the power of sins, and eventually from the very presence of sins.

As Matthew rehearsed the events connected with the royal birth, he realized that a great, new era had dawned. The words of messianic prophecy, long dormant, had now begun to spring to life. He thought especially of Isaiah's cryptic prophecy of a virgin birth and saw it fulfilled in Mary's Child (vv. 22-23). Notice that Matthew claims divine inspiration for the words of Isaiah; the Lord had spoken by the prophet, and therefore his words were truly God-breathed.

The setting of Isaiah's prophecy was as follows: King Ahaz was terrified that the kingdom of Judah might be destroyed by Syria and Israel, and that David's kingly line might be wiped out. God assured him (through Isaiah) that this would not happen, and He gave Ahaz a sign: the virgin birth of the Messiah would be His guarantee that the house of David would never perish. Perhaps the prophecy had some immediate meaning for Ahaz (in connection with the threat of imminent invasion), but the ultimate fulfillment is found in the birth of the Lord Jesus.

Isaiah made this detailed prophecy at least seven hundred years before Christ was born. Matthew adds the explanatory comment that *Immanuel* means "God with us." And so this incomparable Child, born of a human mother, was the eternal God dwelling with mankind. Someone may object that Christ was not called Immanuel when He was here on earth—He was called Jesus. But the name Jesus implies the presence of God with us, because it means Jehovah, the Savior. And there is also the possibility that "Immanuel" will be His characteristic name in His second advent just as "Jesus" was in His first.

———— ❧ ————

This incomparable Child, born of a human mother, was the eternal God dwelling with mankind.

———— ❧ ————

As a result of the angel's interview, Joseph abandoned his plan to divorce Mary. He continued to recognize their betrothal until after Jesus was born. Then he lived with her as husband and wife. Verse 25 disproves the teaching that Mary remained a virgin for the rest of her life. The marriage was consummated after Jesus was born. Other Scriptures indicate that Mary subsequently had children by Joseph; see Psalm 69:7-8; Matthew 12:46; 13:55; Mark 6:3; John 7:3, 5; Acts 1:14; 1 Corinthians 9:5; and Galatians 1:19.

In taking Mary as his wife, Joseph also took her Child as his adopted son. As mentioned already, this is how Jesus became legal Heir to the throne of David. In obedience to the angelic visitor, he called the Baby "Jesus." And thus the Messiah-King was born. The Eternal One entered into time. The Omnipotent became a tiny Infant. The Lord of glory veiled that glory in a human body. And in Him dwelt all the fullness of the Godhead bodily (Col. 2:9).

The King Who Feared a Baby (2:1-12)

Verse 1 in the NET Bible reads, "After Jesus was born in Bethlehem in Judea, in the time of King Herod . . ." This translation helps us conclude that Christ's birth preceded the visit of the wise men by an unspecified period of time.

Herod the Great was a descendant of Esau and therefore a traditional enemy of the Jews. He himself had become a convert to Judaism, but his conversion was more nominal than real. After the death of Julius Caesar, he was promoted from being governor to king of Judea in 40 BC.

It was toward the close of his reign that "wise men" came from the East in search of one who was born king of the Jews. Some think that these men were pagan priests, and that because of their knowledge and predictive powers, they were often chosen as counselors to kings. We do not know where they lived in the East, how many there were, or how long their journey lasted.

It was the star in the East that somehow made them aware of the birth of a king. Possibly they were familiar with the Old Testament prophecies concerning the Messiah's arrival. Perhaps they knew, for instance, Balaam's prediction that a Star would come out of Jacob (Num. 24:17). And perhaps they connected this with Daniel's prophecy of seventy weeks which foretold the time of Christ's first coming (Dan. 9:24-25). But it seems more probable that the knowledge was communicated to them supernaturally via this original Telstar.

Various scientific explanations have been offered to account for this star at this point in history. Some say that it was a conjunction of planets. But the course of this star was highly irregular in that it went ahead of the wise men from Jerusalem till it came to rest over the place where the child was (v. 9). In fact, it was so unusual that it can only be accounted for as a miracle.

When Herod heard that a baby had been born who was to be King of the Jews, he was troubled. Any such baby was a threat to his uneasy crown. All Jerusalem was troubled with him. The city that above all cities should have received the news with delirious joy was disturbed by anything that might upset its current power base or risk the displeasure of the hated Roman rule.

Herod assembled the religious leaders of the Jews to find out where the Messiah was to be born. The chief priests were the high priest and his sons, and perhaps other principal members of his family. The scribes were lay experts in the law of Moses. They preserved and taught the law and served as judges in the Sanhedrin (Jewish religious leaders). These priests and scribes promptly quoted Micah 5:2, where Bethlehem of Judea was named as the future birthplace of the King. Actually, in Micah's prophecy, the city was called "Bethlehem Ephrathah." This identified it part of the tribal territory of Judah. There was more than one Bethlehem in Palestine, and thus the specific city is named with precision. Though one of the smaller hamlets of Judah, it was in no way the least significant, for out of it would come a Ruler in Israel.

Herod then called the wise men secretly to find out when they first saw the star. His secrecy betrayed his sadistic motive; he would need this information later if he was not able to locate the right Child. To cover up his real intention, he sent the wise men to find the Child, then to bring back word so that he too could go and worship. As the men started out, the star which they had seen in the East reappeared! This indicates that the star had not guided them all the way from the East. But now it actually did guide them to the house where Jesus was.

Special mention is made of the great joy of the wise men when they saw the star (v. 10). These Gentiles diligently sought Christ while Herod planned to kill Him, while the knowledgeable priests and scribes were as yet indifferent, and while the people of Jerusalem were troubled. All these attitudes were omens of the way in which the Messiah would be received.

When they entered the house, the wise men saw Jesus with Mary His mother (notice that they were not found in the stable, indicating some length of time had elapsed). They stretched out on the ground in worship before Him, offering costly gifts of gold, frankincense, and myrrh. We should not miss several beautiful touches here. First, let us mark the unusual order: "they saw the child with Mary his mother . . ." We would usually mention the mother first, then her child. But this Child is unique and must be given first place (see also vv. 13-14, 20-21). In that same connection, we should observe that the wise men worshipped Jesus, not Mary or Joseph. (Joseph is not even mentioned here; he will soon disappear entirely from the gospel record.) The lesson for us is simple: wise men still worship Jesus.

Finally, the gifts they brought spoke volumes. Gold is a type or figure of deity and of glory; it speaks of the bright, shining perfection of His divine Person, Frankincense is an ointment, or perfume; it suggests the fragrance of His life of sinless perfection. Myrrh is a bitter herb, sometimes used in embalming; it pictures the sufferings which He would endure in bearing away the sins of the world.

In Isaiah 60:6 we read a prediction that Gentiles would come to the Messiah with gifts, but Isaiah mentions only gold and frankincense, not myrrh. The reason is that Isaiah was speaking of Christ's second coming in power and great glory. There will be no myrrh then, because He will not suffer then. But here in Matthew, the myrrh is included because His first coming is in view. In Matthew we have the sufferings of Christ; in Isaiah 60, the glories that shall follow.

The wise men were warned by God in a dream not to return to Herod and so they obediently returned to their own country by another route. Someone has said that no one who meets Christ with a sincere heart ever returns the same way. True encounter with Him transforms all of life.

Exile in Egypt (2:13-15)

From early childhood the threat of death hung over our Lord. The storm clouds gathered with unprecedented speed and fury. It was clear that He was born to die. But there was an appointed time, and He could not die before then. Any man who walks in the center of God's will is immortal until his work is done.

An angel of the Lord warned Joseph in a dream to flee to Egypt with his family as Herod was ready to embark on his "search and destroy" mission. And so this humble little Jewish family took the long, weary trip to Egypt. We do not know how long they stayed; all we know is that they were refugees until Herod's death. Then the coast was clear for them to return home to Palestine.

And so another prophecy of the Old Testament became clothed with new meaning (v. 15). God had said through the prophet Hosea, "Out of Egypt I called My son" (11:1). In its original context, this referred to Israel's deliverance from Egypt at the time of the exodus. But the statement is capable of a double meaning. The Messiah's history would closely parallel that of the nation of Israel; here the prophecy is fulfilled by His return to Palestine from Egypt.

Massacre in Bethlehem (2:16-18)

When the wise men failed to return to Jerusalem, Herod realized that he had been frustrated in his plot to locate the young King of the Jews. In senseless rage he ordered the death of all male children under two years of age in Bethlehem and its locale. Estimates vary as to the number slain; one writer suggests about twenty-six. It is not likely that hundreds were involved in light of the known population level of the area. Herod set the two-year age limit according to the time when the star first appeared to the wise men. This gives us some clue as to the approximate age of the Baby Jesus at this time.

The weeping which followed the killing of the children was a fulfillment of the prophecy of Jeremiah 31:15. In the prophecy, Rachel, of course, represents the nation of Israel. The grief of the nation is attributed to Rachel, who was buried in a hamlet called Ramah near Bethlehem, where the massacre of the infants took place. As the bereaved parents passed her tomb, she is pictured as weeping with them. It is poetic language.

In his effort to eliminate a potential rival, Herod gained nothing but dishonorable mention in the annals of infamy.

A Nazarene in Nazareth (2:19-23)

After Herod's death an angel of the Lord assured Joseph that it was now safe to return to the land of Israel. When he first reached the land Joseph heard that Archelaus (pronounced Ar-kel-lay-us) had succeeded his father as king of Judea. Joseph knew that the new king had been cruel to the Jews, and so he was hesitant to venture into Judea. His fears were confirmed by a warning from God, so he travelled northward to Galilee and settled in Nazareth.

For the fourth time in this chapter Matthew reminds us that prophecy was being fulfilled. He does not mention any prophet by name but simply says that it had been foretold that the Messiah would be called a Nazarene. There is no verse in the Old Testament that says this in so many words. A more probable explanation is that "Nazarene" is used to describe anyone who lived in Nazareth. The town was viewed with contempt by the rest of the people. Nathaniel expressed this by the proverbial question, "Can anything good come out of Nazareth?" (John 1:46). The scorn which was heaped upon this "unimportant" town naturally fell upon its inhabitants as well. So when verse 23 says, "He shall be called a Nazarene," it means that He would be treated with contempt and mockery. Although we cannot find any prophecy that Jesus would be called a Nazarene, we can find one that says that He would be despised and rejected by men (Isa. 53:3). Another says that He would be a worm and no man; scorned by men, and despised by the people (Ps. 22:6). It is rather amazing that when the Mighty God came to this earth, He was given a nickname of reproach. Those who follow Him are privileged to share His reproach (Heb. 13:13)! Ps 69:9

Rom 15:3

2

MATTHEW 3–4

A Voice in the Wilderness (3:1-12)

B etween chapters 2 and 3 there is an interval of about twenty-eight years. These were the years our Lord spent in Nazareth preparing Himself for the work that lay ahead. They were years in which He performed no miracles, yet a period in which the scrutinizing eyes of God could find nothing but perfect delight (Matt. 3:17). Here in Matthew chapter 3 we come to the threshold of His public ministry.

John the Baptist was six months older than his cousin Jesus (see Luke 1:26, 36). At this crucial moment he stepped onto the stage of human history to serve as forerunner for the King of Israel. His unlikely parish was the wilderness of Judea—an arid area extending from Jerusalem to the Jordan; the region found a parallel in the dry and stony hearts of the people to whom he preached. The substance of his message was, "Repent, for the kingdom of heaven is at hand!" The King would soon appear, but He could not and would not reign over people who clung to their sins. They must change directions, must do an about-face, must confess and forsake their sins. God was calling them from the kingdom of darkness to the kingdom of heaven.

> The King would soon appear, but He could not and would not reign over people who clung to their sins.

In verse 2 we have the first of thirty-two mentions of "the kingdom of heaven" in this gospel. Since a right understanding of this concept is basic, we will pause here to define and describe it.

The Kingdom of Heaven

The kingdom of heaven is the sphere in which God's rule is acknowledged. The word *heaven* is used figuratively for God Himself; this is clearly shown in Daniel 4:25 and 26. In verse 25, Daniel said that the Most High rules the kingdom of men. In the very next verse he says that heaven rules. Thus the kingdom of heaven announces the rule of God and exists wherever people submit to that rule.

There are two aspects of the kingdom of heaven. In its broadest aspect it includes everyone who just *professes* to acknowledge God as the Supreme Ruler. In its inner aspect it includes only those who have been genuinely converted. We may picture this by two concentric circles, a small one inside a large one.

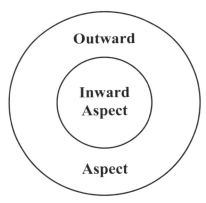

The big circle is the sphere of profession; it includes the true and the false, the wheat and the tares (Matt. 13:24-30). The inner circle includes only those who have been born again through faith in the Lord Jesus Christ. By a synthesis of all the references to the kingdom in the Bible we can trace its historical development in five distinct phases.

First, the kingdom was *prophesied* in the Old Testament. Daniel predicted that God would set up a kingdom that would never be destroyed or yield its sovereignty to another people (Dan. 2:44). He also foresaw Christ's coming to reign and His universal and everlasting dominion (Dan. 7:13, 14; see also Jer. 23:5-6).

Second, the kingdom was described by John the Baptist, Jesus, and the twelve disciples as being *at hand* (Matt. 3:2; 4:17; 10:7), or *present.* In Matthew 12:28, Jesus said, "If I cast out demons by the Spirit of God, surely the kingdom of God has come upon you." And in Luke 17:21 He said, "The kingdom of God is within you." While both these references are to the kingdom of God rather than to the kingdom of heaven, we shall show later that the terms are used interchangeably.

Third, the kingdom is described in an *interim* form. After He was rejected by the nation of Israel, the King returned to heaven. The kingdom exists today in the hearts of all who acknowledge His kingship while the King is absent. This interim phase of the kingdom is described in the parables of Matthew 13.

The fourth phase of the kingdom is what might be called its *manifestation*. This is the literal thousand-year reign of Christ on earth. It was foreshadowed on the Mount of Transfiguration when the Lord was seen in the glory of His coming reign (Matt. 16:28). Jesus referred to it (Matt. 8:11) when He said, "Many will come from east and west, and sit down with Abraham, Isaac, and Jacob in the kingdom of heaven."

The fifth and final form will be the *everlasting* kingdom described in 2 Peter 1:11 as "the everlasting kingdom of our Lord and Savior Jesus Christ."

> The Kingdom is not the same as the church.

The phrase "kingdom of heaven" is found only in Matthew's gospel. The term "kingdom of God" is found in all four gospels. For all practical purposes there is no difference; the same things are said about both. For example, in Matthew 19:23 Jesus said it would be hard for a rich man to enter the kingdom of *heaven*. In Mark 10:23 and Luke 18:24 Jesus is quoted as saying the same thing about the kingdom of *God*. Then Matthew himself also quotes Jesus as saying virtually the same thing with regard to the kingdom of *God* (compare Matt. 19:23 and 24).

One final point is that the kingdom is not the same as the church. The kingdom began when Christ entered on His public ministry; the church began on the day of Pentecost (Acts 2). The kingdom will continue on earth till the earth is destroyed; the church continues on earth till the rapture, then it will return with Christ at His second advent to reign with Him as His bride. At the present time the people who are in the kingdom in its true, inner reality are also in the church.

We return now to our exposition of Matthew 3. John was calling the nation of Israel to turn its back on sin and thus to be in a proper moral and spiritual condition to receive the King. This preparatory ministry of John had been prophesied by Isaiah over seven hundred years previously (v. 3). John called on the people of Israel to prepare the way of the Lord; they could make His paths "straight" by removing from their lives anything that would hinder His complete dominion.

The Baptizer's garment was made of camel's hair, not the soft, luxurious camel's hair cloth of our day, but the coarse, austere fabric of an outdoorsman. He also wore a leather girdle around his waist. This was exactly the same clothing as the prophet Elijah's (2 Kings 1:8) and perhaps was calculated to alert believing Israelites to the similarity of John's mission to that of Elijah (Mal. 4:5; Luke 1:17; Matt. 11:14; 17:10-12).

John's food was locusts and wild honey; he was so consumed by zeal for his mission that the normal comforts and pleasures of life were of much lower priority to him. It must have been a convicting experience to meet John. Here was a man who cared for none of the things that people usually live for. His absorption with spiritual realities must have made others realize how poor they were. His self-renunciation was a stinging rebuke to the worldliness and luxurious living of his day. Yet people flocked out to hear him from Jerusalem, Judea, and the trans-Jordan area (v. 5). A godly remnant of Israelites responded to his message and were baptized by him in the Jordan. They were saying in effect that they were ready to give full allegiance and obedience to the coming King.

With the Pharisees and Sadducees it was a different story. When they stepped forward to be baptized, John knew that they were not sincere. While the Pharisees professed great devotion to the law, they were inwardly corrupt, sectarian, hypocritical, and self-righteous. And John knew that the Sadducees were social aristocrats and religious skeptics who denied such basic doctrines as the resurrection of the body, the existence of angels, the immortality of the soul, and eternal punishment.

John denounced both sects as a brood of vipers who were pretending to desire escape from the onrushing fires of judgment, but who exhibited no signs of true repentance. He challenged them to prove the genuineness of their repentance by the fruit of a transformed life—by faith, sincerity, love, and righteousness (v. 8). And they should stop presuming on their descent from Abraham as a passport to heaven. The grace of salvation is not transmitted in natural birth. God could take the lifeless stones of the Jordan and make them into children of Abraham by a less violent process than the conversion of the Pharisees and Sadducees.

John said that the ax was already laid at the root of the trees (v. 10); in other words, a work of divine judgment was about to begin. Christ's arrival and presence would test all men. Those who were found to be fruitless would be destroyed.

In verses 7-10 John had been speaking exclusively to the Pharisees and Sadducees. In verses 11 and 12 he addressed his entire audience—those who were truly repentant as well as those who were only play-acting. He explained that there was a significant difference between his ministry and the Messiah's. He himself baptized with water for

———— ❧ ————

A work of divine judgment was about to being. Christ's arrival and presence would test all men.

———— ❧ ————

repentance; the water was ceremonial and did not have cleansing value; and the repentance, though real, did not bring a person to full salvation. And so we may say that John's ministry was preparatory and partial. The Messiah would completely overshadow John. As to ability, He would be mightier. As to His Person, He would be worthier. As to His work, it would be more far-reaching; He would baptize with the Holy Spirit and with fire.

The baptism with the Holy Spirit is distinct from the baptism with fire. The former is a baptism of blessing, the latter of judgment. The former took place at Pentecost; the latter is still future. The former is enjoyed by all true believers in the Lord Jesus; the latter will be the fate of all unbelievers. The former would be for those faithful Israelites whose baptism by John was an outward sign of inward repentance; the latter would be for the Pharisees and Sadducees, who showed no evidence of true repentance.

How can we be sure that John was referring to two distinct baptisms? Could not the baptism with fire refer to the tongues of fire that appeared when the Spirit was given at Pentecost? There are at least two indications that the baptism of fire speaks of judgment.

First, when John was speaking to a mixed audience, including those who were genuinely repentant and also the unbelieving Pharisees and Sadducees, he said, "He will baptize you with the Holy Spirit and with fire" (Matt. 3:5-11; Luke 3:7-16). But when, as recorded in Mark 1:5-11, John was speaking only to those who truly confessed their sins, he did not mention the baptism with fire. He simply said, "He will baptize you with the Holy Spirit."

The second main proof that the baptism with fire represents judgment is that immediately following the reference to this baptism, John gave the explanation found in verse 12 (see also Luke 3:17). Here the Lord is pictured using a winnowing fork to toss the threshed grain up into the wind. The wheat (true believers) falls directly to the ground; from there it is carried into His garner (the kingdom). The chaff (unbelievers) is carried a short distance away by the wind; from there it is taken away to be burned "with unquenchable fire." The fire here in verse 12 obviously means judgment. Since verse 12 amplifies verse 11, it is reasonable to conclude that the baptism with fire is a baptism of judgment.

The King Is Baptized and Anointed (3:13-17)

Jesus walked approximately sixty miles from Galilee to that part of the Jordan River near Jericho where John was baptizing. It indicates the importance which He attached to this meaningful ceremony—and should speak volumes to any of His followers who have never followed Him into the water.

Realizing that Jesus had no sins of which to repent, John protested against baptizing Him. It was a true instinct that led the Baptist to suggest that the proper order would be for him to be baptized by Jesus. The Lord

_____ ❧ _____

Jesus' immersion in the Jordan typified His baptism in the waters of God's judgment at Calvary.

_____ ❧ _____

did not deny this; He simply repeated His request for baptism as a fitting way in which to fulfill all righteousness. It was appropriate that in baptism He should identify Himself with those godly Israelites who were coming forward to be baptized by John unto repentance.

But there was an even deeper meaning than this! Baptism for Him was a symbolic ritual depicting the way in which our Lord would, on the cross, fulfill all the righteous claims of God against man's sin. His immersion in the Jordan typified His baptism in the waters of God's judgment at Calvary. His rising out of the water fore-shadowed His resurrection. By death, burial, and resurrection, He would satisfy the demands of divine justice and provide a righteous basis by which sinners could be justified.

As soon as He came out of the water, Jesus saw the Spirit of God descend like a dove from heaven and land on Him (v. 16, a dove is a ground-feeder; it illustrates the Spirit's descent to the earth). In this way Jesus was anointed as Messiah-King. Just as persons and things in the Old Testament were consecrated to sacred purposes by "the oil of holy ointment" (Ex. 30:23-26; 29:27), so He was anointed by the Holy Spirit.

———— ✍ ————

Jesus' baptism was a hallowed occasion, when all three members of the Trinity were seen or heard.

———— ✍ ————

It was a hallowed occasion, when all three members of the Trinity were seen or heard. The beloved Son was there. The Holy Spirit was there. And the Father's voice was heard from heaven, "This is my beloved Son, in whom I am well pleased." It was a memorable event because the voice of God was heard quoting Holy Scripture: "This is my beloved Son" from Psalm 2:7 and "in whom I am well pleased" from Isaiah 42:1. And it was a memorable moment because it was one of three occasions when the Father spoke from heaven in delighted acknowledgment of His unique Son (see also Matt. 17:5 and John 12:28).

The King Is Tested and Approved (4:1-11)

At first, it may seem strange to us that Jesus should be led by the Spirit to be tempted by the devil (v. 1). The reason is that it was necessary to demonstrate Christ's moral fitness for the work to which He had been called. The first Adam proved his unfitness for dominion when he met the adversary in the garden of Eden. Here, the last Adam meets the devil in a head-on confrontation in the wilderness and emerges unscathed.

There is deep mystery connected with the temptation of our Lord. Inevitably the question arises, "Could He have sinned?" If we answer no, then we face the further question, "How could it be a real temptation if He could not yield?" If we answer yes, we are faced with the problem of a God with a capacity to sin.

It is of first importance to remember that Jesus Christ is God and that God cannot sin. It is true that He is also human; however, to say that He could sin as man but not as God is to build a case without scriptural foundation. The New Testament writers jealously guard the sinlessness of Christ. Paul says He "knew no sin" (2 Cor. 5:21); Peter says "He committed no sin" (1 Peter 2:22); and John says, "in Him there is no sin" (1 John 3:5).

Like us, Jesus could be tempted *from without:* Satan could and did come to Him with external suggestions as to what He should do, contrary to the will of God. But unlike us, He could not be tempted *from within:* no sinful lusts or passions could originate in Him. Furthermore, there was nothing in Him that would respond to the devil's seductions (John 14:30).

In spite of the fact that Jesus could not sin, the temptations were real. It was possible for Him to be faced with enticements to sin, but it was morally impossible for Him to yield. He could do nothing of His own will, but only what He saw the Father doing (John 5:19), and it is inconceivable that He would ever see the Father sinning. He could do nothing on His own authority (John 5:30), and the Father would never give Him the authority to yield to temptation.

> **In spite of the fact that Jesus could not sin, the temptations were real.**

The purpose of the temptation was not to see if He would sin, but to prove that even under the most tremendous pressure He could do nothing but obey God's commands. Automobiles are subjected to grueling tests, not to prove that they might be defective, but to show that they will stand up under the most exacting circumstances. The fact that a car can be tested does not necessarily imply that it can fail to meet the standard.

Now we turn to the three specific temptations. After fasting for forty days and nights, Jesus experienced strong craving for food (v. 2). This natural, legitimate appetite provided the devil with an advantage which in many men he could exploit. And so he suggested that Jesus use His miraculous powers to convert the flat, round stones of the desert into loaves of bread, which they closely resembled. The introductory words, "If You are the Son of God . . ." do not imply doubt; they mean, "*Since* You are the Son of God . . ."

The first temptation then was to satisfy a natural appetite and cater to physical comfort by use of divine power in obedience to Satan, and therefore in disobedience to God. It answers to that part of the temptation in Eden, that the fruit of the tree was "good for food" (Gen. 3:6). The apostle John catalogs it as "the lust of the flesh" (1 John 2:16).

The corresponding temptation for us is to live for the gratification of natural desires, to choose a pathway of comfort and ease instead of seeking the kingdom of God and His righteousness (Matt. 6:33). The devil says to us, "You have to live, don't you?" Our Lord's example teaches us that we *don't* have to live, but we *do* have to obey God. He would rather turn stones into children of Abraham for the glory of God (3:9) than turn them into bread for Himself apart from the will of God.

Jesus answered the temptation by quoting the Scriptures (Deut. 8:3). Getting bread is not the most important thing in life. Obedience to every word of God is more important than the satisfaction of physical appetite. As the dependent Man, our Lord did only those things that the Father ordered. He had received no instructions from Him to turn stones into bread; therefore, no matter how intense His hunger might be, He would not act independently or obey Satan.

The second temptation took place in the holy city, Jerusalem, on the pinnacle or wing of the temple (v. 5). The devil challenged Jesus to throw Himself down in a spectacular display of His divine Sonship. Again, the opening clause, "If You are the Son of God," does not express doubt; the adversary used the "if" of argument, not of doubt. This is clear from the fact that he quoted Psalm 91:11-12 (a passage that was generally acknowledged to refer to the Messiah) and applied it to Jesus. In those verses God had promised safety and protection to the Messiah.

The temptation was for Jesus to demonstrate that He was the Christ by performing a sensational stunt. Here was a way for Him to achieve glory without suffering, to reach the throne by by-passing the cross. He would be acting outside the will of God and in collaboration with the evil one. John describes this appeal to the soul as "the pride of life" (1 John 2:16). It resembles a "tree desirable to make one wise" (Gen. 3:6) in the garden of Eden, a means of achieving personal glory in disregard of God's will.

Again Jesus resisted the attack by quoting Scripture, "It is written, 'You shall not tempt the Lord your God'" (see Deut. 6:16). It is true that God had promised to preserve Him, but that guarantee presupposed that the Messiah would be living in the will of God. Outside His will there is no assurance of safety. To claim the promise in an act of disobedience would be tempting God. The time would come when Jesus would be revealed as Messiah to the people at the temple—but the cross must come first. The altar of sacrifice must precede the throne. The crown of thorns must precede the crown of glory. He would await God's time and accomplish God's will.

This temptation comes to us in a desire to attain prominence in the religious world apart from the fellowship of His suffering. We seek great things for ourselves, then run and hide when suffering looms before us. When we stubbornly exalt ourselves in indifference to God's will, we tempt God.

In the third temptation the devil escorted the Lord to a very high mountain, showed Him all the kingdoms of the world and their grandeur, then offered them to Him in exchange for His worship (vv. 8-9). Just as the first temptation was to the body and the second was to the soul, so this one was in the realm of the spirit. It had to do with worship, which is an exercise of the spirit. However, since the reward offered was the kingdoms of the world, it also involved "the lust of the eyes." It was an effort to induce our Lord to gain the scepter of universal empire by worshiping Satan.

— ✑ —

When we stubbornly exalt ourselves in indifference to God's will, we tempt God.

— ✑ —

There is a sense in which the kingdoms of the world do belong to the devil at the present time. He is spoken of as "the god of this world" (2 Cor. 4:4), and John tells us that "the whole world is in the power of the evil one" (1 John 5:19). At His second advent, Jesus will appear as King of kings and Lord of lords (Rev. 19:16). Then the kingdom of this world will become the kingdom of our Lord and His Christ (Rev. 11:15). Jesus would not violate the divine timetable, and certainly He would never worship the devil.

For us the temptation is twofold: it involves exchanging our spiritual birthright for the passing glory of this world and worshiping and serving the creature rather than the Creator.

For the third time, Jesus resisted temptation by using the sword of the Spirit, that is, the appropriate text from the Word of God: "You shall worship the Lord your God, and Him only you shall serve" (cf. Deut. 6:13). Worship and the service that flows from it are for God alone. To worship Satan would be the same as acknowledging him as God.

"Then the devil left Him." Temptation comes in waves rather than in a steady flow. "When the enemy comes in like a flood, the Spirit of the Lord will lift up a standard against him" (Isa. 59:19). What an encouragement for God's tested saints!

We are told that angels came and ministered to Jesus, but no explanation is given concerning this supernatural help. Almost certainly it means that they provided physical nourishment for Him. The passage is one of several that give us a short glimpse behind the curtain of the spirit world. It does not tell us enough to satisfy our curiosity, but we may be sure it tells us all we need to know.

From the temptation of Jesus we learn that the devil attacks those who are filled with the Holy Spirit, but that he is powerless against those who resist him with the Word of God.

Light Dawns in Galilee (4:12-17)

The Judean ministry of our Lord, which lasted almost one year and which is covered in John chapters 1 through 4, is passed over by Matthew between verses 11 and 12. Matthew takes us directly to Jesus' Galilean ministry.

When the Lord heard that John had been arrested and imprisoned, He realized that this was an omen of His own rejection. In rejecting the King's forerunner, the Judeans were, for all practical purposes, rejecting the

> Satan is powerless against those who resist him with the Word of God.

King Himself. But it was not fear that drove Him north to Galilee. Rather, He was giving a vivid demonstration of what His rejection by the Jews would mean: the gospel would go out to the Gentiles. Galilee was a district populated by Gentiles as well as Jews.

Jesus remained in Nazareth until the Jewish populace tried to kill Him for proclaiming the salvation of Gentiles (Luke 4:16-30). Then He moved on to Capernaum by the Sea of Galilee. (It was in this area that the tribal territories of Zebulun and Naphtali were located.) From this time, Capernaum became known as His home town.

Matthew, ever on the alert to link current events with prophecy, records that Jesus' move to Galilee was a fulfillment of Isaiah 9:1-2. The ignorant and superstitious Gentiles who lived in Galilee saw a great light—that is, Christ, the Light of the world. His arrival was like the dawning of day for those who lived in moral and spiritual darkness and death.

From then on Jesus took up the message which John the Baptist had been preaching, "Repent, for the kingdom of heaven is at hand." It was a further call for moral renewal in preparation for His kingdom. The kingdom was at hand in the sense that a genuine offer was about to be made by the King.

"I will make you fishers of men" (4:18-22)

This is actually the second time Jesus called Peter and Andrew. In John 1:35-42, they were called to salvation; here they are called to service. The first call took place in Judea; this one, in Galilee. Before this time, Peter and Andrew had fished for fish; Jesus now called them to be fishers of men. And how would they do this? The formula is simple: "Follow me, and I will make you fishers of men." *Their* responsibility was to follow Christ; that is, to be like Him. *His* responsibility was to make them successful fishermen. If we are living close to the Lord, if we are walking in fellowship with Him, He will see to it that we will catch men.

This is the ministry of character. It means that what we are is more important than what we say. The temptation today is for the would-be personal worker to disregard his own personal life and simply depend on a neat formula, a routine set of questions, human eloquence, a dynamic personality, or clever arguments. These may be very convincing, and may even seem to produce results, but the fact remains that there is no substitute for holiness of life or for true spirituality. We must begin here, for that is where God begins.

> *What we are is more important than what we say.*

In following Christ the disciple learns to go where the fish are running, to use the proper lure, to endure discomfort and inconvenience, to be patient, and to keep himself out of sight. Peter and Andrew heard the call and responded instantly. In true faith they left their nets, which were their means of livelihood. In true commitment and devotion they followed Jesus.

Next, the call came to James and John, the sons of Zebedee. They too became instant disciples. They left not only their means of livelihood but their father as well; thus they acknowledged the priority of Jesus Christ over all earthly ties.

By responding to the call of Christ, these four ordinary fishermen became key figures in the evangelization of the world. Recognition of the lordship of Christ made all the difference in their lives. And if they had remained at their nets, we would never have heard of them.

Christ's Fame Spreads (4:23-25)

The ministry of the Lord Jesus was threefold: He taught God's message in the synagogues; He preached the gospel of the kingdom; and He healed the sick. One purpose of the miracles of healing was to validate His Person and ministry (Heb. 2:3-4). Matthew chapters 5, 6, and 7 are an example of His teaching ministry, and chapters 8 and 9 describe His miracles.

In verse 23 we have the first mention of the gospel in the New Testament—"the gospel of the kingdom." We shall therefore pause here to explain what the gospel is. Basically, the gospel is the good news of salvation from the penalty of sin. In every age of the world's history there has been, is, and will be only one gospel; there is only one way of salvation.

The Gospel of Salvation for All the Ages

As to its *origin,* salvation is by grace (Eph. 2:8). That means that God gives eternal life freely to sinful men who don't deserve it.

As to its *basis,* salvation is through the work of Christ on Calvary's cross (1 Cor. 15:1-4). There the Savior fulfilled all the claims of divine justice and made it possible for God to justify sinners in a righteous way and still be just in doing so. Old Testament believers were saved through the work of Christ,

> The gospel is the good news of salvation from the penalty of sin.

though it was still in their future. They did not know much about it, but God did—and He reckoned the value of Christ's work to their account (Rom. 3:25). In a sense they were saved "on credit." We too are saved through the work of Christ, but in our case the work has already been finished.

As to its *reception,* salvation is by faith (Eph. 2:8). In Old Testament times, people were saved by believing whatever revelation God gave to them. Abraham, for instance, was justified by believing God's promise that he would have a numberless posterity (Gen. 15:5, 6). In this age, men are saved by believing God's testimony concerning His Son as the only way of salvation (1 John 5:11-12).

As to its ultimate *goal,* the gospel looks forward to heaven. The Old Testament saints had this hope (Heb. 11:10, 14-16). We too have the hope of eternity in heaven (2 Cor. 5:6-10).

But while there is only one gospel, yet there are different features of the gospel in different ages. For instance, there is a different emphasis between the gospel of the kingdom and the gospel of the grace of God. The gospel of the kingdom says, "Repent and receive Christ; then you will enter His kingdom when it is set up on earth." The gospel of the grace of God says, "Repent and receive Christ; then you will be taken up to meet Him and to be with Him forever." Fundamentally they are the same gospel—salvation by grace through faith—but they show that there are different administrations of the gospel according to God's plans and purposes. *(dispensations)*

While the simple gospel presents salvation as a gift to be received by believing, in a wider sense the good news includes the whole body of truth which the Lord has committed to us in the Gospels and Epistles. Thus, when Paul spoke of "my gospel" (Rom. 2:16), he included the truth of the church, its calling, and its destiny.

The four gospels (the narratives of the earthly life of Jesus Christ) are not so much a straightforward explanation of the plan of salvation as they are a historical account of the Savior Himself and of the work by which He made salvation available.

———— ❧ ————

All the diseased, demon-possessed, and disabled felt the healing touch of the wonderful Son of God.

———— ❧ ————

Jesus Heals the People (v. 23)

Now to get back to the text. When Jesus preached the gospel of the kingdom, he was announcing His advent as King of the Jews and explaining the terms of admission to the kingdom.

His fame spread through all Syria, the territory north and northeast of Palestine. All the diseased, demon-possessed, and disabled felt the healing touch of the wonderful Son of God. People also thronged to Him from Galilee, the Decapolis (a territory of ten cities with a mostly Gentile population), Jerusalem, Judea, and the region east of the Jordan River.

3

MATTHEW 5

It is no accident that the so-called "Sermon on the Mount" is placed at the beginning of the New Testament. Its position indicates its importance. In it, the King summarizes the character and conduct which He expects of His subjects.

The Sermon on the Mount was never intended to be a presentation of the plan of salvation or to be teaching for unsaved people; it was addressed to the disciples, not the multitude (5:1-2). The standards set forth are impossible as far as human power is concerned; they require divine life.

> The Sermon on the Mount was addressed to the disciples, not the multitude.

For whom was the sermon intended? It was meant for all who acknowledge Christ as King, whether in the past, present, or future. When Christ was on earth it had a direct application to His disciples. During this present age, when our Lord is in heaven, it applies to all who crown Him King in their hearts. Then finally, it will be the code of behavior for Christ's followers during the tribulation period and His glorious reign on earth.

There is no denying that the Sermon has a distinctively Jewish flavor. We see this in allusions to the council (Sanhedrin, 5:22), to the altar (5:24), and to Jerusalem, the city of the great King (5:35). Yet it would not be right to say that its teaching is exclusively for believing Israelites in the past or future; it is for those of every age who acknowledge Jesus Christ as rightful King.

ı of God's Kingdom (5:1-12)

with the Beatitudes, that is, blessings. These set forth
's kingdom. As we will see, the qualities described
ry opposite of those which the world values.

......ing is pronounced on the poor in spirit. This does not
refer to a person's natural disposition but to
deliberate choice and discipline. The poor
in spirit are those who acknowledge their
own weakness and helplessness and who
rely on God's omnipotence. They sense their
spiritual need and find it supplied in the Lord.

—— ᴥ ——

**The Beatitudes set
forth the ideal man
of Christ's kingdom.**

—— ᴥ ——

The kingdom of heaven belongs to this type of people; in that kingdom,
self-sufficiency is not a virtue and self-exaltation is a vice.

Those who mourn are blessed; a day of comfort awaits them. But here it
is not a question of the mourning which everyone in life experiences sooner
or later; the sorrow of this world is more often a curse than a blessing. This
is mourning for the Son of Man's sake; in other words, it is that sorrow
which a person endures in fellowship with the Lord Jesus. As someone
has said, it is "an active sharing and bearing of the world's hurt and sin
like Jesus weeping over Jerusalem." It includes sorrow over one's own sin
and unworthiness, over the appalling conditions in the world, over man's
rejection of the Savior, and over the terrible doom of those who refuse His
mercy. These mourners will be comforted in that coming day when "He
will wipe away every tear from their eyes; there shall be no more death,
nor sorrow, nor crying" (Rev. 21:4). Believers do all their mourning in this
life; for unbelievers, today's grief is only a foretaste of eternal sorrow.

A third blessing is pronounced on the meek; they shall inherit the
earth. By nature these people might be temperamental and harsh. But by
purposefully yielding to Christ's control and learning from Him, they
become meek and lowly in heart (Matt. 11:29). Meekness is the quality
which patiently accepts insults and injuries done to oneself. The meek
person is gentle and mild in his own cause, though he may be a lion in
God's cause or in defending others. The meek do not inherit the earth at
the present time; instead they inherit abuse and dispossession. But they
will literally inherit the earth when Christ the King reigns for a thousand
years of peace and prosperity.

Next, a blessing is pronounced on those who hunger and thirst for righteousness—they shall be satisfied. These people have a passion for uprightness in their own lives first of all. They long to see honesty and justice in political life too. They yearn for integrity in the business world. And they ardently look for practical holiness in the church. They will be abundantly satisfied in Christ's coming kingdom. Righteousness will reign at that time. Corruption will give way to the highest moral standards. The golden rule will be the dominating ethic in all branches of society.

In our Lord's kingdom the merciful are blessed, for they shall obtain mercy. To be merciful means to be actively compassionate. In one sense it means to withhold punishment from offenders who deserve it. But in a wider sense it means to help others who are in need and who cannot help themselves. God showed mercy to us in sparing us from the judgment which our sins deserved and in showing kindness to us through the saving work of Christ. We imitate God when we have compassion on others.

> *To be merciful means to be actively compassionate.*

The merciful will obtain mercy. Here we must understand that Jesus is not referring to the mercy of salvation which God gives to a believing sinner (that mercy is not dependent on man's being merciful to others; it is a free, unconditional gift). Rather, the Lord is speaking of the daily mercy which every child of God needs for Christian living, and also of mercy in that future day when his works will be reviewed and he will be rewarded or suffer loss (1 Cor. 3:12-15). If he has not been merciful, he will not receive mercy; that is, his rewards will decrease accordingly.

The pure in heart are given the enviable assurance that they will see God. Inevitably we link this verse with the majestic words of Psalm 24:3-4: "Who may ascend into the hill of the Lord? Or who may stand in His holy place? He who has clean hands and a pure heart, who has not lifted up his soul to an idol, nor sworn deceitfully." Just as hands refer to outward acts, so the heart points to the inner life. A pure heart is one whose motives are unmixed, whose thoughts are holy, whose conscience is clean.

The expression "they shall see God" may be understood in several ways. First of all, the pure in heart see God now by faith through the Word of God and by the power of the Holy Spirit. Second, they sometimes have what is known as "the beatific vision," a specific, supernatural appearance of the Lord to them. Third, they will see God in the Person of Jesus Christ when He comes again in power and great glory, and also in eternity. This does not contradict John 1:18, which states that "No one has seen God at any time." In His essence God is invisible, but to faith's eye He is always visible; and in the Person of His only Son He will be eternally visible to His glorified saints.

A blessing is pronounced on the peacemakers; they shall be called sons of God. Notice that the Lord is not speaking about people with a peaceful disposition or even those who love peace; He is referring to those who actively intervene to make peace. The natural and easy thing is to watch strife from the sidelines, and sometimes even to gloat over the plight of the unhappy participants. The divine approach is to take positive action toward the cessation of hostilities, even though this may backfire on the peacemaker in abuse and cursing. They shall be called sons of God. This is not how they become sons of God; that can happen only by receiving Jesus Christ as Lord and Savior (John 1:12). But this is how they *demonstrate* themselves as sons of God, and for this type of conduct God will proudly acknowledge them as people who bear the family likeness.

> ———— ❧ ————
> **Men hate a righteous life because it exposes their own unrighteousness.**
> ———— ❧ ————

The next beatitude deals with those who are persecuted, not for their sins but for righteousness' sake; theirs is the kingdom of heaven. These are believers who suffer for doing what is right. Their unshakable integrity condemns the ungodly world and brings out its venomous hostility. Men hate a righteous life because it exposes their own unrighteousness.

The final beatitude seems to be a repetition of the preceding one; it proclaims the blessing of those who are persecuted. But there is a difference. In the previous verse, the subject was persecution for righteousness' sake; here it is persecution for Christ's sake. The Lord clearly foresaw that His disciples would be badly treated because of their association with Him. They would be reviled, persecuted, and slandered for no other reason than their loyalty to Jesus. History has confirmed His prediction; from the outset the world has harassed, persecuted, jailed, and killed members of His little flock. And His prophecy will be fulfilled in a special way during the tribulation period when His faithful Jewish brethren will pass through most acute trials and afflictions.

To suffer for Christ's sake is a privilege that should cause joy and gladness. A great reward awaits those who thus become companions of the prophets in tribulation. These Old Testament spokesmen for God were embodied consciences who stood true to the Lord in spite of the most staggering suffering. All who imitate their loyal courage will share their present exhilaration and their future exaltation.

Here then in the Beatitudes we have a full-length portrait of the ideal citizen in Christ's kingdom. Notice the emphases on righteousness (v. 6), peace (v. 9), and joy (v. 12) and compare with Romans 14:17: "The kingdom of God is not eating and drinking but righteousness and peace and joy in the Holy Spirit."

The Salt of the Earth (5:13)

Jesus likened His disciples to salt; they were to *be* to the world what salt is to us in everyday life. Salt seasons food; it hinders the spread of corruption; it creates thirst. So His followers were to add "flavor" to human society, to serve as a preservative agent, and to make others long for the type of righteousness described in the preceding verses.

> The disciple has one great function— to be the salt of the earth.

If the salt loses its saltiness, how can it be restored? The fact is that there is no way. The salt is useless—except perhaps to be used as a footpath. Barnes' comment on this is illuminating:

"The salt used in this country is a chemical compound—muriate of soda—and if the saltiness were lost, or it were to lose its savor, there would be nothing remaining. In eastern countries, however, the salt used was impure, mingled with vegetable and earthly substances; so that it might lose the whole of its saltiness and a considerable quantity remain. This was good for nothing except that it was used, as it is said, to place in paths, of walks as we use gravel."

The disciple has one great function—to be the salt of the earth. He can do this by living out the terms of discipleship listed in the Beatitudes and in all the Sermon on the Mount. If he fails to exhibit this spiritual reality, men will tread his testimony under their feet. The world has nothing but contempt for a half-hearted believer.

The Light of the World (5:14-16)

Christians are also said to be the light of the world. Jesus spoke of Himself as being the light of the world (John 8:12) while He was in the world (John 12:35-36, 46). The difference is that the Lord is the *source* of all light, while Christians are the *reflection* of His light; that is, of His moral purity and excellence. Their function is to shine for Him just as the moon reflects the glory of the sun.

"A city set on a hill cannot be hidden." This is especially true at night in Palestine. The lights from such a city can be seen for miles around. The Christian is like a city, elevated above its surroundings and shining out in the midst of the world's darkness. Those whose lives exhibit the other-worldly traits of Christ's teaching are conspicuous.

Men do not light a lamp and put it under a bushel. The bushel, of course, is a unit of measure used in business. Christ's followers should not allow the claims of business to douse their witness for Him; better to put the lamp on top of the bushel, that is, to use their business as a means of sharing their Savior with others. Or, as Jesus suggested, put the lamp on a stand so that it will give light to all in the house. He did not intend that we should hoard the light of His matchless teaching to ourselves but that we should share it with family and friends, that is, with everyone that comes into the house. We should let our light shine before men so that as they see our good works, they will glorify our Father in heaven.

The emphasis here again is on the ministry of Christian character. The winsomeness and attractiveness of lives in which Christ is seen speak louder than all the sermons and arguments put together.

The Law Not Abolished, But Fulfilled (5:17-20)

It is the way of most revolutionary leaders to sever all ties with the past and completely repudiate the traditional order. Not so with the Lord Jesus. He consistently upheld the law of Moses and insisted that it must be fulfilled. The law was given by God and was holy, just, and good. The prophetical writings of the Old Testament were likewise God-breathed, and Jesus acknowledged them as the very word of God. He had not come to abolish them but to fulfill them. In the clearest way He insisted that neither a "jot" nor a "tittle" would pass from the law until all was accomplished. The jot here means the smallest letter in the Hebrew alphabet; the tittle was a stroke or small projection that often distinguished one letter from another, much as the bottom stroke of a capital E distinguishes it from a capital F. So Jesus believed not only in the verbal inspiration of the Bible but in its "letter-al" inspiration, if we can coin such a word.

But notice that He did not say that the law would never pass away; He said this would not happen till all was fulfilled.

To be frank, the whole subject of the law and the believer's relation to it is rather complicated. For a summary of the Bible's teaching on it, please turn to page 222 in the appendix.

In Matthew 5:19 Jesus anticipates a natural tendency to relax His commandments. Because they are of such a supernal nature, there is a tendency on our part to explain them away, to rationalize that they cannot mean what they say. The person who thus dulls the sharp edge of Jesus' words and teaches a watered-down brand of discipleship to others shall be called least in the kingdom of heaven. The wonder is that such people are permitted to be in the kingdom at all—but then, entrance into the kingdom is by faith in Christ.

A person's position in the kingdom is determined by his obedience and faithfulness. For instance, the man who takes the words of the Lord at their face value and who obeys them without worrying about the consequences— that man shall be called great in the kingdom of heaven. In terms of being *admitted* into the kingdom, our righteousness must exceed that of the scribes and Pharisees. They contented themselves with religious ceremonies that gave them an outward, ritual cleanness, but never changed their hearts. This external righteousness without inward reality will never do. God requires truth in our inner person; the only righteousness which will satisfy Him is the perfection which He imputes to those who accept His Son as only Lord and Savior (2 Cor. 5:21). Where there is true faith in Christ, there will also be the practical righteousness which our Lord describes in the remainder of the chapter.

———— ✍ ————

God requires truth in our inner person.

———— ✍ ————

The Higher Righteousness Concerning Murder (5:21-26)

The Jews of Jesus' time were all familiar with the fact that murder was forbidden by God, and that the murderer was liable to punishment. This was true before the law was given (Gen. 9:6) and it was later incorporated in the law (Ex. 20:13; Deut. 5:17).

The words "But I say to you . . ." (v. 22) mark a distinct advance in teaching. No longer could a man pride himself because he had never committed the act of murder. Jesus now says, "In my kingdom, you mustn't even have murderous thoughts." He traces the act to its source and warns against three forms of unrighteous anger.

First, the man who is angry with his brother is subject to judgment. That would be equivalent to punishment by a lower court. The NKJV says "angry *without a cause*," but other versions omit the italicized words. Most people can find what they think is a valid cause for their anger. Actually the only times when anger is justified is when God's honor is at stake or whenever someone else is being wronged—but never in retaliation for personal wrongs.

Even more serious is the sin of insulting a brother. In Jesus' day men used the word *Raca,* an obscure Syrian word expressing contempt and abuse. Every generation has its own expressions to accuse men of being stupid. Those who hurl such abuse were subject to trial by the council, that is, the Sanhedrin. This was the highest court among the Jews, the same as our Supreme Court.

> ——— ❧ ———
> **Anger contains the seeds of murder.**
> ——— ❧ ———

Finally, to call a brother a fool makes the offender liable to the hell of fire. Here the word fool means more than just stupid. It signifies a moral fool who ought to be dead and it expresses the wish that he were. Today it is common to hear a man cursing another with the words "Damn you"; he is calling on God to consign the victim to hell. Jesus says that the one who utters such a curse is in danger of "hell fire," that is, of capital punishment. The bodies of executed criminals were often thrown into a burning dump known as *Hinnom.* This was a figure of the fires of hell that shall never be quenched.

There is no mistaking the severity of Jesus' words. He teaches that anger contains the seeds of murder. He states that abusive language contains the spirit of murder. And He warns that cursing language implies the very desire to murder. He mentions three degrees of punishment: the judgment, the council, and hell fire. Sins which were not legally punishable under the law are dealt with in His kingdom—some severely, some more severely, and some most severely.

In verses 23 and 24, a further principle is stated. If a person has been guilty of anger, insult, or cursing, or of any other wrong against a brother, it is useless for him to try to worship God. No Pharisee, either ancient or modern, can gloss over such sins by bringing a gift to the altar as if God's indulgence could be purchased with a bribe. The sin must be confessed to God, then confessed to the offended brother. Only then is the gift acceptable. These words, of course, are written in a Jewish context; the whole idea of bringing a gift to the altar belongs to Judaism. But it is no less applicable in the Christian dispensation. It means, for instance, that we should not go to the Lord's Supper and partake of the bread and the wine if we have sinned against a brother. God gets no worship from a believer who is not on speaking terms with another. First make right the wrong, then come with the "sacrifice of praise to God, that is, the fruit of lips, giving thanks to His name" (Heb. 13:15).

The natural tendency, of course, is to justify oneself. Rather than admit guilt, we stubbornly allow our sins to go unconfessed and unforgiven. It is against this tendency that Jesus warns in verses 25 and 26. It is better to make prompt settlement with an accuser than run the risk of his taking the case into court. If that happens, we are doomed to lose.

It is not necessary to distinguish in these verses between the judge and the guard, or to identify them. The point of the parable is clear. If you are wrong, be quick to admit it and make things right. If you remain unbroken and unrepentant, your sin will eventually catch up with you anyway, and you will not only have to make full restitution but suffer additional penalties as well.

The Higher Righteousness Concerning Adultery (5:27-30)

The Mosaic law was clear in its forbidding of adultery (Ex. 20:14; Deut. 5:18). A man might gloat that he had never broken this particular commandment, and yet he might have "eyes full of adultery and that cannot cease from sin" (2 Peter 2:14). While outwardly respectable, his mind might be constantly wandering down hallways of impurity. So Jesus reminded the disciples that mere abstinence from the physical act was not enough; there must be inward purity. Whoever looks at a woman lustfully has already committed adultery with her in his heart (v. 28). The law forbade the act of adultery; Jesus forbids the desire.

It is a well-known fact that sin begins in the mind and that if we nourish and enjoy it long enough, the probability is that eventually we will commit the act.

> ➢ Sow a thought and you reap an act.
> ➢ Sow an act and you reap a habit.
> ➢ Sow a habit and you reap a character.
> ➢ Sow a character and you reap a destiny.

Maintaining a clean thought life demands strict self-discipline. Thus Jesus taught that if any part of our body causes us to sin—whether the eye for seeing or the hand for doing—it would be better to lose that member for time than to lose one's soul for eternity (vv. 29-30).

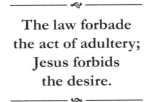

The law forbade the act of adultery; Jesus forbids the desire.

Must we take Jesus' words here literally? Was He actually advocating self-mutilation? The words are literal to this extent: *if it was necessary* to lose a member rather than lose one's soul, then we should gladly part with the member. *Fortunately it is never necessary!* The Holy Spirit can empower the believer to live a holy life. Someone has said, "It takes a passion to conquer a passion."

The Higher Righteousness Concerning Divorce (5:31-32)

Under the Old Testament law, if a man divorced his wife, he was required to give her a divorce certificate (Deut. 24:1-4). Jesus refers to this in verse 31. The passage in Deuteronomy refers to the specific cases where one man divorced his wife because he found some indecency in her or another because he disliked her. There is no suggestion that she had committed adultery; that offense would have been punishable by death (Deut. 22:22). In the kingdom of Christ, anyone who divorces his wife except for unfaithfulness makes her an adulteress. This does not mean that she automatically becomes an adulteress when she leaves his home. But it presupposes that, having no means of support, she is forced to go to live with another man. In doing so she becomes an. adulteress. Also in Christ's kingdom, whoever marries the woman who is thus divorced commits adultery because in God's eyes she is another man's wife.

The subject of divorce and remarriage is one of the most complicated in the Bible. It is virtually impossible to answer all the questions that arise. For a summary of what the Scriptures teach on the topic, see page 217 in the appendix.

The Higher Righteousness Concerning the Use of Oaths (5:33-37)

The law contained several prohibitions against taking the name of the Lord in vain; that is, swearing by the name of God and then failing to tell the truth or to do what was promised (Lev. 19:12; Num. 30:2; Deut. 23:21). It was not so much a question of profanity as of perjury.

The Jews sought to evade this by swearing by heaven or by earth or by Jerusalem or by their head. They reasoned that as long as they did not use God's name, He was not involved, and therefore they did not have to tell the truth. Here the Lord condemns such skirting of the law as sheer hypocrisy and forbids any form of swearing or oath in ordinary conversation. He knew that oaths were of no use; a good man would not need one and a bad man would not heed one. He brushed them aside, for He knew that nothing extraneous will produce truth if a man is not inwardly truthful.

> *Nothing extraneous will produce truth if a man is not inwardly truthful.*

Also, Jesus knew that God is involved, no matter what you swear by—His throne, the earth, the royal capital, or even one's own head, because He is its Creator, the One Who determines and changes the color of our hair.

For a Christian, an oath is unnecessary. His *yes* should mean *yes,* and his *no* should mean *no.* Any attempt to get around this basic truth comes from the evil one. There are no circumstances under which it is ever proper for a Christian to lie. This passage, incidentally, forbids such common expressions as *Jeez* (Jesus) and *Good Heavens.* And it forbids any shading of the truth or exaggeration. It does not, however, forbid taking an oath in a court of law: Jesus Himself testified under oath before the high priest (Matt. 26:63). And apparently it did not forbid an oath by those who transmitted the Scriptures to us, because Paul, writing by divine inspiration, twice called God to witness the truth of what he was saying (2 Cor. 1:23; Gal. 1:20).

The Higher Righteousness Concerning Retaliation (5:38-42)

The law said, "An eye for an eye and a tooth for a tooth." In other words, it stipulated that a crime be punished with an equal penalty. This was both a command to punish and a limitation on punishment—the penalty must not exceed the crime. Authority to take revenge was vested in the government, of course, and not in the private victim.

Jesus went beyond the law to a higher righteousness by abolishing retaliation altogether. He showed His disciples that whereas revenge was once legally permissible, now non-resistance was graciously possible. They were to shock the world by introducing a hitherto unknown behavior. They would not resist an evil person. If struck on one cheek, they would turn the other. If sued for their suit-coat, they would give their overcoat as well. If compelled to carry an official's luggage one mile, they would carry it two.

They were instructed to give to a person who asked for help, and not to refuse a borrower. The reason this command seems so impractical to us is that we possess so much and hold on to it so steadfastly. If we followed Christ's other commands to forsake all, to lay up our treasures in heaven, to be content with food and clothing, we would accept these words more literally and willingly.

Of course, the words of the Lord presuppose that the person who asks for help has a genuine need, and that the borrower wants money for a legitimate cause. It would be wrong to give to a beggar if in so doing we were subsidizing drunkenness or encouraging laziness. The Bible never commands us to do anything that would be harmful to another person's best interests. Sometimes it is impossible to know whether the need is legitimate; in such cases it is better, as someone has said, "to help a score of fraudulent beggars than to risk turning away one man in real need."

Humanly speaking, of course, such behavior as the Lord calls for here is impossible. It is only as a person is indwelt and empowered by the Holy Spirit that he can live this other-worldly kind of life. Only as Christ is allowed to live His life in the believer can insult, injustice, and inconvenience be repaid with love. This is "the gospel of the second mile."

The Higher Righteousness Concerning Treatment of One's Enemies (5:43-48)

Our Lord's final example of the higher righteousness demanded in His kingdom concerns the treatment of one's enemies. The law had taught the Israelites to love their neighbors and hate their enemies. In Leviticus 19:18 they were clearly commanded to love their neighbors as themselves. Though they were never explicitly told to hate their enemies, this spirit underlay much of their indoctrination. Were they not given detailed instructions about going to war (Deut. 20:1-20)? Were they not taught to exterminate the Canaanites (Deut. 7:24; 9:3)? It was a righteous hostility, directed against the enemies of God; and it justified the use of military weapons in order to kill.

But now a different day has dawned. Jesus announces that we are to love our enemies and pray for our persecutors. The fact that love is commanded shows that it is a matter of the will and not primarily of the emotions. Obviously it is not the same

> *We are to love our enemies and pray for our persecutors.*

as natural affection, because it is not natural to love those who hate and harm you. It is a supernatural grace and can be manifested only by those who have divine life.

Jesus said that His followers should return good for evil so that they might be sons of their Father in heaven. He did not mean that this is the way by which we *become* sons of God; that can take place only by spiritual birth. Rather, He meant that this is how we *demonstrate* we are sons of God. We demonstrate that we are His sons by behaving like Him. He sends the sun and the rain on the just and unjust alike, so we should deal graciously with all. There is no reward for loving those who love us. Unconverted tax-collectors do that. It does not require divine power. Nor is there any virtue in greeting our relatives and friends. Pagans can do that; there is nothing distinctively Christian about it. If our standards are no higher than the heathen's, it is certain that we will never make an impact on the world.

The Lord closes this section with the admonition, "Therefore you shall be perfect, just as your Father in heaven is perfect." The word "perfect" here must be understood in light of the context. It does not mean sinless or flawless. The previous verses explain that to be perfect means to love those who hate us, to pray for those who persecute us, and to show kindness to both friend and foe. Perfection here is that spiritual maturity which enables a Christian to imitate God in dispensing blessing to the just and to the unjust without partiality.

4

MATTHEW 6–7

Don't Parade Your Piety (6:1)

In verse 1 Jesus warns against the temptation to parade our piety—that is, to perform deeds of righteousness just to be seen by others. It is not the deed He condemns but the motive. If public notice is the motive, then it is also the only reward, because God will not reward hypocrisy.

In the verses that follow, three areas are specified where practical righteousness must be done with a pure motive:

Giving (vv. 2-4)	→	Manward
Prayer (vv. 5-15)	→	Godward
Fasting (vv. 16-18)	→	Selfward

Don't Trumpet Your Giving (6:2-4)

It seems incredible to us that people of Jesus' day noisily attracted attention to themselves as they were about to leave an offering in the synagogue or give a handout to beggars on the street. How the Lord must have despised it! He dismissed their conduct with the terse comment "they have their reward," that is, they gain a reputation among men as being generous and that is their reward.

To not let your left hand know what your right hand is doing means that our good works should be done for God and not to gain fame. The passage should not be pressed to forbid any gift that might be seen by men. It is virtually impossible to make all one's contributions strictly anonymous, what with government requirements concerning receipts for income tax purposes, etc. But it certainly does condemn the practice of giving in order to have one's name inscribed on a bronze plaque or on a list of donors.

The name "Father" is found ten times in the first eighteen verses of this chapter and is the key to understanding them. Practical deeds of righteousness should be done for Him, not for man's approval. Only then will He reward them.

Don't Pray for Publicity's Sake (6:5-6)

Next, Jesus warns His disciples against hypocrisy in prayer. They should not purposely position themselves in public areas, either religious or secular, so that others will see them praying and be impressed by it. If the motive of prayer is to satisfy the love of prominence, then the prominence gained is its only reward.

> Practical deeds of righteousness should be done for God, not for man's approval.

In verse 6 the personal pronoun changes to the singular (in verses 5 and 7 the "you" is plural). The emphasis is on personal, private communion with God. If our real motive is to get through to God, He will hear and answer. The point is not *where* we pray; Paul taught that the men should pray "in every place" (1 Tim. 2:8). The point is *why* we pray—to be seen of men or to be heard by God?

A commentator named Eucker says that "the greatest danger to religion is that the old self-life, after being put out by repentance and renunciation, comes back again and takes over new forms in the service of the old self. The old self becomes religious."

Don't Pray Empty Phrases (6:7-15)

Prayer should not be the unthinking repetition of certain stock sentences or empty phrases. God is not impressed by many words, however articulate or religious they might be. He wants to hear the sincere expressions of our heart. We have a Father who knows what we need before we ask Him. So if that is so, why should we pray at all? The reason is that in prayer we acknowledge our need and our dependence on Him. In prayer we commune with Him. And in prayer we grow in faith.

In verses 9 to 13 we have what is generally termed The Lord's Prayer. In using this title, however, we should always remember that Jesus never prayed it Himself; as the sinless One it was neither necessary nor appropriate for Him to pray for forgiveness (v. 12). This was given as a prayer for His disciples.

It was given as a pattern for prayer. It seems clear from verse 7 that our Lord did not intend these exact words to be repeated by rote; they would then become empty phrases. Rather He intended this to be a suggested outline as to the form or order our prayers should take.

Our Father in heaven. Prayer should be addressed to God, the Father, and should acknowledge Him as the enthroned Sovereign of the universe. In Ephesians 2:18 we further learn that prayer is *to* the Father, *through* the Son, and *in* the Spirit.

Hallowed be Your name. This teaches us that we should begin our prayers with worship, ascribing praise and honor to Him who is so worthy of it.

> **We should begin our prayers with worship.**

Your kingdom come. After worship, we should pray for the advancement of God's cause. We should put His interests first. Specifically, we should pray for the day when our Savior-God, the Lord Jesus, will set up His kingdom on earth and reign in righteousness.

Your will be done. In this petition we acknowledge that God knows what is best and that we surrender our own will to His. It also expresses a longing to see His will acknowledged throughout the world.

On earth as it is in heaven. This phrase modifies all the three preceding petitions. His name is hallowed in heaven. He is undisputed King in heaven. His will is done-perfectly in heaven. The prayer is that all these conditions might exist on earth as they do in heaven.

Give us this day our daily bread. After putting God's interests first, we are permitted to present our own needs. This petition acknowledges our dependence on God for the supply of our daily food, both spiritual and physical.

> "This seems a very small thing to ask—only bread for a day. Why are we not taught to pray for bread enough to last a week, or a month, or a year? For one thing, Jesus wanted to teach us a lesson of continual dependence. He taught us to come each morning with a request simply for the day's food, that we might never feel we can get along without our Father. Another lesson he wanted to teach us was that the true way to live is by the day. We are not to be anxious

even about the supply of tomorrow's needs. When tomorrow comes it will be right for us to take up its cares. The same great lesson was taught in the way the manna was given-just a day's portion at a time." (J. R. Miller)

And forgive us our debts, as we forgive our debtors. This obviously does not refer to *judicial* forgiveness from the penalty of sin, because that type of forgiveness is obtained by placing faith in Christ on a once-for-all basis. Rather, this refers to *parental* forgiveness, which is necessary if fellowship with our Father is to be maintained. If believers are unwilling to forgive their debtors, how can they expect to be in fellowship with their Father who has freely forgiven them all their debts? To be in fellowship with a person implies similarity of interests and attitudes. God's forgiving spirit must be manifest in those who would live in happy fellowship with Him.

> ———— ✺ ————
> **Parental forgiveness is necessary if fellowship with our Father is to be maintained.**
> ———— ✺ ————

And do not lead us into temptation. This request has proved puzzling to many because they know that God would never tempt anyone to sin (James 1:13). That is true, but it is also true that God does allow His people to be tested and tried. And this petition expresses a healthy distrust of one's own ability to resist temptation or to stand up under trial. It acknowledges complete dependence on the Lord for preservation. While the words in themselves might present theological problems, they are tremendously meaningful to all who are conscious of their own frailty.

But deliver us from the evil one. This is the prayer of all who desperately desire to be kept from sin by the mighty power of God. It is the heart's cry for daily salvation from the power of sin in the life.

Verses 14 and 15 serve as sort of an explanatory footnote to verse 12. They are not part of the prayer but explain and emphasize that the parental forgiveness mentioned in verse 12 is conditional. They do not have anything to do with the divine Judge's forgiveness of a sinner from the penalty of sin. They deal with the forgiveness which God the Father grants to sons in His family. This family forgiveness depends on our willingness to forgive one another.

Before leaving the pattern prayer, we should mention that the Lord Jesus later amended it somewhat. In John 16:23-27, He reminded the disciples that up till that point in time they had prayed to God, but that from then on they would pray to God in His (Jesus') name and authority.

Don't Fast to Impress (6:16-18)

The third form of religious pretense which Jesus denounced was the deliberate attempt to create the appearance of fasting. The hypocrites disfigured their faces when they fasted in order to look sad, haggard, and serious. It was a ridiculous attempt to appear holy.

True believers should fast in secret, giving no outward appearance of it. To anoint the head and wash the face means to give the appearance of normal life. It is enough that God knows the exercise of soul we are experiencing; His reward will be better than people's approval.

To fast is to abstain from gratifying any physical appetite. It may be voluntary, as in this passage, or involuntary, as in Matthew 15:32 and other passages (Acts 27:33; 2 Cor. 6:5; 11:27). In the New Testament, it is associated with mourning (Matt. 9:14, 15; Mark 2:18-20; Luke 5:33-35) and prayer (Luke 2:37; Acts 13:2-3; 14:23). In these passages it appears that fasting accompanied prayer as an acknowledgment of deep earnestness in discerning the will of God and of a solemn awareness of the responsibility of obeying His guidance.

> "The exercise of fasting stands in immediate connection with prayer, and we think the connection is most instructive. Fasting implies abstention from things natural and earthly; prayer implies occupation with things spiritual and heavenly. The former closes the channel of communications between nature and the scene around; the latter opens the channel between the spiritual man and the scene above." (C. H. Mackintosh)

Fasting has no merit as far as salvation is concerned, or as far as giving a person standing before God. A Pharisee once boasted that he fasted twice a week (Luke 18:12) but it failed to make him right with God (v. 14). But when a Christian fasts secretly as a spiritual exercise, God sees and rewards him. So while fasting is not clearly commanded in the New Testament, it is encouraged by the promise of reward.

The practice of fasting can help one's prayer life, delivering him from dullness and drowsiness. It can help the preacher, promoting clarity and alertness. It is valuable at special times of crises when one wishes to discern the will of God. It is generally agreed to be good for one's physical well-being (if not carried to excess). And it is of value in promoting self-discipline—which most of us need. It is largely a matter of one's individual exercise of soul before God, and, as with everything else in the Christian life, it should be done to the glory of God and with a desire to please Him and to serve Him more effectively. It loses its value when it is imposed legalistically or done to impress.

Where Is Your Treasure? (6:19-21)

We come now to some of the most revolutionary teachings of our Lord—and therefore some of the most neglected. The rest of the chapter deals with a simple theme, namely, security for the future and how to find it.

In verses 19-21 Jesus completely reverses every known plan for insuring a secure future financially. He clearly says, "Do not lay up for yourselves treasures on earth, where moth and rust destroy and where thieves break in and steal." His words cut across everything we have been taught to be prudent and practical. Almost any insurance agent or investment counselor will tell you that the only way to be sure of your future is to adopt some lay-away plan now.

> The only investments that are not subject to loss are the treasures laid up in heaven.

Jesus says that the only investments that are not subject to loss are treasures laid up in heaven. Inflation cannot affect them there. Nor is there danger of theft, corrosion, or corruption. Then He adds the underlying reason for this radical investment policy: "Where your treasure is, there your heart will be also." If your treasures are in a safe-deposit box, your heart will be there. If your treasures are in heaven, your interests will be centered there. Each of us must decide if Jesus meant what He said. If He did, then we face the question, "What are we going to do with our earthly treasures?" If He didn't, then we face the question, "What are we going to do with our Bible?"

How Is Your Vision? (6:22-23)

Jesus realized that it would be difficult for His followers to see how His unconventional teaching on security for the future could possibly work, so He used the human eye to teach a lesson on *spiritual* sight.

He stated first that the eye is the lamp of the body. In other words, it is through the eye that the body receives its illumination and can see things as they are. If the eye is healthy, the whole body is flooded with illumination; that is, a person can see things in their proper perspective. But if the eye is diseased or damaged, then vision is impaired. Instead of light, there is darkness.

The spiritual application is this: the healthy eye belongs to the man whose motives are pure, who has a simple desire for God's interests, and who is willing to accept Christ's teachings literally. His whole life is flooded with illumination. He believes Jesus' words, forsakes earthly riches, lays up his treasures in heaven, and then sees that this is the only true security.

The man with the diseased eye has double vision. He is trying to live for two worlds. He doesn't want to let go of his earthly treasures, yet he wants treasures in heaven too. The teachings of Jesus seem impractical and impossible to him. He cannot see their wisdom. He lacks clear guidance; the whole subject is darkness to him.

In the latter part of verse 23 Jesus said, "If the light that is in you is darkness, how great is that darkness!" In other words, if you know that Christ forbids trusting earthly treasures for security, yet you go ahead and do it anyway, the teaching you have failed to obey becomes darkness—a very intense form of spiritual blindness. You cannot see riches in their true perspective.

Who Is Your Master? (6:24)

The impossibility of living for God and for money is stated here in terms of masters and slave. No man can serve two masters. One will inevitably take precedence in his loyalty and obedience. So it is with God and mammon. They present rival claims to every man, and a choice must be made. Either we must put God first and reject the rule of materialism or we must live for temporal things and refuse God's claims on our lives.

What Is Your Goal? (6:25-34)

In this passage the Lord Jesus hits out at the common tendency to make life revolve around food and clothing and thus miss its real meaning. And the problem is not so much what we shall eat and wear *today,* but ten, twenty, or thirty years from now. We worry about the future. This worry drives us to devote our finest energies to making sure we will have enough to live on. Then before we know it, our lives have passed and we have missed the central purpose for which we were made. Such worry is sin for, as someone has said, it denies the love of God by implying that He doesn't care for us; it denies the wisdom of God by implying that He doesn't know what He's doing; and it denies the power of God by implying that He isn't able to provide for us.

> Our bodies are intended to be our servants, not our masters.

And such worry completely overlooks the fact that life is more than food, and the body than clothing. Did God create us in His own image and likeness with no higher destiny than that we should consume food? Were our bodies made to be nothing more than clotheshorses? We are here for bigger business than that. We are here to worship, love, and serve Him and to represent His interests. Our bodies are intended to be our servants, not our masters.

The birds illustrate God's care for His creature's food. They preach to us silently how unnecessary it is for us to worry. Jesus said that "they neither sow nor reap nor gather into barns, yet your heavenly Father feeds them. Are you not of more value than they?" We should not infer from this that we need not work for the supply of our present needs. The Lord's dictum on this is, "If any one will not work, let him not eat" (2 Thess. 3:10). And actually, the birds have to scratch around for their daily food. Neither should we infer that it is wrong for a farmer to sow, reap, and gather his crops. Up to a point, that is a necessary part of his providing for his current necessities. What the Bible forbids is the multiplication of barns and silos in an attempt to provide future security in independence of God. This practice is condemned in the Lord's story of the rich farmer (Luke 12:16-21).

The argument is that if God takes care of creatures of a lower order *without* their conscious participation, He will all the more take care of those for whom creation took place *with* their active participation.

The main lessons that emerge from verse 26 are that:

1. In His ordering of the universe, the Lord provides food for the birds on a day by day basis. No matter how tiny or insignificant they are, they do not have to build barns in order to be sure of food a year ahead.

2. If God cares for the birds so much, how much more does He care for His children. Therefore, how irrational it is for us to make the future our concern.

Worry about the future is not only irrational and dishonoring to God; it is also pointless. The Lord demonstrates this with a question, "Which of you by worrying can add one cubit to his stature?" In the companion passage in Luke 12:25-26 He adds the question, "If you then are not able to do the least, why are you anxious about the rest?" A short person cannot worry himself eighteen inches taller, and a dying person cannot add eighteen minutes to the length of his life by being anxious about it. Yet relatively speaking it would be a lot easier to perform either of these feats than it would to anxiously provide in advance for all possible future needs.

Next, the Lord dealt with the unreasonableness of worrying that we will not have enough clothes in the future. In this area, the flowers teach us a lesson on trust. The lilies of the field (probably wild anemones) never work, yet their beauty surpasses that of Solomon's royal garments. The closer we inspect them, the more beautiful they appear. The point is that God clothes flowers which have a very brief existence and are then used as fuel in the baking oven. If He can provide such elegant covering for short-lived wild-flowers, He will certainly care more for His people who worship and serve Him and who are destined to live with Him forever.

> **We should not spend our lives in anxious pursuit of sufficient food, drink, and clothing for the future.**

The conclusion is that we should not spend our lives in anxious pursuit of sufficient food, drink, and clothing for the future. That is not our business. The unconverted Gentiles spend their lives in the mad accumulation of material things. They live as if food, drink, and clothing were all of life. All their activities revolve around these three things. But it should not be so with the Christian. He has a heavenly Father who knows that He has these basic needs.

If a disciple were responsible to provide in advance for his future needs, then all his time and energy would have to be devoted to amassing financial reserves. He could never be sure that he had saved enough, because there is always the danger of market collapse, inflation, catastrophe, prolonged illness, paralyzing accident, etc. All of life would be spent in laying up treasures on earth because there is no answer to the nagging question, "How much is enough?" And this means, of course, that God would be robbed of the service of His people. The real purpose for which they were created and converted would be missed. Men and women bearing the divine image would be living for an uncertain future on this earth when they should be living with eternity's values in view. There would be little or no time for Christian service.

The Lord, therefore, makes a tremendously important covenant with His followers in verse 33. He says in effect, "If you will put God's interests first in your life, I will guarantee your future needs. If you seek first the kingdom of God and His righteousness, I will see that you will never lack the necessities of life."

It is God's revolutionary social security program. The believer's responsibility is to live first and foremost for the Lord, at the same time working to provide for his current needs and those of his family. His calling is to be an ambassador of Jesus Christ; his job is a means of providing bread and butter. He invests everything above current needs in the work of the Lord and trusts God for the future with unshakable confidence that the Lord will provide. In the final analysis, God is the believer's only security anyway. This being the case, the believer should walk by faith in Him rather than in material stockpiles.

Because of God's covenant to care for the future needs of those who put Him first in life, there is no need to worry about tomorrow (v. 34). We are called to live a day at a time. Let tomorrow worry about itself. And let the day's own troubles be enough for the day. In other words, live every day to the hilt for God. Face the problems and challenges as they come. And leave the future in the hands of the One who controls it.

Do Not Judge (7:1-5)

We should notice that this section about judging others comes immediately after our Lord's provocative teaching concerning earthly riches. There is an important connection. Those who accept His words and seek to obey them literally are inclined to be critical of wealthy Christians. On the other hand, those who feel it to be their Christian duty to provide for the future needs of themselves and their families tend to be critical of those who give up everything to follow Jesus. Such censoring is out of order. The Lord calls all His people to a life of faith. Some venture timidly into this life. Others walk with moderation. Still others march confidently. No one lives completely by faith. The principle is, "According to your faith be it unto you." No matter how much we may live by faith we still have to say, "We are unprofitable servants." And yet the more we rest on the promises of God, the more rewarding it is. As someone has said, "Once you start walking on water, you never want to ride in a boat again."

There are several areas in the Christian life where judging of others is forbidden:

1. It goes without saying that we should not judge motives; only God can read them.

2. We should not judge by outward appearances or show respect of persons (John 7:24; James 2:1).

3. We should not judge others who have a conscience about matters that are not in themselves right or wrong (Rom. 14:3-13).

4. We should not judge the service of another Christian (1 Cor. 4:1-5).

5. We shouldn't judge a brother by speaking evil against him (James 4:11-12) or murmuring against him (James 5:9).

In general the Lord forbids the habit of finding fault with others, of being harsh, critical, and judgmental. Sometimes these words of our Lord are used by people to ban all forms of judging. No matter what happens, they piously say, "Well, we mustn't judge."

> ❧
>
> **The Lord forbids the habit of finding faults with others.**
>
> ❧

It is as if we should throw away our moral and spiritual standards and our powers of discernment. The truth is that there are many areas in which Christians are *commanded* to judge. For example:

1. When disputes arise between believers, they should be settled in the church and not taken to a civil court (1 Cor. 6:1-8).

2. The local church is required to judge certain forms of sin and to excommunicate the guilty offender (Matt. 18:17; 1 Cor. 5:9-13).

3. Believers are required to judge the doctrinal teaching of preachers (Matt. 7:15-20; 1 Cor. 14:29; 1 John 4:1). The standard by which they judge it, of course, is the Word of God.

4. Christians must judge whether other people are truly born again. The command, "Do not be unequally yoked together with unbelievers" (2 Cor. 6:14), requires such judgment.

5. Those in the church must judge which men have the qualifications of elders and of deacons (1 Tim. 3:1-13).

6. We have to judge those who are lazy, fainthearted, weak, and disobedient, and treat them as directed in the Word (1 Thess. 5:14; 2 Thess. 3:14).

Therefore in His warning against judging, Jesus did not intend that we should abandon our critical faculty. The New Testament has many illustrations of legitimate judgment of the condition, conduct, and teaching of others. In making such judgments, the scriptural principle is that charges must be confirmed by the testimony of two or three witnesses (Matt. 18:16).

In verse 2, Jesus warned that unrighteous judgment would be repaid in kind. This principle of reaping what we sow is built into all human life and affairs. We shall be measured by our own yardstick. In Mark 4:24 the principle is applied to our appropriation of the Word, and in Luke 6:38 to our liberality.

> We must remedy our own faults before criticizing them in others.

Then the Savior exposed the natural tendency to see a small fault in someone else and not to see the same fault in ourselves, even though we may have it to a much greater degree. He used a figure of speech known as *hyperbole* (pronounced hy-per-bo-lee) in which a statement is purposely exaggerated in order to drive home the point. A man with a log in his own eye often finds fault with a speck in another person's eye and doesn't even notice the log in his own eye. Certainly he is in a very poor position to help the man with a speck while a log is protruding from his own, which means, of course, that we cannot help someone else with a personal fault if we ourselves have that fault to a greater extent. We must remedy our own faults before criticizing them in others.

Do Judge (7:6)

This verse proves that Jesus did not intend to forbid *all* kinds of judging. He here warned the disciples not to give holy things to dogs or throw pearls before swine. Under the Mosaic law, dogs and pigs were unclean animals. Here they obviously depict wicked men. In a broad sense we are obligated to share the gospel with all people, even if they do not want to hear us. The fact that they may neglect it or reject it for a while need not put us off. But there is a class of vicious, "unclean" men who treat divine truths with utter contempt. If we continue to set the claims of Christ before them, they respond with abuse and violence. In such cases we are not obligated to continue. We have discharged our responsibility. To press the matter only brings vile contempt to the Word of God, needless harm to ourselves, and increased condemnation to the offenders.

Needless to say, it requires spiritual perception to discern these people. Perhaps that is why the next verses take up the subject of prayer, by which we can ask for wisdom.

———— ❧ ————

Wisdom and power for the Christian life will be given to all who earnestly and persistently pray for it.

———— ❧ ————

Ask, Seek, Knock (7:7-11)

If we think we can live the Sermon on the Mount in our own strength, then obviously we have failed to realize the supernatural character of the life to which Jesus calls us. We do not have the wisdom or power for such a life; it must be given to us from above. And so here we have an invitation to keep pursuing it. Wisdom and power for the Christian life will be given to all who earnestly and persistently pray for it (vv. 7-8).

Taken out of context, these verses might seem like a blank check for believers—in other words, we can get anything we ask for. This is not true. The verses must be understood in their context. Here, they guarantee the adequate dynamics for obeying Christ's words, but they must be understood in the light of all the other verses in the Bible dealing with prayer. What seem to be unqualified promises concerning prayer are actually qualified in other passages. For instance, the person praying must have no unconfessed sin in his life (Ps. 66:18). He must pray in faith (James 1:6-8). He must pray in conformity with the will of God (1 John 5:14-15). He must pray sincerely (Heb. 10:22a). He must persevere in prayer (Luke 11:5-10; 18:1-8).

When the conditions for prayer are met, the Christian can have complete confidence that God will hear and answer. This assurance is based on the character of God our Father. On the human level, we know that if a son asks his father for bread, he will not give him a stone. The loaves in Bible times were small, flat and brownish-gray; they closely resembled stones. To give a stone for a loaf would be to deceive. If an earthly father would not deceive a hungry son, it is unthinkable that our heavenly Father would do so. We know also that a father would not give a serpent for a fish. The fish provides wholesome nourishment, whereas the serpent inflicts pain and perhaps death. So God will never give us anything that would be harmful or cause needless pain.

> *God will never give us anything that would be harmful or cause needless pain.*

The Lord Jesus argues from the lesser to the greater. If sinful men reward their children's requests with what is best for them, how much more will our heavenly Father do so?

In the parallel passage in Luke, Jesus said, "How much more will your heavenly Father give the Holy Spirit to those who ask Him!" (11:13). In one sense, this promise was fulfilled at Pentecost when the Holy Spirit was given; now, all believers are indwelt by the Holy Spirit. But in another sense we need to pray continually for the *power* of the Holy Spirit to live out the teachings of Christ through us.

The Golden Rule (7:12)

The immediate connection of this verse with the preceding seems to be this: our Father is a Giver of good things to us. We should imitate Him in showing kindness to others. The way to test whether an action is good is whether we would want to receive it ourselves.

Other religious leaders had given a similar ethic in negative form. They said, "Do not do to others what you would not want them to do to you." But our Lord's words go beyond passive restraint to active benevolence. Christianity is not simply a matter of abstaining from sin; it is positive goodness.

Jesus added that this so-called Golden Rule "is the law and the Prophets," that is, it expresses in condensed form all the moral teachings of the law and the Prophets. The righteousness demanded by the Old Testament Scriptures is fulfilled in those born-again believers who thus walk according to the Spirit (Rom. 8:4). This is probably one of the most revolutionary verses in the Bible. If it were universally obeyed, think what the results would be in international relations, in labor-management negotiations, in family life, in the church, and in every other sphere of life!

Two Gates and Two Ways (7:13-14)

Now the Lord Jesus forewarns His followers that the gate of Christian discipleship is a narrow one and the road is hard. But those who faithfully follow His teachings find the abundant life. On the other hand, there is the wide gate and the easy way—the life of self-indulgence and pleasure. The end of such a life is destruction. Here it is not a question of losing one's soul but of failure to live out the purpose of one's existence.

Of course, these verses also have a gospel application. They depict the two roads and two destinies of the human race. There is the wide gate and the broad road that leads to destruction (Prov. 16:25); it is a popular, well-traveled highway. Then there is the narrow gate and way that leads to life; the Lord Jesus is both the gate and the way (John 10:9; 14:6). Relatively few take Him as the way to heaven. People are born on the broad way; they can transfer to the narrow way only by the new birth. But while this is a valid *application* of the passage, the *interpretation* seems to be for those who are already believers. Jesus is saying, in effect: "To follow Me will require discipline, perseverance, self-denial, faith, and endurance. But this is the only life worth living. If you choose the easy way through life, you will have plenty of company, but you will miss God's best for you." The passage does not deal primarily with the salvation of the soul but with the salvation of one's life.

False Prophets (7:15-20)

Wherever the stern demands of true discipleship are taught, there are false prophets who advise the wide gate and the easy way. They water down the truth until, as Spurgeon said, "There is not enough left to make soup for a sick grasshopper." Jesus warns His disciples against these men who profess to be God's mouthpieces. They come in sheep's clothing; that is, they give the outward appearance of being true believers. But inwardly they are ravening wolves; that is, they are vicious unbelievers who prey on the immature, the unstable, and the naive.

Verses 16-20 deal with the detection and doom of false prophets: "You will know them by their fruits." The lives and teachings of these men betray them. A tree or plant produces fruit in accordance with its own character. For instance, a thorn bush cannot bear grapes, and a thistle cannot produce figs. Thorns and thistles picture the curse of God on man because of sin (Gen. 3:18); grapes and figs are clean food for man's nourishment and welfare. A healthy tree bears good fruit, whereas an unsound tree bears corrupt fruit. This principle is never violated in nature (v. 18) or in the spiritual realm. The corrupt tree bearing corrupt fruit is cut down and burned. The doom of the false teachers is "swift destruction" (2 Peter 2:1).

The life and teachings of those who claim to speak for God should be tested according to the Word of God: "To the law and to the testimony! If they do not speak according to this word, it is because there is no light in them" (Isa. 8:20). "Thus you will know them by their fruits" (v. 20).

False Professors (7:21-23)

Next, the Lord Jesus warns against those who claim to acknowledge Him as Lord but who have never been genuinely converted. Mere profession is not enough; there must be the outward manifestation of the new birth in obeying the will of God. Not everyone who calls Him Lord will enter into the kingdom of heaven in its inner reality; they are in the kingdom as far as outward profession is concerned, but are not true subjects of the King. (See notes on the kingdom, ch. 3:2.) Only those who do the will of God enter that kingdom. The first step in doing the will of God is believing on the Lord Jesus (John 6:29).

> The first step in doing the will of God is believing on the Lord Jesus.

In that coming day when unbelievers will stand before Christ for judgment (Rev. 20:11-15), many will remind Him that they prophesied, cast out demons, and did mighty miracles, all in His name. But they will protest in vain. He will remind them that He never knew them with favor or acknowledged them as His own. We should learn from this verse that not all miracles are of divine origin and that not all miracle workers are divinely accredited. A miracle simply means that a supernatural power is at work. That power may be divine or it may be satanic.

Wise and Foolish Builders (7:24-27)

Jesus closes His sermon with a parable that drives home the importance of obedience. It is not enough to hear His words; we must put them into practice. First He speaks of a wise man who built his house upon rock (having dug down to rock, see Luke 6:48). The house was battered from every direction by a storm but it stood firmly. Then there was the foolish man who built his house on a foundation of sand (just on the ground, the surface, see Luke 6:49). When the storm came, the house collapsed because it had no solid base.

We are not left to guess the identity of the wise man. It is the disciple who not only hears these teachings (chapters 5-7) but does them (v. 24). His life has a solid foundation. When the inevitable trials come from all directions, he is able to endure because his life is firmly grounded.

The foolish man is the disciple who hears Christ's teachings but instead of practicing them lives like the rest of the people around him. This man will not be able to stand against the storms of adversity. He buckles under the severe stresses of life. Though he may be saved as far as his soul is concerned, his life is wasted, his testimony is zero, and he suffers loss of reward at the judgment seat of Christ.

"The eternal salvation of the builder is not the issue. The lesson is this: That every man . . . is spending his life—his time, strength, and means—in building a life structure, a character, an exhibition of himself; and this product of his energy will be severely tested, as a building, by a tempest. If it stands the test, the builder will have permanent advantage from his life-work; if it collapses, he will find that he has lived and toiled in vain." (G. H. Lang)

If a man lives according to the principles of the Sermon on the Mount, the world calls him a fool; Jesus calls him a wise man. The world considers a wise man to be one who lives by sight, who lives for now, and who lives for self; Jesus calls such a man a fool.

It is legitimate to use the wise and foolish builders to illustrate the gospel. The wise man puts his full confidence in the Rock, Christ Jesus, as Lord and Savior. The foolish man refuses to repent and rejects Jesus as his only hope for salvation. But the interpretation of the parable actually carries us beyond salvation to its practical outworking in the Christian life.

Astonishment! (7:28-29)

When Jesus concluded His message, the multitude was astonished. If we can read the Sermon on the Mount and not be astonished at its revolutionary character, then we have failed to grasp its meaning. The people recognized a difference between Jesus' teaching and that of the scribes. *He* spoke with authority; *their* words were powerless. His was a voice; theirs was an echo.

5

MATTHEW 8–9

Beginning with chapter 8 and continuing through chapter 12, we find the Lord Jesus presenting conclusive evidence to the nation of Israel that He was indeed the Messiah of whom the prophets had written. Isaiah, for instance, had foretold that the Messiah would open the eyes of the blind, unstop the ears of the deaf, cause the lame man to leap like a deer, and make the tongue of the dumb to sing (Isa. 35:5-6). Jesus fulfilled all these prophecies. Israel, therefore, should have had no difficulty in identifying Him as the Christ—but none are so blind as they that will not see.

The events recorded in these chapters are not necessarily in chronological order; the order is moral rather than chronological. What's more, this is not a complete account of the Lord's ministry, but isolated events selected by the Holy Spirit as representative of Christ's miracles.

There are certain threads to look for:

➤ Christ's absolute authority over disease, demons, death, and the elements.

➤ His claim to absolute lordship in the lives of those who would follow Him.

➤ The mounting rejection of Jesus by the nation of Israel, particularly by the religious leaders.

➤ The ready reception of the Savior by individual Gentiles.

Power Over Leprosy (8:1-4)

Although the teaching of the Lord Jesus was radical, it had a drawing power—so much so that great crowds followed Him. Truth is self-verifying; and though men may not like it, they can never forget it.

A Jewish leper knelt before Jesus with a desperate appeal for healing. Leprosy is an appropriate "type" of sin because it is loathsome, destructive, easily transmitted, and, in some forms, humanly incurable. (Certain forms of leprosy mentioned in the Bible are not the same as the leprosy now known as Hansen's disease.) This leper had faith that the Lord could cure him, and such faith is never disappointed.

Lepers were untouchables. Physical contact with them might expose a person to infection. And in the case of the Jews, it made a person ceremonially unclean—that is, unfit to worship with the congregation of Israel. But when Jesus touched the leper and spoke the healing words, the leprosy vanished instantly. He has power to cleanse from sin and to qualify the cleansed person to be a worshiper.

Jesus commanded the leper to tell no one. There were at least two reasons for this:

1. The man must first go to the priest, as the law directed. There should be no delay in obeying what God says.

2. The Lord was aware of the danger of a popular movement to make Him king by a people who were interested only in deliverance from Roman control. The Jews were ready to revolt. This would only result in needless bloodshed, and Jesus would not be party to it. He knew that Israel was unrepentant, that the nation would reject His spiritual leadership, and that He must first go to the cross.

Under the law of Moses, the priest also served as a physician. When a leper was cured, he was obligated to appear before the priest in order to be pronounced clean. He was also ordered to bring an offering (Lev. 14:4-6, 10). It was probably a very rare event for a leper to be healed. In fact it was so rare that it should have alerted this priest, causing him to investigate further whether the Messiah had appeared at last. But we do not read of any such reaction.

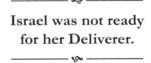

Israel was not ready for her Deliverer.

The spiritual implications of the miracle are clear. The Messiah had come to Israel with power to heal the nation of its "leprosy." He presented this miracle as one credential. But the priest and the people were insensitive to His presence in their midst. Israel was not ready for her Deliverer.

Power Over Paralysis (8:5-13)

The faith of a Gentile centurion is now introduced in striking contrast to the unreceptive attitude of the Jews. If Israel will not welcome her King, the despised pagans will acknowledge Him. The centurion was a Roman military officer in charge of about one hundred men, and was stationed in or near Capernaum. He came to Jesus to seek healing for his servant who had suffered a violent and painful attack of paralysis. This was an unusual display of compassion—most officials of that day would not show such concern for a servant boy.

When the Lord Jesus offered to visit the sick boy, the centurion showed the reality and depth of his faith. He said, in effect, "I am not worthy that you should enter my house. And anyway, it isn't necessary, because you could just as easily heal him by saying the word. I know something about authority and obedience to authority. I take orders from my superiors, and I give orders to those under me. My commands are obeyed implicitly. How much more would your words have power over the illness that now afflicts my servant!"

Jesus marveled at the faith of this Gentile centurion. This is one of two times when Jesus is said to have marveled (the other time being when He marveled at the unbelief of the

> The reward of faith is proportionate to its confidence in the character of God.

Jews [Mark 6:6]). He had not found such faith among God's chosen people, Israel. This led Him to point out that in His coming kingdom, Gentiles would flock from all over the world to enjoy fellowship with the Jewish patriarchs, while the sons of the kingdom would be thrown into the outer darkness. "Sons of the kingdom" are those who were Jews by birth who professed to acknowledge God as their King but who were never truly converted. But the principle applies today as well. Many children who are privileged to be born and raised in Christian families will perish in hell because they reject Christ, while jungle savages will enjoy the eternal glories of heaven because they believed the gospel message when they first heard it.

Jesus said to the centurion, "Go your way; and as you have believed, so let it be done for you" (v. 13). The reward of faith is proportionate to its confidence in the character of God. The servant was instantly healed, even though Jesus was some distance away.

We may see in this a picture of Christ's present ministry: healing the non-privileged Gentiles from the paralysis of sin, even though He Himself is not bodily present.

Power Over Fever (8:14-15)

Entering Peter's house, Jesus found his mother-in-law sick with a fever. As soon as He touched her, the fever vanished. Usually fever leaves a person greatly weakened, but this cure was so instantaneous and complete that she was able to get out of bed and serve Him. This was a fitting expression of gratitude for what Jesus had done for her. We should imitate her, whenever we are healed, by serving Him with renewed dedication and vigor.

Power Over Demons and Various Sicknesses (8:16-17)

At evening, when the Sabbath was over (see Mark 1:21-34), the people surged to Him with many victims of demon-possession. These pathetic individuals often exhibited superhuman knowledge and power; at other times they were tortured and tormented. Their behavior sometimes resembled that of insane persons, but the cause was demonic rather than physical or mental. Jesus drove the demons out with a word.

He also healed all that were sick, fulfilling the prophecy of Isaiah (53:4): "He Himself took our infirmities and bore our diseases" (v. 17). This verse is often used by faith-healers to show that healing is in the atonement, and that therefore physical healing is something the believer can claim by faith. 4. But here the Spirit of God applies the prophecy to our Savior's earthly healing ministry and not to His work on the cross.

The Miracle of Human Refusal (8:18-22)

We have seen Christ exercising authority over disease and demons. It is only when He comes in contact with men and women that He meets with resistance. Here we have the miracle of human refusal.

As Jesus prepared to cross the Sea of Galilee from Capernaum to the east side, a self-confident scribe stepped forward with a voluntary pledge to follow Him "all the way." The Lord's answer challenged him to count the cost; it would mean a life of self-denial. In His public ministry, He did not have a home of His own; however, there were homes where He was a

MATTHEW 8–9 ❖ 67

welcome guest and, in the physical sense, He usually had a place to sleep. The true force of His words seems to be spiritual: this world could not provide Him with true, lasting rest. He had a work to do and He could not rest until it was accomplished. The same is true of those who would be His followers; this world is not their resting place—or at least, it shouldn't be.

Another well-meaning follower expressed a willingness to follow Him, but there was a higher priority in his life: "Lord, let me first go and bury my father." Whether the father had already died or whether his departure was still future makes little difference. The basic trouble was expressed in the contradictory words: "Lord . . . me first." He put self ahead of Christ. While it is perfectly proper to provide a decent burial for one's father, it becomes wrong when such a worthy act takes precedence over the Savior's call.

Jesus answered him, in effect, as follows: "Your first and foremost duty is to follow Me. Let the spiritually dead bury the physically dead. An unsaved person can do that kind of work just as well as you. But there is a work which you alone can do. Give the best of your life to that which is enduring. Don't waste it on trivia."

We are not told how these two disciples responded. There is a strong implication that they left Christ to make a comfortable place for themselves in the world and to spend their lives hugging the subordinate. Before we condemn them, we should test ourselves on the two terms of discipleship enunciated by Jesus in this passage.

Power Over the Elements (8:23-27)

The Sea of Galilee is noted for sudden and violent storms that whip it into a churning froth. Winds sweep down the valley of the Jordan from the north, picking up speed in the narrow gorge. When they hit the Sea, they make it extremely unsafe for navigation.

On this particular occasion, Jesus was crossing from the west side to the east. At the time the storm broke, He was asleep in the boat. The terrified disciples awoke Him with frantic pleas for help. It can be said to their credit that they went to the right Person. After rebuking them for their puny faith, He rebuked the winds and the waves. When a great calm descended, the men were amazed that even the elements obeyed their humble Passenger. How little they understood that the Creator and Sustainer of the universe was in the boat that day!

All disciples encounter "storms" sooner or later. At times it seems we are going to be swamped by the waves. What a comfort it is to know that Jesus is in the boat with us. As an old hymn puts it, "No water can swallow the ship where lies the Master of ocean and earth and skies." And no one can calm life's storms like the Lord Jesus.

"Depart from us" (8:28-34)

On the east side of the Sea of Galilee was a city called Gadara; its people were known as Gadarenes. When Jesus arrived there, He met two unusually violent cases of demon possession. These demoniacs lived in cave-like tombs and were so fierce, they made travel in that area unsafe.

As Jesus approached, the demons cried out, "What have we to do with You, Jesus, You Son of God? Have you come here to torment us before the time?" (v. 29). They knew who Jesus was, and that He would finally destroy them. In these respects their theology was more accurate than that of many modern liberals. Then, sensing that Jesus was going to cast them out of the men, they asked that they might transfer to a herd of swine feeding nearby. Strangely enough, Jesus granted their request—but why? Why should the Sovereign Lord satisfy the request of demons? To understand His action, we must remember two important facts. First, demons shun the disembodied state; they want to indwell human beings, or, if that is not possible, animals or other creatures. Second, the purpose of the demons is always to destroy; there is no exception to this rule. Now, if Jesus had simply cast them out of the maniacs, the demons would have been a menace to the other people of the area. By allowing them to go into the swine, He prevented their entering humans and confined their destructive power to animals. It was not yet time for their final destruction by the Lord.

As soon as the transfer took place, the swine ran headlong down a steep incline into the sea and drowned. This demonstrates the principle that the ultimate aim of demons is always to destroy. Also it underlines the terrifying possibility that two men can be indwelt by the number of demons it takes to destroy two thousand swine (Mark 5:13).

The herdsmen ran back into the city with news of what had happened to the pigs and to the demoniacs. The result was that some hostile citizens came out to Jesus and asked Him to leave the area. Ever since then, Jesus has been criticized for the needless slaughter of pigs and has been asked to leave because He values human life above animals. We can scarcely conceive of any person asking Jesus to go away. He had come to their coasts to bring them rich blessings. He had begun His work of grace as soon as He landed by curing their most terrible cases of demon-possession. He would have gone on performing other works of mercy and love if they had not urged Him to depart. It was all because of the loss of the pigs. If that was the way Christ's work was going to affect them, they did not want Him to go any further. Some people feel the same way when a work of grace begins in their community. They are opposed to Christianity because it interferes with their (illicit) business. Such men are against Christianity because Christianity is against them.

> ——— ❧ ———
> **Have you turned Jesus away because you value something of this world more than Him?**
> ——— ❧ ———

If these Gadarenes were Jews, then it was unlawful for them to raise pigs. But whether or not they were Jews, their condemnation is that they valued a herd of pigs more than the healing of two demoniacs. What about you? Have you turned Him away because you value something of this world more than Him?

Power to Forgive Sins (9:1-8)

Rejected by the Gadarenes, the Lord Jesus recrossed the Sea of Galilee and came to Capernaum, which is here called "his own city" (see Mark 2:1-12). This became His own city after the people of Nazareth had attempted to destroy Him (Luke 4:29-31); it was here that He performed some of His mightiest miracles.

Four men came to Him carrying a paralyzed man on a mat. Mark's account tells us that because of the crowd, they had to tear up the roof and lower the man into Jesus' presence (2:1-12). When Jesus saw their faith, He said to the paralytic, "Take heart, my son; your sins are forgiven" (v. 2). Notice that He saw *their* faith. Faith prompted the four men to bring the invalid to Jesus. And the faith of the invalid went out to Jesus for healing.

Our Lord first rewarded this faith by pronouncing his sins forgiven. Here the Great Physician removed the cause before treating the symptoms; He gave the greater blessing first. This raises the interesting question whether Christ ever healed a person physically without also imparting salvation.

As soon as the scribes heard Jesus declare the man's sins forgiven, they accused Him of blasphemy among themselves. After all, only God can forgive sins—and they were certainly not about to receive Him as God! The omniscient Lord Jesus read their thoughts, rebuked them for their evil hearts of unbelief, then asked them whether it was easier to say, "Your sins are forgiven" or "Rise and walk." Actually, it's as easy to *say* one as the other, but that's not the point. Which is easier to *do?* The fact is that both are humanly impossible. The difference between them is that the results of the first command are not visible, whereas the effects of the second are immediately discernible.

In order to show the scribes that He had authority on earth to forgive sins (and should therefore be honored as God), Jesus condescended to give them a miracle they could *see.* Turning to the paralytic, He said, "Arise, take up your bed, and go to your house."

When the crowd saw him walking home with his pallet they registered two emotions—fear and wonder. They were afraid in the presence of what was obviously a supernatural visitation. They glorified God for giving such authority to men, but they completely missed the significance of the miracle. The *visible* healing of the paralytic was designed to confirm that the man's sins had been forgiven—an *invisible* miracle. From this they should have realized that what they had witnessed was not a demonstration of God giving authority to men, but of God being present among them in the Person of the Lord Jesus Christ. They did not understand, however.

As for the scribes, we know from later events that they only became more hardened in their unbelief and hatred.

The Call of Matthew (9:9)

The tense atmosphere building up around Christ is now temporarily relieved by Matthew's simple and humble account of his own call. By occupation he had been a tax-collector, or a custom house officer. He and his fellow officials were hated by the Jewish populace because of their crookedness, because of the oppressive taxes that they exacted, and, most of all, because they served the interests of the Roman Empire, Israel's overlord.

As Jesus passed the tax office, He said to Matthew, "Follow Me." The response was instantaneous; he rose and followed. Matthew left a traditionally dishonest job to become an instant disciple of Jesus. As someone has said, "He lost a comfortable job, but he found a destiny. He lost a good income but he found honor. He lost a comfortable security, but he found an adventure the like of which he had never dreamed." Among his rewards were becoming one of the Twelve and being an instrument through whom the Holy Spirit moved to pen the gospel which bears his name.

Jesus Eats with Sinners (9:10-13)

The meal described here was arranged by Matthew in honor of Jesus (Luke 5:29). It was the converted tax-collector's way of confessing Christ publicly and of introducing his associates to the Messiah. The guests were therefore tax-collectors and others who were generally known to be sinners.

It was the practice in those days to eat reclining on couches and facing the table. When the Pharisees saw Jesus associating in this way with the social "scum," they went to His disciples and charged Him with "guilt by association." They could not imagine that any true prophet would eat with sinners. Jesus overheard and answered, "Those who are well have no need of a physician, but those who are sick. The Pharisees considered they were "healthy" and were unwilling to confess their need for Jesus. (Actually they were extremely ill spiritually and desperately needed healing.) The tax collectors and sinners, by contrast, were more willing to acknowledge their true condition and to seek Christ's saving grace.

> God is not pleased with rituals that are divorced from personal godliness.

So the charge was true! Jesus did eat with sinners. If He had eaten with the Pharisees, the charge would still have been true—perhaps even more so. If Jesus hadn't eaten with sinners in a world like ours, He would always have eaten alone. But it is important to remember that when He ate with sinners, He never indulged in their evil ways or compromised His testimony for God. He used the occasion to call people to truth and holiness.

The trouble with the Pharisees was that although they followed the prescribed rituals of Judaism very carefully, their hearts were hard, cold, and merciless. So Jesus dismissed them with a challenge to learn the meaning of Jehovah's words, "I desire mercy and not sacrifice" (quoted from Hosea 6:6). This means that although God had instituted the sacrificial system and had ordered Israel to offer sacrifices, He did not want the rituals to become a substitute for inward righteousness. God is not pleased with rituals that are divorced from personal godliness. This is precisely what the

Pharisees had done. They observed the letter of the law but had no mercy or compassion for those who needed spiritual help. They associated only with self-righteous people like themselves.

In contrast, the Lord Jesus pointedly told them, "I did not come to call the righteous, but sinners, to repentance" (v. 13). He perfectly fulfilled God's desire for mercy as well as sacrifice. In one sense, there are no righteous people in the world, so He came to call everyone to repentance. But here the thought is that His call is only effective for those who agree with God that they are sinners. He can dispense no healing to those who are proud, stiff-necked, self-righteous, and unrepentant—like the Pharisees.

> God's call is only effective for those who agree with God that they are sinners.

The Old and the New (9:14-17)

By this time John the Baptist was probably in prison. His confused disciples came to Jesus with a problem. They had seen the Pharisees fasting, and they themselves fasted, but Jesus' disciples did not. Why not?

The Lord answered with an illustration: He was the Bridegroom and His disciples were the wedding guests. As long as He was with them, there was no reason for fasting as a sign of mourning. But He would be taken from them, and then His disciples would fast. He *was* taken from them—in death and burial. And since His ascension He has been bodily absent from His disciples. While Jesus' words do not command fasting, they certainly approve it as an appropriate exercise for those who wait for the Bridegroom's return.

The question raised by John's disciples further prompted Jesus to point out that John marked the end of one dispensation and He the beginning of another. In two illustrations, He draws the curtain on the legal dispensation and announces the new age of grace. And He shows that the principles of each cannot be mixed. To try to mix law and grace would be like using a piece of new, unwashed, unshrunk cloth to patch an old garment. When washed, the patch would shrink, ripping itself away from the old cloth. The disrepair would be worse than ever. Or the mixture would be like putting new wine in old wineskins. The pressure caused by the fermentation of the new wine would burst the old skins because they had lost all their elasticity. "The life and liberty of the gospel destroys the wineskins of ritualism"

(Williams). The introduction of the Christian era would inevitably result in tension. The joy which Christ brought could not be contained within the forms and rituals of the Old Testament. There must be an entirely new order of things.

"Thus does the King warn His disciples against the admixture of the old . . . and the new. . . . And yet this is what has been done throughout Christendom. Judaism has been patched up and adapted everywhere among the churches and the old garment is labeled "Christianity." The result is a confusing mixture, which is neither Judaism nor Christianity, but a ritualistic substitution of dead works for a trust in the living God. The new wine of free salvation has been poured into the old wineskins of legalism, and with what result? Why, the skins are burst and ruined and the wine is spilled and most of the precious life-giving draught is lost. The law has lost its terror, because it is mixed with grace, and grace has lost its beauty and character as grace, for it is mixed with law-works." (Pettingill)

Power to Raise the Dead, Part I (9:18-19)

Jesus' discourse on the change of dispensations was interrupted by a distraught ruler of the synagogue whose daughter had just died. He knelt before Jesus, requesting Him to come and restore her to life. It was rather exceptional that this man should seek help from Jesus; most of the Jewish leaders would have feared the scorn and contempt of their associates for doing so. At any rate, Jesus honored his faith by starting out with His disciples toward the ruler's home.

Power to Heal the Incurable (9:20-22)

Another interruption! This time it was a woman who had suffered from a hemorrhage for twelve years. But Jesus was never annoyed or irritated by such interruptions; He maintained perfect poise at all times and was always accessible and approachable.

Medical science had not been able to help this woman; in fact, her condition was getting worse (Mark 5:26). In her extremity she met Jesus—or at least she saw Him surrounded by a crowd. She believed that He was able to heal her, so she edged through the crowd and touched the fringe of His garment. True faith never went unnoticed by Him. He turned and pronounced her healed; His power flowed instantly and she was well for the first time in twelve years.

Power to Raise the Dead, Part II (9:23-26)

The narrative now returns to the ruler whose daughter had died. When Jesus reached the house the professional mourners were wailing. He ordered the room to be cleared of visitors, at the same time announcing that the girl was not dead but asleep. Most Bible students believe that the Lord was using *sleep* here in a figurative sense for death. Often in the New Testament the body of a believer is said to sleep in death.

> ─── ❧ ───
> **True faith never went unnoticed by Jesus.**
> ─── ❧ ───

Some believe, however, that the girl may have been in a coma. This interpretation does not deny that Jesus could have raised her if she had been dead. But it emphasizes that Jesus was too honest to take credit for raising the dead when actually the girl had not died. Sir Robert Anderson held this view. He pointed out that the father and all the others said she had died, but Jesus said she had not. So Anderson says it all depends on whom you want to believe. In any case, the Lord took the girl by the hand and the miracle occurred—the girl got up. It didn't take long for the news of the miracle to spread throughout the entire district.

Power to Give Sight 9:27-31

As Jesus left the ruler's neighborhood, two blind men followed Him, pleading for sight. Though blind in the physical sense, these men had acute spiritual discernment. In addressing Jesus as Son of David, they showed that they recognized Him as the long-awaited Messiah and the rightful King of Israel. And they knew that when the Messiah came, one of His credentials would be that He would give sight to the blind (Isa. 61:1). This, therefore, was their moment of destiny and they seized it. When Jesus tested their faith by asking if they believed He could give them sight, they immediately responded, "Yes, Lord." The Great Physician touched their eyes and assured them that because they believed, they would see. Immediately their eyes became completely normal.

Man says, "Seeing is believing." God says, "Believing is seeing." Jesus said to Martha, "Did I not say to you that if you would believe you would see . . ." (John 11:40). The writer to the Hebrews wrote, "By faith we understand . . ." (11:3). The apostle John wrote, "These things I have written to you who believe . . . that you may know . . ." (1 John 5:13). God is not pleased with the kind of faith that demands a prior miracle; He wants us to believe Him simply because He is God.

Why did Jesus sternly charge the healed men to tell no one? In the notes on 8:4, we suggested that probably He did not want to bring about a fickle, premature movement to enthrone Him as king. The people were as yet unrepentant; He could not reign over them until they were born again. Also, a revolutionary uprising in favor of Jesus would bring terrible reprisals from the Roman government on the Jews. Besides all this, the Lord Jesus had to go to the cross before He could reign; anything that blocked His pathway to Calvary was at variance with the predetermined plan of God.

In their delirious gratitude for eyesight, the two men spread the news of their miraculous cure throughout the district. While we might be tempted to sympathize with them, and even to admire their zealous testimony, the hard fact is that they were disobedient and inevitably did more harm than good, probably by stirring up a shallow curiosity rather than a Spirit-inspired interest. Not even gratitude is a valid excuse for disobedience.

—————— ❧ ——————

Not even gratitude is a valid excuse for disobedience.

—————— ❧ ——————

Power to Give Speech (9:32-34)

There seems to be a spiritual sequence in the miracles here. First Jesus gave life to the dead girl, then sight to the blind, now speech to the dumb. The order is life first, then understanding, and then testimony.

An evil spirit had stricken this man with dumbness. Someone was concerned enough to bring the demoniac to Jesus. God bless the noble band of the anonymous who have been His instruments in bringing others to Jesus! As soon as Jesus cast out the demon, the man spoke. It is probably no stretch of the imagination to assume that he used his restored power of speech from then on in worship and witness for the One who had so graciously healed him.

The common people acknowledged that Israel was witnessing unprecedented miracles. The Pharisees answered by saying that Jesus cast out demons by the prince of demons. This is what Jesus later labeled the unpardonable sin (12:32). To attribute the miracles which He performed by the power of the Holy Spirit to the power of Satan was blasphemy against the Holy Spirit. While others were being blessed by the healing touch of Christ, the Pharisees remained spiritually dead, blind, and dumb.

The Need for Harvest Workers (9:35-38)

This verse begins what is known as the Third Galilean Circuit. The Lord Jesus traveled throughout the cities of Galilee, preaching the good news of the kingdom, namely, that He was the King of Israel, and that if the nation repented and acknowledged Him, He would reign over them. This does not overlook the fact that He would still have had to die as the Savior of the world, but it emphasizes the fact that a genuine offer of the kingdom was being made to Israel at that time. What would have happened if Israel had welcomed Jesus as their Messiah-King? The Bible does not answer the question. We do know that Christ would still have had to die to provide a righteous basis by which God could justify sinners of all ages!

As Christ taught and preached, He healed all kinds of sicknesses. Just as miracles characterized the first advent of the Messiah, in lowly grace, so they will mark His second advent, in power and great glory (compare Hebrews 6:5: "the powers of the age to come").

As Jesus gazed on Israel's multitudes, stressed and helpless, He saw them as sheep without a shepherd. His great heart of compassion went out to them. Oh, that we too might know more of that passionate yearning for the spiritual welfare of the lost and dying around us. How we need to pray constantly:

> Let me look on the crowd, as my Savior did,
> till my eyes with tears grow dim;
>
> Let me view with pity the wandering sheep,
> and love them for love of Him.

A great work of spiritual harvest needed to be done, but the laborers were few. The problem has persisted to this day, it seems; the need is always greater than the work-force. The Lord Jesus told the disciples to ask the Lord of the harvest to send out laborers into His harvest. Notice here that the need does not constitute a call. Workers should not *go* until they are *sent*.

Jesus did not identify "the Lord of the harvest." Some think it is the Holy Spirit. In chapter 10:5, Jesus Himself sends out the disciples, so it seems clear that He Himself is the One to whom we should pray in this matter of world evangelization.

6

MATTHEW 10–12

Jesus Appoints Twelve Disciples (10:1-4)

The chapter break here is unfortunate. In the last verse of the preceding chapter, the Lord had instructed His disciples to pray for more laborers. To pray that request sincerely, believers must be willing to go themselves, so here we find the Lord calling the Twelve. The uniqueness of Jesus is seen here. Other men had performed miracles, but no other man ever conferred the power on others (v. 1).

The twelve disciples were:

1. *Simon Peter.* Someone has described Peter as "Gallant, generous-hearted, affectionate, impetuous soul that he was, he was a born leader of men."

2. *Andrew.* He was introduced to Jesus by John the Baptist (John 1:36), then brought his brother Peter to Him. He made it his business thereafter to bring men to Jesus.

3. *James.* A son of Zebedee, he was later slain by Herod (Acts 12:2)—the first of the Twelve to die as a martyr.

4. *John.* Also a son of Zebedee. We are indebted to him not only for the fourth gospel, but for three epistles and the book of Revelation.

5. *Philip.* A citizen of Bethsaida, he brought Nathanael to Jesus. He is not to be confused with Philip, the evangelist, in the book of Acts.

6. *Bartholomew.* Believed to be the same as Nathanael, the Israelite in whom Jesus found no guile (John 1:47).

7. *Thomas*, also called Didymus, meaning twin. Commonly known as "Doubting Thomas," his doubts gave way to a magnificent confession of Christ (John 20:28).

8. *Matthew*. The former tax-collector who wrote this gospel.

9. *James, the son of Alphaeus*. Little else is known about him.

10. *Thaddaeus*. He is also known as Lebbaeus and Judas the son of James (Luke 6:16). His only recorded utterance is found in John 14:22.

11. *Simon* the Cananaean, whom Luke calls the Zealot (Luke 6:15).

12. *Judas Iscariot*, the betrayer of our Lord.

The Twelve were probably in their twenties at this time. Taken from varied walks of life and probably young men of average ability, their true greatness lay in their association with Jesus.

The Mission to Israel, Part I (10:5-15)

The remainder of the chapter contains Jesus' instructions to His disciples concerning a special preaching tour to the people of Israel. This is not to be confused with the later sending of the seventy (Luke 10:1) or with the Great Commission (Matt. 28:19-20). This was a temporary mission, and while some of the principles are of lasting value for God's people in all ages, some were not intended to be permanent. This is proved by the fact that they were later revoked by the Lord Jesus (Luke 22:35-36).

First the *route* is given (vv. 5-6). They were not to go to the Gentiles or to the Samaritans (a half-breed race who were hated by the Jews). Their ministry was to be limited at this time to the lost sheep of the house of Israel. The *message* was the glorious proclamation that the kingdom of heaven was at hand, or available (v. 7). If Israel refused, there would be no excuse, because an official announcement was being made exclusively to them. The kingdom had drawn near in the Person of the King. Israel must decide whether to accept or reject Him. The disciples were given *credentials* to confirm their message (v. 8). They were to heal the sick, raise the dead, cleanse lepers, cast out demons. The Jews demanded signs (1 Cor. 1:22) so God graciously condescended to give them signs.

As to *remuneration*, the Lord's representatives were to make no charge for their services. They had received their blessings without cost and were to dispense them on the same basis. They would not be required to make advance *provision* for the journey (vv. 9-10). After all, they were Israelites preaching to Israelites, and it was a recognized principle among the Jews that the laborer deserves his food. The general idea is that their needs would be supplied on a day by day basis.

What arrangements were they to make for *housing?* When they entered a city, they were to look for one who would receive them as disciples of the Lord and who would be open to their message (v. 11). Once they found such a host, they were to stay with him as long as they were in the city. If a household seemed inclined to receive them, the disciples were to show courtesy and gratitude in accepting such

> In rejecting Christ's disciples, people were rejecting Him.

hospitality. But if a house refused to host the Lord's messengers, they were not obligated to pray for God's peace on it. Not only that, they were to dramatize God's displeasure by shaking the dust off their feet. In rejecting Christ's disciples, they were rejecting *Him.* He solemnly warned that such rejection would bring down more severe punishment in the Day of Judgment than the sexual perversion of Sodom and Gomorrah.

Verse 15 proves that there will be degrees of punishment in hell; otherwise how could it be more tolerable for some than for others?

The Mission to Israel, Part II (10:16-23)

In this section Jesus counsels the Twelve concerning their *behavior in the face of persecution.* They would be surrounded by vicious men bent on destroying them. They must be wise as serpents; that is, they should avoid giving needless offense or being tricked into compromising situations. And they must be innocent as doves, protected by the armor of a righteous character.

They should be on guard against unbelieving Jews who would bring them into both civil and religious courts. But God's cause would triumph over man's evil as it always does. When the time came, they would be given divine aid, both as to what to speak in such a way as to glorify Christ and utterly confuse and frustrate their accusers. Two extremes should be avoided in interpreting verse 19. The first is the naive assumption that a Christian need never prepare a message in advance. The second is the view that the verse has no relevance for us today. It is proper and desirable for a preacher to prayerfully wait before God for the appropriate word for a specific occasion. But it is also true that in moments of crisis, all believers can claim God's promise that they will be given wisdom to speak with divine intuition. They become mouthpieces for the Spirit of their Father.

Jesus forewarned His disciples that they would have to face treachery and betrayal from within their families. The disciples would be hated by all—not by all without exception, but by all classes of men—men of all cultures, nationalities, etc. We can take the perspective that, as someone has put it, "There is a cost for being identified with Him—or should we call it a 'reward'?"

> **Endurance is the hallmark of those who are genuinely saved.**

Verse 22, taken by itself, this seems to imply that salvation can be earned by steadfast endurance. We know that this cannot be the meaning because throughout the Scriptures salvation is presented as a free gift of God's grace through faith (Eph. 2:8-9). Neither can the verse mean that those who remain faithful to Christ will be saved from physical death; the previous verse predicts the death of some faithful disciples. The simplest explanation is that endurance is the hallmark of those who are genuinely saved; a mark of true faith is that it has the quality of permanence. The ones who endure to the end in times of persecution show by their perseverance that they are true believers (compare Matthew 24:13).

Those who study Bible passages dealing with the future find that the Spirit of God often shifts from the immediate future to the distant future. A prophecy may have a partial and immediate significance and also a complete and more distant fulfillment. For instance, the two advents of Christ may be merged in a simple passage without explanation (Isa. 52:14, 15; Micah 5:2-4). In verses 22 and 23 the Lord Jesus makes this kind of prophetic transition. He first warns the twelve disciples of the sufferings they would have to undergo for His sake. Then He seems to see them as a type of His devoted Jewish followers during the great tribulation.

The first part of verse 23 could refer to the twelve disciples. They were not obligated to remain under the tyranny of their enemies if there was an honorable way to escape. The latter part of verse 23 carries us forward to the days preceding Christ's coming to reign: ". . . You will not have gone through the cities of Israel, before the Son of Man comes." This could not refer to the mission of the Twelve because the Son of Man had already come.

It seems far more likely that this is a reference to Christ's second coming. During the great tribulation, Christ's faithful Jewish brethren will go forth with the gospel of the kingdom. They will be persecuted and pursued. Before they can reach all the cities of Israel with the message, the Lord Jesus will return to judge His foes and set up His kingdom. In Matthew 24:14 Christ says that the gospel of the kingdom will be preached in *all the world* before His second advent—but there really is no contradiction. The gospel will be preached in all nations though not necessarily to every individual. But this message will meet stiff resistance in Israel, and the messengers will be severely persecuted and hindered. Thus, not all the cities of Israel will be reached.

"Fear Not" (10:24-33)

The disciples of the Lord would often have occasion to wonder why they should have to endure ill-treatment. If Jesus was the true Messiah, why were His followers suffering instead of reigning? In verses 24 and 25 He anticipates their question and answers it by reminding them of their relationship to Him: Teacher / disciple, Master / servant, Householder / member. The meaning of discipleship is following the Teacher, not being superior to Him. The servant should not expect to be treated better than his Master. If men call the worthy Master of the house "Beelzebul" (meaning "lord of the dwelling," that is, the dwelling of evil spirits), they will hurl even greater insults at the members of His household.

Three times the Lord told His followers not to fear (vv. 26, 28, 31). First, they should not fear the seeming victory of their foes; His cause would be gloriously vindicated in a coming day. Up till now the gospel had been presented in a low-key way. But soon the disciples must boldly proclaim it.

Second, the disciples should not fear the murderous rage of men. The worst that men can do is kill the body. Physical death is to be with Christ, to have deliverance from sin, sorrow, sickness, suffering, and death; it is translation into eternal glory. The disciples should not fear men but should have a reverential fear of God, who can destroy both soul and body in hell. This is the greatest loss—to suffer eternal separation from God, from Christ, and from hope.

When going through great trials, the disciples could be confident of the unceasing care of God. The Lord Jesus teaches this from the common sparrow. Two of these insignificant birds were sold for a penny, and yet not one of them dies outside the will of God, or without His knowledge, or presence. The same God who takes a personal interest in the tiny sparrow keeps an accurate count of the number of hairs in the head of each of His children. This conveys the supreme care God has for each of His people.

In view of the foregoing considerations, what is more reasonable than that the disciples of Christ should openly and fearlessly confess Him before men? Any shame or reproach they might bear on earth will be abundantly rewarded in heaven when the Lord Jesus confesses them before His Father. Confession of Christ here involves commitment to Him as Lord and Savior and the resulting acknowledgment of Him by life and by lips. It includes, of course, all that true belief in Christ may involve. In the case of most of the Twelve, this led up to the ultimate confession of the Lord in martyrdom.

Denial of Christ on earth will be repaid with denial before God in heaven. To deny Christ in this sense means to refuse to recognize His claims over one's life. Those whose lives say, in effect, "I never knew You" will hear Him say one day, "I never knew you." The Lord is not referring to a temporary denial of Him under pressure, as in Peter's case, but to that kind of denial that is habitual and final.

Not Peace, But a Sword (10:34-39)

Our Lord's words in verse 34 must be understood as a figure of speech in which the visible results of His coming are stated as the apparent purpose of His coming. He says He did not come to bring peace but a sword. Actually, in a very real sense He did come to make peace (Eph. 2:14-17). But the point here is that whenever individual men and women would become His followers, their families would turn against them. One of the costs of discipleship is to experience tension and strife from one's own family. This household hostility is often more bitter than is encountered in other areas of life.

And so a choice must often be made between Christ and family. No ties of nature can be allowed to deflect a disciple from complete allegiance to the Lord. But there is something else that is even more apt to rob Christ of His rightful place than family—that is, the love of one's own life. So Jesus added, "and he who does not take his cross and follow Me is not worthy of Me." The cross, of course, was a means of execution; it spoke of condemnation and death. To take up one's cross and follow Christ means to live in such devoted abandonment to Him that even death itself is not too high a price to pay. Not all disciples are required to lay down their lives for the Lord, but all are called on to value Him so highly that they do not count their lives precious to themselves.

> The greatest use of a life is to spend it in the service of Christ.

Love of Christ must overmaster the instinct of self-preservation. The strong temptation is to hug one's life by trying to avoid the pain and loss of a life of total commitment. But this is the greatest waste of a life—to spend it gratifying self. The greatest use of a life is to spend it in the service of Christ.

Even a Cup of Cold Water (10:40-11:1)

Not everyone would refuse the message of the disciples. Some would recognize them as representatives of the Messiah and would receive them graciously. The disciples, however, would have limited ability to reward such kindness. But they need not worry; anything done for them would be reckoned as being done for the Lord Himself and would be rewarded accordingly. And to receive Him, of course, was the same as receiving the Father who sent Him. The reason for this is that the one who is sent represents the sender. And anyone who receives a prophet because he is a prophet will receive a prophet's reward.

"The Jews regarded the reward of the prophet as the greatest; while kings bore rule in the name of the Lord, and priests ministered in the name of the Lord, the prophet came from the Lord to instruct both priest and king. Christ says that if you do no more than receive a prophet in the capacity of a prophet, the same reward that is given to the prophet will be given to you, if you help the prophet along. . . . Say, 'Is this message of God for me? Is this man a prophet of God to my soul?' If he is, receive him, magnify his word and work, and get part of his reward." (A. T. Pierson)

No small act of kindness shown to a follower of Jesus will go unnoticed.

And thus the Lord closes His special charge to the Twelve by investing them with regal dignity. Let them never forget that they were representatives of the King and that their glorious privilege was to speak and act for Him.

Having sent the Twelve on the special, temporary mission to the house of Israel, Jesus departed to preach and teach in the cities of Galilee where the disciples had previously lived.

John the Baptist Reassured (11:2-6)

By now John had been imprisoned by Herod. Discouraged and lonely, he began to wonder. If Jesus were truly the Messiah, why did He allow His forerunner to be in prison? Like many great men of God, John suffered a temporary lapse of faith. So he sent some of his disciples to ask if Jesus really was the One the prophets had promised, or if they should still be looking for the Messiah. Jesus answered by reminding John that He was performing the miracles predicted of the Messiah, and more, so there was no room for doubt (the dead being raised up was not prophesied of the Messiah; it was greater than the miracles that were predicted.)

Jesus also reminded John that the gospel was being preached to the poor, in striking fulfillment of the messianic prophecy in Isaiah 61:1. Ordinary religious leaders often concentrate their attention on the wealthy and aristocratic. The Messiah brought good news to the poor. Then the Savior added, "And blessed is he who is not offended because of Me." God's blessing would rest on those who, by spiritual insight, recognized Jesus of Nazareth as the promised Messiah. Verse 6 should not be interpreted as a rebuke to John the Baptist. Everyone's faith needs to be confirmed and strengthened at times. It is one thing to have a temporary lapse of faith and quite another to be permanently stumbled as to the true identity of the Lord Jesus. No single chapter is the story of a man's life. Taking John's life in its totality, we find a record of faithfulness and perseverance.

Jesus Praises John (11:7-19)

As soon as John's disciples had left with Jesus' words of reassurance, the Lord turned to the multitude with words of glowing praise for him. This same crowd had gone out to the desert when John was preaching there. Had they gone to see a weak man, shaken by every passing wind of human opinion? No! John was a fearless preacher, an embodied conscience, who would rather suffer than be silent, and rather die than lie. Had they gone out to see a well-dressed palace courtier who loved comfort and ease? No! John was a simple, frugal man of God whose austere life was a rebuke to the enormous worldliness of the people.

Had they gone out to see a prophet? Well, in fact John was the greatest of the prophets. But in what sense? He was the greatest because of his position as forerunner of the Messiah-King. This is made clear in verse 10; John fulfilled Malachi's prophecy (3:1)—the messenger who would prepare the people for Messiah's coming. It has been well said, "John opened the way for Christ and then he got out of the way for Christ." The statement in verse 11, "But he who is least in the kingdom of heaven is greater than he," proves conclusively that Jesus was speaking about John's privilege and not his character. A person who is least in the kingdom of heaven does not necessarily have a better character than John, but he does have greater privilege. To be a citizen of the kingdom is greater than to announce its arrival.

The statement in verse 12 is capable of two interpretations. First of all, the enemies of the kingdom did their best to take the kingdom with the purpose of destroying it. Their rejection of John foreshadowed the rejection of the King Himself and thus of the kingdom. But it may also mean that those who were ready for the King's coming responded enthusiastically to the announcement and strained every muscle to enter. This is the meaning in Luke 16:16: "The law and the prophets were until John; since that time the kingdom of God has been preached, and everyone is pressing into it." Here the kingdom of God is pictured as a besieged city, with all classes of men hammering at it from the outside, trying to get in. A certain spiritual violence is necessary. Whichever meaning you adopt, the thought is that John's preaching touched off a violent reaction, with widespread and deep inward effects.

The entire Old Testament predicted the coming of the Messiah (v.13). Then John stepped out upon the stage of human history, announcing that He had come. John's role was unique. His ministry was not just prophecy; it was announcing the fulfillment of prophecy. Malachi had predicted that before Messiah's appearance, Elijah would come as a forerunner (Mal. 4:5-6). That is what the Lord refers to in verse 14. If the people had been willing to accept Jesus as Messiah, John would have filled the role of Elijah. Not that John actually was Elijah in reincarnation—he disclaimed being Elijah in John 1:21. But he went before Christ in the spirit and power of Elijah (Luke 1:17).

When Lord said, "He who has ears to hear, let him hear!" He meant, don't miss the deep significance of what you are hearing. If John fulfilled the prophecy concerning Elijah, and was the forerunner of the Messiah, then Jesus Himself was the promised Messiah. In thus accrediting John the Baptist, Jesus was reaffirming His own claim to be the Christ of God. To accept one would lead to acceptance of the other. The generation of Jews to whom Jesus was speaking, however, was not interested in accepting either. Jesus compared them to spoilt children playing in the market places who refused to be satisfied with any appeals. If their friends wanted to pipe so they could dance, they refused. If their friends wanted to play-act a funeral, they refused to mourn.

If John's asceticism made them uncomfortable, then surely they would be pleased with Jesus' more ordinary eating habits. But no! They called Him a glutton, a drunkard, a friend of tax-collectors and sinners. It goes without saying that Jesus never indulged in food or drink to excess; their charge was a total lie. It is true that He was a friend of tax-collectors and sinners, but not in the way they meant. He befriended sinners in order to save them from their sins, but He never shared or approved their sins.

"Yet wisdom is justified by her children" (v. 19). The Lord Jesus, of course, is Wisdom personified (1 Cor. 1:30). Though unbelieving men might slander Him, yet He is vindicated in His works and in the lives of those who

——— ✿ ———
The Lord Jesus is Wisdom personified.
——— ✿ ———

follow Him. Though the mass of the Jews might refuse to acknowledge Him as Messiah-King, yet His claims were completely verified by His miracles and by the spiritual transformation of His devoted disciples.

The Unrepentant Cities of Galilee (11:20-24)

Privilege brings responsibility. The greater the privilege, the greater the responsibility. No cities were ever more privileged than Chorazin, Bethsaida, and Capernaum. The incarnate Son of God had taught their favored people, and had performed most of His mighty miracles within their walls. In the face of the most overwhelming evidence, they had stubbornly refused to repent. Little wonder, then, that the Lord should pronounce the most solemn doom upon them.

Chorazin and Bethsaida had heard the gracious entreaties of their Savior-God, yet they willfully and stubbornly turned Him away. He compared them to the coastal cities of Tyre and Sidon which had fallen under God's judgment because of their idolatry and wickedness. If they had been privileged to see the miracles of Jesus, they would have humbled themselves in the deepest repentance. In the day of judgment, therefore, Tyre and Sidon would fare better than Chorazin and Bethsaida.

The words "it shall be more tolerable . . . in the day of judgment" (v. 22) indicate that there will be degrees of punishment in hell, just as there will be degrees of reward in heaven (1 Cor. 3:12-15). The single sin that consigns men to hell is refusal to submit to Jesus Christ (John 3:36b). But the depth of suffering in hell is conditional on the privileges rejected and the sins committed.

Some of Christ's most extraordinary miracles were performed in Capernaum (which had become Jesus' hometown after Nazareth rejected Him). Its people should have repented in deep contrition and should

> There will
> be degrees of
> punishment in hell.

have gladly acknowledged the Lord. If the vile city of Sodom, the capital of homosexuality, had been so privileged, it would have repented and would have been spared. But Capernaum missed the day of its unparalleled opportunity. Jesus had actually lived there and presented the most irrefutable evidences of His Messiahship. Sodom's sin was great. But Capernaum's sin was greater; it rejected the holy Son of God. No sin is greater than that. Therefore, Sodom's punishment will not be as severe as Capernaum's in the Day of Judgment.

If all this is true of Capernaum, how much more true is it of our country where Bibles abound, where the gospel is broadcast, and where few, if any, are without excuse.

In the days of our Lord, there were four prominent cities in Galilee: Chorazin, Bethsaida, Capernaum, and Tiberias. He pronounced woes against the first three but not against the fourth. What has been the result? The destruction of Chorazin and Bethsaida has been so complete that their exact sites are unknown. The location of the ruins of Capernaum is uncertain. Tiberias is still standing. This remarkable fulfillment of prophecy is one more proof of Jesus Christ's omniscience and the Bible's inspiration.

Christ's Reaction to Rejection (11:25-30)

The three cities of Galilee did not have eyes to see nor heart to love the Christ of God. And He knew that their attitude was but a foretaste of rejection on a wider scale. But how did He react to their lack of repentance? Not with bitterness, or cynicism, or vindictiveness. Rather, He lifted His voice in thanksgiving to God that nothing could frustrate His sovereign purposes. "I thank You, Father, Lord of heaven and earth, that You have hidden these things from the wise and prudent and have revealed them to babes" (v. 25). In considering this prayer, we should avoid two possible misunderstandings. First, Jesus was not expressing pleasure in the inevitable judgment of the Galilean cities. Second, He did not imply that God had high-handedly withheld the light from the wise.

The cities had had every chance to welcome the Lord Jesus. They deliberately refused to submit to Him. When they refused the light, God withheld the light from them. But God's plans will not fail. If the intelligentsia will not believe, then God will reveal Him to humble hearts. He fills the hungry with good things and sends the rich away empty (Luke 1:53).

Those who consider themselves to be too wise and understanding to need Christ become afflicted with judicial blindness. But those who readily admit their lack of wisdom receive a revelation of Him "in whom are hidden all the treasures of wisdom and knowledge" (Col. 2:3). Jesus thanked the Father for so ordaining that if some would not have Him, others would. In the face of enormous unbelief He found consolation in the overruling plan and purpose of God. Christ was not rejoicing in the fate of the proud, but that God's revelation did not depend on human attainments for being received.

All things had been delivered to Christ by His Father. This would be an outstanding claim if it came from anyone else, but in the lips of the Lord Jesus it is a simple statement of truth. At that moment, with opposition mounting, it did not appear that He was in control, but He was. The program of His life was moving on toward eventual glorious triumph.

"No one knows the Son except the Father" (v. 27). There is incomprehensible mystery about the Person of Christ. The union of deity and humanity in one Person raises problems that boggle the human mind. For instance, there is the problem of death. God cannot die, yet Jesus is God and Jesus died. And yet His divine and human natures are inseparable. So although we can know Him and love Him and trust Him, there is a sense in which only the Father can truly understand Him.

In the ultimate sense, only God is great enough to understand God. Man cannot come to know Him by his own strength or intellect. But the Lord Jesus can and does reveal the Father to those whom He chooses. As the only begotten of the Father, He makes Him known to those who believe (John 1:18; 14:7). When we read in verse 27 that the Father is revealed only to those whom the Son chooses, we might be tempted to think of an arbitrary selection of a favored few. But the following verse guards against such an interpretation. The Lord issues a universal invitation to all who are weary and heavy laden to come to Him for rest. As we examine this invitation of infinite tenderness, let us remember that it was issued after the blatant rejection of Jesus by the favored cities of Galilee. Man's hate and obstinacy could not extinguish His love and grace.

Come . . . To come means to believe (Acts 16:31); to receive (John 1:12); to eat (John 6:35); to drink (John 7:37); to look (Isa. 45:22); to confess (1 John 4:2); to hear (John 5:24, 25); to enter a door (John 10:9); to open a door (Rev. 3:20); to touch the hem of His garment (Matt. 9:20-21); and to accept the gift of eternal life (Rom. 6:23).

to Me. . . The object of faith is not a church, or a creed, or a clergyman, but the living Christ. Salvation is in a Person and His name is Jesus. Those who have Jesus are as saved as God can make them.

All you who labor and are heavy laden . . . . In order to truly come to Jesus, a person must be willing to admit that he is burdened with the weight of sin. Only those who acknowledge they are lost can be saved. Faith in the Lord Jesus Christ is preceded by repentance toward God.

and I will give you rest. . . Notice that rest here is a gift; it is unearned and unmerited. This is the *rest* of salvation that comes from realizing that Christ finished the work of redemption on Calvary's Cross. It is the rest of conscience that follows the realization that the penalty of one's sins has been paid once for all and that God will not demand payment twice.

In verses 29 and 30 the invitation changes from salvation to service.

Take My yoke upon you . . . This means to enter into submission to His will, to turn over control of one's life to Him (Rom. 12:1-2).

and learn from me . . . As we acknowledge His lordship in every area of our lives, He trains us in His ways.

for I am gentle and lowly in heart . . . In contrast to the Pharisees who were harsh and proud, the true Teacher is meek and lowly. Those who take His yoke (who are harnessed, or bound, to Him) will learn to take the lowest place.

and you will find rest for your souls . . . Here it is not the rest of conscience but the rest of heart that is found by taking the lowly place before God and man. It is also the rest that one experiences in the service of Christ when he stops trying to be great.

For My yoke is easy and My burden is light . . . Once again there is a striking contrast with the Pharisees. Jesus said of them, "They bind heavy burdens, hard to bear, and lay them on men's shoulders; but they themselves will not move them with one of their fingers" (Matt. 23:4). Jesus' yoke is easy; it does not chafe. His burden is light. This does not mean that there are no problems, trials, labor, or heartaches in the Christian life. But it does mean that we do not have to bear them alone. We are yoked with One who gives sufficient grace for every time of need. To serve Him is not bondage, but perfect freedom.

> To serve Jesus is not bondage, but perfect freedom.

The Sabbath Controversy (12:1-8)

This chapter records the mounting crisis of rejection. The malice and hostility of the Pharisees have been rising. Now they are ready to spill over. The issue that opens the floodgates is the Sabbath question.

On this particular Sabbath day, Jesus and His disciples were passing through the grain fields. The disciples began to pick ears of grain and to eat them. The law permitted them to help themselves to grain from their neighbor's field as long as they did not use a sickle (Deut. 23:25). But the Pharisees were legalists; they charged that the Sabbath had been broken. Though their specific charges are not stated it is likely that they accused the disciples of harvesting (picking the grain), threshing (rubbing it in their hands), and winnowing (separating the grain from the chaff).

Jesus replied to their ridiculous complaint by reminding them of an incident in the life of David (read 1 Samuel 21:1-6). God never found fault with David eating the showbread. Why not? The reason is that God's law was never intended to inflict hardship on His faithful people. Also we should remember that it was not David's fault that he was in exile. A sinful nation had rejected him. If he had been given his rightful place, he and his followers would not have had to eat the showbread. Because there was sin in Israel, God permitted an act that was otherwise forbidden. The analogy is clear. The Lord Jesus was the rightful King of Israel, but the nation would not acknowledge His claim as Sovereign. If He had been given His proper place, His followers would not have been reduced to eating in this way on the Sabbath or on any other day of the week. History was repeating itself. Once again there was sin in Israel. The Lord did not reprove His disciples as they had not done anything wrong.

Then again, Jesus reminded the Pharisees that the priests profaned the Sabbath by killing and sacrificing animals and by performing many other servile duties (Num. 28:9-10). Yet they were guiltless because they were engaged in the service of God. The Pharisees knew that the priests worked every Sabbath in the temple without desecrating the temple. Why then should they criticize the disciples for acting as they did in the presence of One who was greater than the temple?

The Pharisees never understood the heart of God. In Hosea 6:6 He had said, "I desire mercy and not sacrifice," meaning that God puts compassion before ritual. He would rather see His hungry people picking grain on the Sabbath to satisfy their need than observing the day so strictly as to inflict physical distress. If the Pharisees had only realized this, they would not have condemned the innocent disciples.

Then Jesus added, "For the Son of Man is Lord even of the Sabbath." It was He who had instituted the law in the first place, and therefore He was the One most qualified to interpret its true meaning. For a short review on the scriptural teaching on the Sabbath, see page 220 in the appendix.

Jesus Heals on the Sabbath (12:9-14)

From the grain fields Jesus went to the synagogue. Luke tells us that the scribes and Pharisees were there to watch Him so that they might find some charge against Him (Luke 6:6-7).

Inside the synagogue was a man with a withered hand who suddenly became valuable to the Pharisees as a means through which to trap Jesus. They knew that Jesus was always predisposed to reduce human misery. If He would heal on the Sabbath, then they would catch Him in a punishable offense, they thought. So they began by asking: is it lawful to heal on the Sabbath?

Jesus answered by asking if they would pull one of their sheep out of a pit on the Sabbath day. Of course they would—but why? Perhaps their pretext was that it was a work of mercy—but another consideration might be that the sheep was worth money to them and they would not want to incur financial loss, even on the Sabbath. Our Lord then reminded them that a man is of greater value than a sheep. If it is right to show mercy to an animal, how much more justified is it to do good to a human being on the Sabbath.

Having trapped the Jewish leaders in the pit of their own greed, Jesus healed the withered hand. It is interesting to hear Him tell the man to stretch forth his hand. Faith and the human will were called into action. Obedience was then rewarded with healing. You would think that the Pharisees would have been happy that the man was healed—a man they had neither the power nor the inclination to help. They responded by instigating a plot to kill Him.

Healing for All (12:15-21)

Knowing the thoughts of His enemies, Jesus withdrew. Yet wherever He went, the crowds gathered; and wherever the sick gathered, He healed them. But He charged them not to publicize their miraculous cures. Was He trying to shield Himself from danger? No, He wanted to avoid any movement to make Him a popular revolutionary hero. The divine schedule must be kept. His revolution would come, not by the shedding of Roman blood, but by the shedding of His own blood.

His gracious ministry was in fulfillment of the prophecy of Isaiah 41:9; 42:1-4. The prophet foresaw the Messiah as a gentle conqueror, bringing justice to victory without force or fanfare.

The prophecy pictures Jesus as the Servant whom Jehovah had chosen, the Beloved One in whom God's soul was well pleased. God would put His Spirit upon Him—a prophecy fulfilled at the baptism of Jesus. And His ministry would reach out beyond the confines of Israel; He would proclaim justice to the Gentiles. This latter note becomes more dominant as Israel's "NO" grows louder.

Isaiah further predicted that the Messiah would not wrangle or cry aloud and His voice would not be heard in the streets. In other words, He would not be a political trouble maker, stirring up the populace with fiery ranting. He would not break a bruised reed or quench a smoldering wick—that is,

He would not trample on the dispossessed or underprivileged in order to reach His goals. If He found a broken-hearted, oppressed person, He would encourage and strengthen him. If He found even a spark of faith, He would fan it into a flame. His ministry would continue till He would bring justice to victory. His humble, loving care for others would not be extinguished by the hate and ingratitude of men.

"...And in His name Gentiles will trust" (v. 21). In Isaiah this expression is translated "and the coastlands shall wait for His law," but the meaning is the same. The coastlands refer to the Gentile nations. They are pictured as waiting for His reign so that they might be His loyal subjects.

Jesus Is Charged with being Empowered by Satan (12:22-30)

When Jesus healed a blind and dumb demoniac, the common people began to think seriously that He might be the Son of David; that is, the Messiah of Israel. This enraged the Pharisees; they could not tolerate any suggestion of sympathy with Jesus. So they exploded with the awful charge that the miracle had been performed by the power of Beelzebul, the prince of the demons. This ominous indictment was the first open accusation that the Lord Jesus was demon-empowered. Having read their thoughts, Jesus proceeded to expose their folly. He pointed out that no kingdom, city, or house divided against itself can continue successfully. If He was casting out Satan's demons by the power of Satan, then Satan was working against himself. This, of course, would be absurd on the face of it. Satan would be bringing about his own defeat.

Our Lord had a second devastating answer for the Pharisees. Some of their Jewish associates, known as exorcists, claimed to have the power to cast out demons. Jesus neither admitted nor denied their claim. He simply used the claim to point out that if He cast out demons by Beelzebul, then the Pharisees' sons (i.e., these exorcists) also cast out demons by Beelzebul. The Pharisees would never admit this, but they could not escape the logic of the argument. Their own associates would condemn them for implying that they exorcised as agents of Satan.

The truth, of course, was that Jesus cast out demons by the Spirit of God. His entire life as a Man on earth was lived by the power of the Holy Spirit. He was the Spirit-filled Messiah Whom Isaiah had foretold (Isa. 11:2; 42:1; 61:1-3). Therefore He said to the Pharisees, "If I cast out demons by the Spirit of God, surely the kingdom of God has come upon you" (v. 28). This announcement must have been a crushing blow to them because they prided themselves on their theological knowledge. Yet the kingdom of God *had* come upon them because the King was among them and they hadn't even realized it.

Far from being in league with Satan, the Lord Jesus was Satan's Conqueror. He illustrates this by the story of the strong man (v. 29). The strong man is Satan. His house is the sphere he controls. His goods are his demons. Jesus is the One who binds the strong man, enters his house, and plunders his goods. Actually the binding of Satan takes place in stages. It began during Jesus' public ministry. It was decisively guaranteed by the death and resurrection of Christ. It will be true to a more marked degree during the King's thousand-year reign (Rev. 20:2). It will be eternally true when he is cast into the lake of fire (Rev. 20:10). At the present time the devil does not seem to be bound; he still exercises considerable power. But his doom is determined and his time is short.

Referring to the blasphemous attitude of the Pharisees, Jesus then said, "He who is not with Me is against Me, and he who does not gather with Me scatters abroad" (v. 30). By their attitude, the Pharisees showed that they were not with the Lord; therefore, they were against Him. By refusing to harvest with Him, they were scattering the grain. They had accused Jesus of casting out demons by the power of Satan while actually they themselves were the servants of Satan, seeking to frustrate the work of God.

In Mark 9:40, Jesus said, ". . . He that is not against us is on our side." This seems to be a flat reversal of His words here in Matthew 12:30. The difficulty is resolved when we see that in Matthew, it is a matter of *salvation*. A man is either for Christ or against Him; there is no neutrality. In Mark, the subject is *service*. There are wide differences among the disciples of Jesus—differences in local church fellowship, differences in methods, and differences in interpretation of non-fundamental doctrines. But here the rule is that if a man is not against the Lord, he is for Him and should be respected accordingly.

The Unpardonable Sin (12:31-32)

Verses 31 and 32 mark a crisis in Christ's dealings with the leaders of Israel. Here He accuses them of committing the unforgivable sin by blaspheming against the Holy Spirit.

The unpardonable sin was the charge that Jesus performed His miracles by the power of Satan when actually He did them by the power of the Holy Spirit. It was blasphemy against the Holy Spirit because it was calling Him Beelzebul, the prince of the demons. There is forgiveness for other forms of sin and blasphemy, but to blaspheme the Holy Spirit is a sin for which there is no forgiveness in this age or in the millennial age to come. When Jesus said "in this age," He was speaking of the days of His public ministry on earth. The unpardonable sin was committed when He was performing miracles on earth. There is a reasonable doubt whether this sin can be committed today, because He is not bodily present performing miracles.

The unpardonable sin is not the same as rejecting the gospel; a man may reject the Savior for years, then repent, believe, and be saved. (Of course, if a man dies in unbelief, then there is no forgiveness for him.) The unforgivable sin is not the same as backsliding; a believer may wander far away from the Lord, yet be restored to fellowship in God's family.

> The unpardonable sin is not the same as rejecting the gospel.

Many people today worry that they have committed the unpardonable sin. Supposing for the moment that it is a sin that can be committed during this period, the fact that a person is concerned is evidence that he is not guilty of it. Those who committed it were hard and unrelenting in their opposition to Christ. They were not concerned about insulting the Spirit and did not hesitate to plot the death of the Son. They showed neither remorse nor repentance.

Every Careless Word (12:33-37)

Even the Pharisees would have had to admit that the Lord had done good by casting out demons. Yet they accused Him of being evil. In verse 33, He exposes their inconsistency and says, in effect, "Make up your minds. If a tree is good, its fruit is good, and vice versa." The quality of the fruit is a reflection of the tree that produced it. The fruit of His ministry had been good. He had healed the sick, given sight to the blind, caused the deaf to hear, made the dumb to talk, cast out demons, and raised the dead. Could a corrupt tree have brought forth such good fruit? Utterly impossible! Why then did they so stubbornly refuse to acknowledge Him?

The reason was that their poisonous words against the Son of man was the outflow of their evil hearts. A heart filled with goodness will be evidenced by words of grace and righteousness. A wicked heart expresses itself in blasphemy, bitterness, and abuse. Then Jesus solemnly warned them (and us) that people will give account for every careless word they say. That being so, how much greater will be their condemnation for the vile, contemptuous words which they spoke against God's holy Son! The words men have spoken are an accurate gauge of their lives and will thus form a suitable basis for condemnation or acquittal. In the case of believers, the penalty for all such sins has been paid through the death of Christ; but our careless speech, unconfessed and unforgiven, will result in loss of reward at Christ's judgment seat.

The Sign of the Prophet Jonah (12:38-42)

In spite of all the miracles Jesus had performed, the scribes and Pharisees had the nerve to ask Him for a sign. They implied, of course, that they would believe if He would prove Himself to be the Messiah. But their hypocrisy was transparent. If they had not believed as a result of so many wonders, why would they be convinced by one more?

The attitude that demands miraculous signs as a condition for belief is not the attitude that pleases God. As Jesus said to Thomas, "Blessed are those who have not seen and yet have believed" (John 20:29). In God's economy, seeing follows believing.

They were evil because they were willfully blind to their own Messiah. They were adulterous because they were spiritually unfaithful to their God. They sought a sign when He, their Creator-God, stood in their midst. A unique Person, combining absolute deity and perfect humanity was speaking to them, and they dared to ask Him for a sign. He told them that no sign would be given to them except the sign of the prophet Jonah. By this He referred to His own death, burial, and resurrection. Jonah's experience of being swallowed by the fish and then disgorged (Jonah 1:17; 2:10) prefigured the Lord's burial and resurrection. His rising from among the dead would be the great, final, climactic sign of His ministry to the nation of Israel.

Just as Jonah was three days and three nights in the belly of the big fish, so our Lord predicted that He would be three days and three nights in the heart of the earth. This, of course, raises a problem. If, as generally believed, Jesus was buried on Friday afternoon and rose again on Sunday morning, how can it be said that He was three days and nights in the tomb?

The answer is that, in Jewish reckoning, any part of a day and night counts as a complete period.

The guilt of the Jewish leaders is now depicted by two contrasts. First, the Gentile inhabitants of Nineveh were far less privileged, yet when they heard Jonah's preaching, they repented with deep grief. They will rise at the judgment to condemn the men of Jesus' day for failing to receive Someone greater than Jonah—the incarnate Son of God.

The Queen of Sheba was a Gentile. At great effort and expense, she traveled from the south for an interview with King Solomon. By way of contrast, the Jews of Jesus' day did not have to travel at all to see Him; He had traveled from heaven to their petty neighborhood to be their Messiah-King. Yet though He was infinitely greater than Solomon, they had no room in their lives for Him. A Gentile queen will condemn them in the judgment for such carelessness.

In this chapter our Lord has been presented as greater than the temple (v. 6), greater than Jonah (v. 41), and greater than Solomon (v. 42).

The Empty House (12:43-45)

Now Jesus gives, in parabolic form, a summary of the past, present, and future of unbelieving Israel. The man represents the Jewish nation. The unclean spirit was the idolatry which characterized the nation from the time of its slavery in Egypt to the Babylonian captivity. The captivity temporarily cured Israel of its idolatry. It was as if the unclean spirit had gone out of the man. From the end of the captivity to the present day, the Jewish people have not been idol-worshipers. They are like a house that is "empty, swept, and put in order." Two thousand years ago, Jesus Christ sought admittance to that empty house. He was the rightful Occupant, the Master of the house. But the people refused to let Him in. Though they no longer worshiped idols, they would not worship the true God either.

The empty house speaks of spiritual vacuum. It is a dangerous condition, as the sequel shows. Reformation is not enough. There must be the positive acceptance of the Savior. In a coming day, the spirit of idolatry will decide to return to the house. He will be accompanied by seven other spirits more evil than himself. Since seven is the number of perfection or completeness, this probably refers to idolatry in its fully developed form. Israel will be possessed by the worst form of idolatry. This looks forward, of course, to the tribulation period when the apostate nation will worship the Antichrist. To bow down to the man of sin and to worship him as God is a more terrible form of idolatry than the nation has ever been guilty of in the past. And so the last state of that man becomes worse than the first. Unbelieving Israel will suffer the awful judgments of the great tribulation, and their suffering will far exceed that of the Babylonian captivity. The idolatrous portion of the nation will be utterly destroyed at Christ's second coming.

"So shall it be also be with this wicked generation" (v. 45). The same apostate Christ-rejecting race that rejected the Son of God at His first advent will suffer severe judgment at His second.

"Who is My mother?" (12:46-50)

These verses describe a seemingly ordinary incident in which Jesus' family comes to speak to Him. But the incident is full of spiritual significance; it marks a distinct turning point in His dealing with Israel. Someone told the Lord that His mother and His brothers were waiting outside, wishing to talk with Him. Why had they come? Mark may give us a clue. Some of Jesus' family decided He was out of His mind (Mark 3:21, 31-35). Jesus responded by asking, "Who is My mother and who are My brothers?" Then pointing to His disciples, He said in effect, "These who do the will of my Father in heaven are my brothers, and sisters, and mother."

What a startling announcement! What did it mean? Mary and her sons represented the nation of Israel, Jesus' blood relations. Up to now He had limited His ministry largely to the lost sheep of the house of Israel. But it was becoming abundantly clear that His own people would not have Him. Instead of bowing to Him as their Messiah, the Pharisees had accused Him of being controlled by Satan. So now Jesus announces a new order of things. From now on, His ties with Israel would no longer be the controlling factor in His outreach. Now, human relationships would take lower priority to spiritual considerations. It was obedience to God that would bring men and women into vital relationship with Him—and it wouldn't matter if they were Jews or Gentiles. Although the compassionate heart of Christ would continue to plead with His people, the Jews, it is clear that chapter 12 clearly signals a break with Israel.

The die is cast. Israel will not have Him, and so, He will turn to those who will.

7

MATTHEW 13–14

We have come to a crisis point in Matthew's gospel. At the close of the previous chapter the Lord indicated that earthly relationships were now superseded by spiritual ties, that it was no longer a question of Jewish birth but of obedience to God, the Father. The King had been rejected by the scribes and Pharisees. In rejecting the King, they were rejecting the kingdom. Now, by a series of parables, the Lord Jesus gives a preview of the new form the kingdom would take during the period between His rejection and His eventual manifestation as King of kings and Lord of lords.

> ———— ❧ ————
> **Earthly relationships were now superseded by spiritual ties.**
> ———— ❧ ————

As will be seen, these parables describe the kingdom of heaven. Six of them begin with the words, "The kingdom of heaven is like . . ." Let us review at this point some explanatory facts about the kingdom. First of all, the kingdom of heaven is the sphere where the rule of heaven is acknowledged. And since heaven is God's throne, it is the sphere where God's rule is acknowledged.

The Scriptures teach that the kingdom has two aspects which we may describe as outward profession and inward reality. In the first instance, it includes everyone who says that he recognizes God as rightful Ruler. But in its inner reality, it includes only those who are born-again, those who have entered the kingdom by being converted. In its broadest sense we could call it Christendom, but in its narrow sense it embraces only true Christianity.

We mentioned that the kingdom is found in five phases; every Bible reference to it should fit into one of these phases.

> ➤ It was *prophesied* in the Old Testament.

> ➤ It was announced by John the Baptist as being *at hand* or *present* in the Person of the King.

> ➤ It has an *interim* form. This is what we will be considering here in chapter 13. Following His rejection, the King returns to heaven, but the kingdom continues on earth wherever men profess to be His subjects.

> ➤ It will be followed by the kingdom in *manifestation*—the literal, thousand-year reign of Christ on earth.

> ➤ There is the *everlasting* kingdom of our Lord and Savior, Jesus Christ.

It must be emphasized once again that the kingdom is not the same as the church. The kingdom began before the church and will continue on earth after the church has been removed. The only identity between the kingdom and the church is this: the kingdom in its inward reality (i.e., consisting only of true believers) during the period from Pentecost to the rapture is composed of the same people as the church. With this background in mind, let us look at the parables.

The Parable of the Four Soils (13:1-9)

Jesus went out of the house where He had healed the demoniac and sat by the shore of the Sea of Galilee. Many Bible students see this as a symbolic act. The house pictures the nation of Israel and the sea represents the Gentiles. Thus the Lord's movement depicts a distinct break with Israel; during its interim form, the kingdom will be preached to the nations.

A parable is a story which has an underlying spiritual or moral teaching.

As a great multitude gathered on the beach, He entered a boat and began to teach the people by parables. A parable is a story which has an underlying spiritual or moral teaching which is not always clear immediately. The seven parables that follow tell us what the kingdom will be like during the time between Christ's first and second advents. The first four were spoken to the multitude; the last three were given only to the disciples. The Lord explained the first three and the seventh to the disciples, leaving them (and us) to interpret the others with the keys He had already given.

The first parable concerns a man who planted his seed in four different types of soil. As might be expected the results were different in each case. Read Matthew 13:3-8. Jesus closed the parable with the cryptic admonition, "He who has ears to hear, let him hear!" By use of the parable He was conveying an important message to the multitude, and a different message to the disciples. None should miss the significance of His words.

Since the Lord Himself interprets the parable in verses 18-23, we will restrain our curiosity until we reach that paragraph.

The Rationale of Parables (13:10-17)

The disciples were puzzled that the Lord should speak to the people in the veiled language of a parable, so they asked Him to explain His method. In His reply, Jesus distinguished between the unbelieving crowd and the believing disciples. The Jewish crowd, a cross-section of the nation, was quite obviously rejecting Him, even if their rejection would not be complete until the cross. They would not be permitted to know "the mysteries of the kingdom of heaven," whereas His true followers would be helped to understand.

The term *mystery* in the New Testament is (1) a fact which had never previously been known by man; (2) a fact that man could never learn apart from divine revelation; and (3) a fact that has now been revealed.

The mysteries of the kingdom were truths, unknown up till that time, concerning the kingdom in its interim form. The very fact that the kingdom would *have* an interim form had been a secret up to now. The parables describe some of the features of the kingdom during the time when the King would be absent. Some people therefore call this "the mystery form of the kingdom"—not that there is anything mysterious about it, but simply that it was never known before.

Now it may seem high-handed that these secrets should be withheld from the multitude and revealed to the disciples. But the Lord gives the reason in verse 12: "For whoever has, to him more will be given, and he will have abundance; but whoever does not have, even what he has will be taken away from him." The disciples had faith in the Lord Jesus; therefore, they would be given the capacity for more. They had accepted the light, therefore they would receive more light. The Jewish nation, on the other hand, had rejected the Light of the world; they would therefore not only be prevented from receiving more light, but would actually lose what little light they had.

It was not at all a matter of whim on the Lord's part. It was simply the outworking of a principle which is built into all of life, that willful blindness is followed by judicial blindness. That is why He spoke to the Jews in parables. They professed to see, that is, to be familiar with divine truth, but Truth Incarnate (that is, Jesus Christ) stood before them and they resolutely refused to see Him. They were unwilling to understand the wonderful fact of the Incarnation, so the capacity to understand was taken from them.

They were a living fulfillment of the prophecy of Isaiah 6:9-10. Israel's heart had grown dull, and their ears were insensitive to God's voice. They deliberately refused to see with their eyes. They knew that if they saw, and heard, and understood, and repented, God would heal them. But in their sickness and need, they refused His help. Therefore, their punishment was that they should hear but never understand, and see but not perceive (v. 14).

The disciples were tremendously privileged, because they were seeing what no one had seen before. The prophets and righteous men of the Old Testament had longed to be living when the Messiah actually arrived, but their desire had not been fulfilled. The disciples were favored to live at that crisis moment in history, to see the Messiah, to witness His miracles, and to hear the incomparable teaching which came from His lips.

The First Parable Explained (13:18-23)

Having explained why He used parables the Lord now proceeds to expound the parable of the four soils. He does not identify the sower, but we can be sure that it refers either to Himself (v. 37) or to those who preach the message of the kingdom for Him. He defines the seed as the word of the kingdom (v. 19). The soils represent those who hear the message:

1. The hard-packed pathway speaks of people who refuse to receive the message. They hear the gospel but do not understand it —not because they can't but because they won't. The birds are a picture of Satan; he snatches away the seed from the hearts of these hearers. He cooperates with them in their self-chosen barrenness. The Pharisees were hard-soil hearers.

2. When Jesus spoke of rocky ground, He undoubtedly had in mind a thin layer of earth covering a ledge of rock. This represents people who hear the word and respond enthusiastically and joyfully. At first the sower might be elated that his preaching is so successful. But soon he learns a deeper lesson; namely, that it is not good when the message is received with smiles and cheers. First there must be conviction of sin, contrition, and repentance. It is far more promising to see an inquirer weeping his way to Calvary than to see him walking down the aisle light-heartedly and exuberantly. The shallow earth yields a shallow profession; there is no depth to the root. His profession is tested by tribulations and persecutions that are as scorching as the sun. He decides it isn't worth it and abandons any profession of subjection to Christ.

3. The thorn-infested ground represents another class who hear the word and appear outwardly to be genuine subjects of the kingdom. But with the passing of time, their interest is choked out by the cares of the world and by their delight in riches. There is no fruit for God in their lives.

4. The good soil represents true believers. They hear the word receptively and understand it through obeying what they hear. Although they do not all bring forth the same amount of grain, they all show by their fruit that they have divine life. Fruit here is probably the manifestation of Christian character rather than souls won to Christ. When the word *fruit* is used in the New Testament, it generally refers to the fruit of the Spirit (Gal. 5:22-23).

What was the parable meant to say to the crowds? Obviously it was a warning against the danger of hearing without obeying. It was calculated also to encourage individuals to receive the Word sincerely, then to prove their reality by bringing forth fruit for God.

As for the disciples, the parable prepared them and all future followers of Jesus for the otherwise discouraging fact that relatively few of those who hear the message are genuinely saved. It saves Christ's loyal subjects from the delusion that all the world will be converted through the spread of the gospel. The disciples are also warned in this parable against the three great antagonists to the spread of the gospel: (1) the devil (the birds: the evil one); (2) the flesh (the scorching sun: tribulation or persecution); and (3) the world (the thorns: cares of the world and the delight in riches).

Finally the disciples are given a vision as to the tremendous returns from investing in human personality.

- ➢ Thirty fold is 3,000 percent return on the investment.
- ➢ Sixty fold is 6,000 percent return on the investment.
- ➢ One hundred fold is 10,000 percent return on the investment.

There is actually no way of measuring the results of a single case of genuine conversion. An unknown Sunday school teacher invested in D. L. Moody. Moody won others. They in turn won others. That Sunday school teacher started influences that will never stop.

The Parable of Wheat and Tares (13:24-30)

In the preceding parable we had a vivid illustration of the fact that the kingdom of heaven includes those who give only lip service to the King as well as those who are His genuine disciples. The first three soils typify the kingdom in its widest circle—outward profession. The fourth soil represents the kingdom as a smaller circle, including only those who have been converted.

> There is no way of measuring the results of a single case of genuine conversion.

This second parable—that of the wheat and the tares—also sets forth the kingdom in these two aspects. The wheat depicts true believers, whereas the tares are mere professing believers.

Jesus here compares the kingdom to a man who sowed good seed in his field. But while men slept, his enemy came and sowed weeds among the wheat. Unger says that the most common tare found in grain fields in the Holy Land is bearded darnel, "a poisonous grass, almost indistinguishable from wheat while the two are growing into blade. But when they come into ear, they can be separated without difficulty."

When the slaves saw the tares mixed in with the grain, they asked the householder how this happened. He immediately recognized it as the work of his enemy. The slaves were ready to pull the weeds immediately. But the farmer ordered them to wait till harvest, at which time the reapers would separate the two. The grain would be gathered into the barns and the darnel would be burned. Why did the farmer order this delay in separation?

In nature the roots of the grain and darnel so intertwine that it is virtually impossible to pull up one without the other.

This parable is explained by our Lord in verses 37-43, so we will forego further comment till then.

The Parable of the Mustard Seed (13:31-32)

Next, the Savior likens the kingdom to a mustard seed which is the smallest of seeds. When a man planted one of these seeds, it grew into a large shrub—so large that it is here called a tree. The smallest of seeds became the greatest of herbs. Though it was not a huge tree, it was large enough for birds to lodge in its branches.

The seed represents the humble beginning of the kingdom. In its early days the kingdom was kept relatively small and pure as a result of persecution. But with the patronage and protection of the state, it suffered abnormal growth. Then the birds of the air came and roosted in it. The same word for birds is used here as in verse 4; Jesus explained the birds as meaning the evil one (v. 19). And so the kingdom became a nesting place for Satan and his agents. Today the umbrella of Christendom covers such Christ-denying systems as Unitarianism, Christian Science, Mormonism, and Jehovah's Witnesses.

So here the Lord forewarned the disciples that during His absence the kingdom would experience a phenomenal growth. But they should not be deceived nor equate growth with success. It would be unhealthy growth. Though the tiny seed would become a large shrub, its largeness would become "a dwelling place of demons, a prison for every foul spirit, and a cage for every unclean and hated bird!" (Rev. 18:2).

The Parable of Leaven in the Meal (13:33)

The Lord Jesus then compared the kingdom to leaven (yeast) which a woman hid in three measures of meal (grain). Eventually all the grain became leavened. A common interpretation is that the meal is the world and the leaven is the gospel. The gospel will be preached throughout the world until eventually everyone will be saved. This view, however, is contradicted by Scripture, by history, and by current events.

Leaven is always used as a "type" of evil in the Bible. When God commanded His people to rid their houses of leaven (Ex. 12:15), they understood that leaven was a type of evil. If anyone ate what was leavened from the first day till the seventh day, that person would be cut off from Israel (Ex. 12:15). In the New Testament Jesus warned against the leaven of the Pharisees and Sadducees (Matt. 16:6, 12) and the leaven of Herod (Mark 8:15). In 1 Corinthians 5:6-8 leaven is defined as malice and wickedness, and the context of Galatians 5:9 shows that there it means false teaching. In general, leaven means either evil doctrine or evil behavior.

And so in this parable the Lord warns against the permeating power of evil working in the kingdom of heaven. Just as the parable of the mustard seed shows evil in the external character of the kingdom, so this parable shows the inward corruption that would take place.

We believe then that the interpretation of the parable is this. The grain, a staple food commodity, represents the food of God's people as it is found in the Bible. The leaven is evil doctrine. The woman is a false prophetess who teaches and tricks (Rev. 2:20). Is it not significant that women have been the founders of several of the false cults? Forbidden by the Bible to teach in the church (1 Cor. 14:34; 1 Tim. 2:12), they have defiantly taken the place of doctrinal authorities and have defiled the food of God's people with destructive heresies.

A Fulfillment of Prophecy (13:34-35)

The first four parables were spoken to the multitudes. The use of this teaching method by the Lord Jesus was in fulfillment of the prophecy of Asaph in Psalm 78:2, where the seer prophesied that the Messiah would speak in parables about things that were hidden from the foundation of the world. These features of the kingdom of heaven in its interim form were secret up until this time. Now they were being made known.

Explanation of the Second Parable (13:36-43)

The remainder of the Lord's discourse was spoken to the disciples, inside the house. Here the disciples may represent the believing remnant of the nation of Israel. The renewed mention of the house reminds us that God has not rejected forever His people whom He foreknew (Rom. 11:2).

In His interpretation of the wheat and tares parable, Jesus identified Himself as the sower. He was the sower directly during His earthly ministry, and He is the sower indirectly through His servants in all succeeding ages.

The field is the world. It is very important to emphasize this. The field is not the church; the field is the world. The good seed means the sons of the kingdom, the point being that these sons of the kingdom were "sown" in the world. During His three years of public ministry, Jesus sowed the world with disciples who were loyal subjects of the kingdom.

> Satan has a counterfeit for every divine reality.

The weeds are the sons of the evil one. Satan has a counterfeit for every divine reality. He sows the world with those who look like disciples, talk like disciples, and, to some extent, walk like disciples. But they are not genuine followers of the King. The enemy, of course, is Satan. He is the enemy of God and of all who are the people of God.

The harvest is the close of the age; that is, the end of the kingdom age in its interim form. This age will end when Jesus Christ returns in power and glory to reign as King. The Lord is not referring to the end of the church age; it leads only to confusion to introduce the church here.

The reapers are the angels (see Rev. 14:14-20). During the present phase of the kingdom, no forcible separation is made of the wheat and the darnel. They are allowed to grow together. But at the second advent of Christ, the angels will round up all causes of sin and all evildoers and throw them into the furnace of fire, a place of torment. The wheat gathered into barns simply means that the righteous kingdom subjects who are on earth during the tribulation will enter the glorious kingdom to enjoy the millennial reign of Christ.

Again Jesus adds the cryptic advice, "He who has ears to hear, let him hear!"

This parable does not justify, as some mistakenly suppose, the toleration of ungodly people in a local Christian church. Remember that the field is the world, not the church. Local churches are explicitly commanded to put out of their fellowship all who are guilty of certain forms of wickedness (1 Cor. 5:9-13). The parable simply teaches that in its mystery form, the kingdom of heaven will include both the real and the counterfeit, and that this condition will continue till the end of the age. Then God's messengers will separate the false from the true. The former will be taken away in judgment; the latter will be left to enjoy the glorious reign of Christ on earth.

The Parable of the Hidden Treasure (13:44)

All the parables so far have taught that there will be good and evil in the kingdom, righteous and unrighteous subjects. The next two parables concentrate on the righteous subjects and show that there will be two classes of them:

1. Believing Jews during the periods before and after the church age. These make up a godly remnant of Israelites, represented by the treasure hidden in the field.

2. Believing Jews and Gentiles during the present age. These make up the church, represented by the pearl of great price.

In the parable of the treasure, Jesus compares the kingdom to a treasure hidden in a field. A man finds it, covers it up, then gladly goes and sells all that he has to buy the field. We would suggest that the man is the Lord Jesus Himself. (He was the man in the parable of the wheat and tares, v. 37.) The treasure represents a godly remnant of believing Jews such as existed during Jesus' earthly ministry and will exist again after the church is raptured. These believing Jews are hidden in the field in the sense that they are dispersed throughout the world and in a real sense unknown to any but God. Jesus is pictured as discovering this treasure, then going to the cross and giving all that He had in order to buy the world (2 Cor. 5:19; 1 John 2:2) where the treasure was hidden. Redeemed Israel will be brought out of hiding when her Deliverer comes out of Zion and sets up the long-awaited messianic kingdom.

The parable is sometimes applied to a sinner, giving up all in order to find Christ, the greatest Treasure. But this interpretation violates the doctrine of grace which insists that salvation is without money and without price (Isa. 55:1; Eph. 2:8-9).

The Parable of the Costly Pearl (13:45-46)

The kingdom is also likened to a dealer searching for fine pearls. When he finds a pearl of unusually great value, he goes and sacrifices all he has to buy it. There is a hymn that says, "I've found the Pearl of greatest price." In the hymn, the finder is the sinner and the Pearl is the Savior. But once again we protest that the sinner does not have to sell all and does not have to buy Christ. We believe that the merchantman is the Lord Jesus. The pearl of great price is the church. At Calvary He sold all that He had to buy this pearl.

It is interesting that in the parable of the treasure, the kingdom is likened to the treasure itself. Here the kingdom is not likened to the pearl but to the merchantman. Why this difference? In the preceding parable, the emphasis is on the treasure—redeemed Israel. The kingdom is very closely linked with the nation of Israel. It was originally offered to that nation and, in its future form, the Jewish people will be the main subjects of the kingdom.

In this parable, the emphasis is on Christ, not the church. As we have already mentioned, the church is not the same as the kingdom. All who are in the church are in the kingdom in its interim form, but not all who are in the kingdom are in the church. The church will not be in the kingdom in its future form but will reign with Christ over the renewed earth. The emphasis here is on the King Himself and on the tremendous price He paid to woo and win a bride that would share His glory in the day of His manifestation.

The sea in Scripture is linked with the Gentiles, just as the land is linked with Israel. As the pearl comes out of the sea, so the church comes largely, though not exclusively, from the nations. This does not overlook the fact that there are converted Israelites in it, but it merely states that the dominant feature of the church is that it is a people called out from the nations for His name.

The Parable of the Dragnet (13:47-50)

The final parable in the series likens the kingdom to a net which was thrown into the sea and gathered fish of every kind. The fishermen sorted out the fish, keeping the good in containers and discarding the bad.

Our Lord interprets the parable. The time is the end of the age; that is, the end of the tribulation period. It is the time of the second advent of Christ. The fishermen are the angels. The good fish are the righteous; that is, saved people, both Jews and Gentiles. The bad fish are the unrighteous; that is, unbelieving people of all races. A separation takes place, as we also saw in the parable of the wheat and tares. The righteous enter the kingdom of their Father, whereas the unrighteous are sent to a place of fire where there is weeping and gnashing of teeth. This is not the final judgment, of course; this judgment takes place at the outset of the millennium; the final judgment occurs at the end of the thousand years (Rev. 20:7-15).

Disciples, Scribes, Householders (13:51-52)

As soon as He finished telling the parables, the Master Teacher asked His disciples if they understood. They replied, "Yes." This may surprise us, and may even make us slightly jealous of them. Perhaps we cannot answer yes so confidently.

> Disciples are to be channels—not terminals—of blessing.

Because they understood, they were obligated to share with others. Disciples are meant to be channels—not terminals—of blessing. The twelve were now scribes trained for the kingdom of heaven; that is, teachers and interpreters of the truth. They were like a householder who brings out of his treasure things old and new. In the Old Testament they had a rich deposit of what we might call old truth. In the parabolic teaching of Christ, they had just received what was completely new. From this vast storehouse of knowledge they should now impart the glorious truth to others.

A Prophet Without Honor (13:53-58)

Having finished His discourse on the parables, Jesus left the shores of Galilee and went to Nazareth for His last visit there. As He taught in the synagogue, the people were astonished at His wisdom and His reported miracles. To them He was only the son of Joseph the carpenter. They knew His mother by name, and His brothers, James, Joseph, Simon, and Judas. And His sisters—they were still living there in Nazareth! How then could one of their own home town boys say and do the things for which He had become so well known? It puzzled them, and they found it easier to cling to their ignorance than to acknowledge the truth. They took offense at Him.

This prompted Jesus to point out that a genuine prophet is generally more appreciated away from home. As the saying goes, "familiarity breeds contempt." This unfortunate twist in fallen human nature never brought sadder consequences than when the Son of God visited Nazareth. "He did not do many mighty works there because of their unbelief" (v. 58). It was not because He could not do them; man's wickedness cannot restrain the power of God. But He did not do the miracles because He would have been blessing where there was no desire for blessing. He would have been meeting needs where there was no consciousness of need.

Herod's Uneasy Conscience (14:1-12)

News of Jesus' ministry flowed back to Herod the tetrarch. This infamous son of Herod the Great was also known as Herod Antipas. It was he who had ordered the execution of John the Baptist. When he heard of Christ's miracles, his conscience began to stab him awake. The memory of the slain prophet kept coming before him. He told his servants, "It's John. He has come back from the dead. That explains these miracles."

In verses 3-12 we have what is known as a literary flashback. Matthew interrupts the narrative to review the circumstances surrounding John's death. This is how it had happened: Herod had abandoned his own wife and had been living in an adulterous, incestuous relationship with his brother's wife, Herodias. As a prophet of God, John could not let this pass without rebuke. Indignantly and fearlessly, he pointed his finger at Herod and denounced him for his immorality.

The king was angry enough to kill him but the people acclaimed John as a prophet, and they would have reacted, perhaps violently, against John's execution. So the tyrant satisfied his rage momentarily by having John imprisoned. Later, on his birthday, the daughter of Herodias so pleased the king by her dancing that he impulsively offered her anything she wanted. Prompted by her ungodly mother, she asked for John's head on a platter. By now the king's anger against John had calmed down somewhat; perhaps he even admired the prophet for his courage and integrity. But it was too late for regret. Though he was sorry, he felt he had to fulfill his promise. The order was given. John was beheaded and the gruesome request of the dancing girl was granted.

> In times of persecution, suffering, and sorrow, we too should go and tell it to Jesus.

John's disciples gave their master's body a respectful burial, then they went and told Jesus. They could not have gone to anyone better to pour out their sorrow, grief, and indignation. Nor could they have left us a better example. In times of persecution, oppression, suffering, and sorrow, we too should go and tell it to Jesus.

As for Herod, his crime was finished but the memory lingered on. Now when he heard of Jesus' activities, the entire episode returned to haunt him.

Five Thousand Are Fed (14:13-21)

When Jesus heard that Herod was troubled by reports of His miracles, He withdrew by boat to go to a secluded area by the Sea of Galilee. We can be sure He did not go because of fear; He knew that nothing could happen to Him before His time came. We do not know the main reasons for His move, but a lesser reason was that His disciples had just returned from their preaching mission (Mark 6:30; Luke 9:10) and needed a time of rest and quietness. However, the crowds flocked out to Him on foot. As He went ashore, they were waiting for Him. Far from being annoyed by this intrusion on His privacy, our compassionate Lord set to work immediately, healing their sick.

When evening came, the disciples felt that a crisis was brewing. So many people, and nothing for them to eat! So they asked Jesus to send the people to the villages where they could get food. How little they understood the heart of Christ or discerned His power!

The Lord quietly assured them that there was no need for the people to leave. Then He completely caught the disciples off guard by saying, "You give them something to eat." They were staggered. "Give them something to eat? We have nothing but five loaves and two fish." They had forgotten that they also had Jesus. Patiently He replied, "Bring them here to me."

We can picture the Lord directing the crowds to sit down on the grass. Taking the loaves and fish, He gave thanks, broke the loaves, and gave them to the disciples for distribution to the hungry crowds. There was plenty for all. When they were all satisfied, the disciples gathered up twelve baskets of leftovers. When Jesus finished there was more left over than when He began—ironically, enough for a basket for each unbelieving disciple. And a multitude of perhaps 10,000 to 15,000 had been fed (5,000 men plus women and children).

The miracle was intended as a spiritual lesson for disciples of every generation. The hungry multitude is always present. There is always a little band of disciples with seemingly pitiful resources. And ever and always there is the compassionate Savior. When disciples are willing to give Him what little they have, He multiplies it to feed thousands. The notable difference is this: The 5,000 men who were fed that day had their hunger satisfied only for a short time; those today who feed upon the living Christ are satisfied forever (see John 14:12).

In his description of this miracle, John tells us that "when the people saw the sign which he had done, they said, 'This is truly the prophet who is to come into the world!'" (John 6:14).

A Storm on Galilee (14:22-33)

The previous miracle assured the disciples that they were following One who could abundantly provide for their needs. Now they learn that they have One who can protect them and empower them as well.

While He was dismissing the multitude, Jesus told the disciples to get in the boat and start back to the other side of the lake. Then He Himself went up on a hillside to pray. When evening came He was there alone. (In Jewish reckoning there were two evenings. One began in mid-afternoon and the other at sunset. The first is referred to in verse 15 and the second here.)

In the meantime the boat was far from land and battling a contrary wind. As the boat was being battered by the waves, Jesus saw the plight of the disciples. In the fourth watch of the night, that is, between 3 and 6 a.m., He came to them walking on the water. Thinking it was a ghost, the disciples panicked. But immediately they heard the reassuring voice of their Master and Friend, "Be of good cheer! It is I; do not be afraid" (v. 27).

How true to our own experience! We are often storm-tossed, tried, concerned, in despair. The Lord seems far away. But all the time He is praying for us. When the night seems darkest, He is near at hand. We often mistake Him even then and push the panic button. Then we hear His comforting voice and remember that the waves that caused us to fear are under His feet.

When Peter heard the well-known and well-loved voice, his affection and enthusiasm bubbled over. "Lord, if it is you, command me to come to You on the water." Rather than magnify Peter's "if" as a sign of small faith, we should instead see his bold request as a mark of great trust. Peter sensed that Jesus' commands are His enablings; that He gives strength for whatever He orders.

As soon as Jesus said "Come," Peter jumped out of the boat and began walking toward Him. As long as he kept his eyes on Jesus, he was able to do the impossible; but the minute he became occupied with the strong wind, he began to sink. Frantically he cried, "Lord, save me." Then the Lord took him by the hand, gently rebuked his little faith, and brought him to the boat. As soon as Jesus went on board, the wind ceased. A worship meeting took place in the boat with the disciples saying to Jesus, "Truly you are the Son of God."

> The Christian life is like walking on water. It is humanly impossible.

The Christian life is like walking on water. It is humanly impossible. It can only be lived by the power of the Holy Spirit. As long as we look away from every other object and to Jesus only (Heb. 12:2), we can experience a supernatural life. But the minute we become occupied with ourselves or our circumstances, we begin to sink. Then we must cry to Christ for restoration and for divine enablement.

Jesus Heals in Gennesaret (14:34-36)

The boat docked at Gennesaret (pronounced Ge-nes-a-ret), a city located on the northwest shore of the Sea of Galilee. As soon as the men spotted Jesus, they scoured the area for all that were sick and brought them to Him. They simply asked that the sick might touch the fringe of His garment; as many as did were healed. For a while, at least, there were no sick people in that area. The district experienced health and healing through a visit by the Great Physician.

8

MATTHEW 15–17

It is often pointed out that Matthew's gospel does not follow a chronological order during the early chapters. But from the beginning of chapter 14 to the end, the events are largely given in the order in which they happened.

In this chapter a dispensational order also emerges, as follows:

1. The continued haggling and bickering of the Pharisees and scribes (vv. 1-20) anticipates Israel's rejection of the Messiah.

2. The faith of the Canaanite woman (vv. 21-28) pictures the gospel going out to the Gentiles in this present age.

3. The healing of great crowds (vv. 29-31) and the feeding of 4,000 (vv. 32-39) point us to the future millennial age with its world-wide blessings of health and prosperity.

What Is Clean and Unclean? (15:1-20)

The Pharisees and scribes were tireless in their efforts to trap Jesus. A delegation of them came to Him from Jerusalem, charging His disciples with uncleanness for eating with unwashed hands and therefore violating the tradition of the elders. In order to appreciate this incident, we must understand the references to clean and unclean, and we must also know what the Pharisees meant by washing.

First of all, the whole concept of clean and unclean goes back to the Old Testament Scriptures. It had nothing to do with physical, moral, or spiritual cleanness, but was entirely a ceremonial matter. If a person touched a dead body, for instance, he was ceremonially unclean. Or, if he ate certain things, he contracted ceremonial defilement. This meant that he was not ritually fit to worship God. Before he could approach God, the law required him to go through a cleansing ritual. This was not the tradition of the elders, but the law of God.

The elders, however, had added tradition to the cleansing rituals. They insisted, for instance, that before a Jew ate, he should put his hands through an elaborate cleansing process. It wasn't enough just to wash his hands, as we do and as the disciples of Jesus probably did. They required the washing of the arms up to the elbows and added other details without which cleansing was not official. Thus, when the Pharisees criticized the disciples, it was for their failure to observe these additional rules.

The Lord Jesus reminded His critics that what *they* were transgressing was "the commandment of God," not simply the tradition of the elders. Then He went on to give an example of how they did this. The law commanded the Jews to honor their parents (v. 4). This would include supporting them financially if the parents were in need. But the scribes and Pharisees (and many others) did not want to spend their money for the support of their aged parents. So they devised a tradition by which to avoid their responsibility. When asked for help by father or mother, all they had to do was recite such words as these: "Any money which I have and which could be used to support you has been dedicated to God, and therefore I cannot give it to you." Having recited this formula (v. 5), they were free from financial responsibility to their parents.

Thus by following this devious tradition, they had robbed the Scriptures of its authority in its command to them to take care of their parents. And in doing so they fulfilled the prophecy of Isaiah 29:13 in that they professed to honor God with their lips, but their hearts were far from Him. Their worship was worthless because they were giving higher priority to the traditions of men than to what God said.

Turning to the multitude, Jesus made a very significant pronouncement. He declared that what goes into the mouth doesn't defile a man, but rather what comes out. This was a revolutionary statement. Under the Levitical code, what went into the mouth *did* defile a man. The Jews were forbidden to eat the meat of any animal which did not chew the cud or have cloven hooves. They were not allowed to eat fish unless it had scales and gills. Detailed instructions were given by God as to foods that were clean and unclean.

Now, the Law-giver paved the way for dissolving the whole system of ceremonial defilement. He said that the food which His disciples ate with unwashed hands did not defile them. But as for the hypocrisy of the scribes and Pharisees—that was truly defiling.

When the disciples brought word that the Pharisees were offended by this denunciation, Jesus answered by comparing them to plants which had not been divinely planted. They were tares rather than wheat, and would eventually be uprooted (that is, destroyed). Then He added, "Let them alone; they are blind leaders of the blind." Although they professed to be authorities in spiritual matters, they were blind to spiritual realities. The people they were leading were blind also. It was inevitable that leaders and followers would fall into a pit.

The disciples were undoubtedly shaken by this complete reversal of all they had been taught about clean and unclean foods. It was like a parable to them—obscure and veiled. Peter put their unsettlement into words when he asked for an explanation of the parable.

─────── ❧ ───────
True defilement is moral, not physical.
─────── ❧ ───────

The Lord first expressed wonder that they were so slow to understand. Then He explained that true defilement is moral, not physical. Edible foods are not clean or unclean in and of themselves. In fact, no material thing is essentially evil in itself; it is the abuse of a thing that is wrong. The food man eats enters his mouth, goes into his stomach for digestion, then the unassimilated residue is evacuated. His moral being is not affected—only his body.

If food doesn't defile, then what does? Jesus answered, "Those things which proceed out of the mouth come from the heart, and they defile a man." Here "the heart" is not the organ that pumps the blood, but the evil, corrupt source of human motives and desires. This part of man's moral nature manifests itself by impure thoughts, then by depraved words, then by evil acts, of which the Lord lists some examples in verse 19.

The Pharisees and scribes were extremely careful when it came to the showy and detailed observance of hand-washing ceremonies. But their inner lives were polluted. They majored in minors and overlooked the matters of real importance. They could criticize the disciples for failure to keep manmade traditions, yet plot to kill the Son of God and be guilty of that whole catalog of sin.

The Faith of a Gentile (15:21-28)

Jesus withdrew to the region of Tyre and Sidon, on the Mediterranean coast. As far as we know, this was the only time during His public ministry that He was outside Jewish territory. Here in Phoenicia, a Canaanite woman asked Him to heal her demon-possessed daughter.

It is important to realize that this woman was a Gentile, not a Jewess. She was descended from the Canaanites, an immoral race which God had marked for utter extinction. Through Israel's disobedience, some had survived the invasion of Canaan under Joshua, and this woman was a descendant of the surviving remnant. As a Gentile, she did not enjoy the privileges of God's chosen earthly people. She was an alien, a stranger, having no hope, and without God in the world (Eph. 2:12). As far as her status was concerned, she had no claim on God or on His Messiah. But when she spoke to Jesus, she addressed Him as the Lord, the Son of David. This was a title which the Jews used in speaking of the Messiah. Although Jesus *was* the Son of David, a Gentile had no right to approach Him on that basis. That is why He did not answer her at first.

The disciples urged Him to send her away; to them she was a nuisance. To Him she was a welcome example of faith and a vessel in whom His grace would shine. But first He must prove and educate her faith! He reminded the woman that His mission was to Israel, not to Gentiles, and certainly not to Canaanites. She was not put off by this apparent refusal. Dropping the title "Son of David," she worshiped Him, saying, "Lord, help me." If she couldn't come to Him as a Jew to her Messiah, she would come as a creature to her Creator.

In order to prove further the reality of her faith, Jesus told her that it was not right for Him to turn aside from feeding the Jewish children in order to give bread to Gentile dogs. If this sounds harsh to us, we should remember that, like the surgeon's scalpel, it was not intended to hurt but to heal. She *was* a Gentile. The Jews looked upon the Gentiles as scavenging dogs, prowling around the streets for scraps of food. However, Jesus here used the word for pet dogs. The question was, would she acknowledge her unworthiness to receive the least of His mercies?

Her reply was magnificent. She agreed with His description completely. Taking the place of an unworthy Gentile, she cast herself on His mercy, compassion, and grace. She said, in effect, "You are right! I am only a dog under the table. You are feeding your chosen people at the table. But I notice that crumbs sometimes drop from the table to the floor. Won't you let me have some crumbs? I am not worthy that you should heal my daughter, but I beseech you to do it for one of your undeserving creatures."

Jesus commended her for her great faith. While the unbelieving children had no hunger for the bread, here was a self-confessed dog who was crying out for it. Her faith was rewarded; her daughter was healed instantly. The fact that our Lord healed this Gentile daughter at a distance suggests His present ministry at God's right hand, bestowing spiritual healing on Gentiles during this age when His ancient people are set aside nationally.

Healing for the Multitudes (15:29-31)

In Mark's gospel (7:31) we learn that Jesus left Tyre, then traveled north to Sidon, eastward across the Jordan, and south through the region of the Decapolis (meaning "ten cities"). There, near the Sea of Galilee, He healed the lame, the maimed (amputees), the blind, the dumb, and many others. The crowd, probably Gentile, was astonished; they glorified the God of Israel. The people naturally associated Jesus and His disciples with Israel, therefore they correctly deduced that the God of Israel was working in their midst.

Four Thousand Are Fed (15:32-39)

Careless readers, confusing the following incident with the feeding of the 5,000, have accused the Bible of error. The fact is that the two incidents are quite distinct, and they supplement rather than contradict each other.

After three days with the Lord, the multitude had run out of food. He would not let them go away hungry; they might collapse on the way. Again the disciples became frustrated at the impossible task of feeding such a mob; this time they had only seven loaves and a few fish.

As in the case of the 5,000, Jesus seated the people, gave thanks, broke the loaves and fishes and handed them to the disciples for distribution. He expects His disciples to do what they can; then He steps in and does what they cannot. After the people had had enough, there were seven baskets of surplus food. The number fed was 4,000 men, plus women and children. In the next chapter we shall see that the statistics relating to the two feeding miracles are significant (16:8-12). Every detail of the Bible narrative is charged with meaning.

After dismissing the crowd, Jesus went by boat to Magadan, or Magdala, located on the west shore of the Sea of Galilee.

Signs of the Times (16:1-4)

The Pharisees and Sadducees held very different doctrinal beliefs, but they were now united in a common aim to trip up the Lord Jesus. To test Him they asked Him to demonstrate a sign from heaven. In doing so, perhaps they were implying an opposite source for His previous miracles. Or perhaps they wanted some supernatural sign in the sky. All Jesus' miracles had been performed on the earth; could He do celestial miracles as well?

Jesus replied by continuing the theme of the sky. They knew how to interpret the weather from the appearance of the sky, but they could not interpret the signs of the times. What *were* the signs of the times? First, the prophet who announced the advent of the Messiah had appeared in the person of John the Baptist. Second, they had witnessed miracles which were prophesied of the Messiah. They saw Him do things that no other man had ever done, like giving sight to people born blind and raising the dead to life. Another sign of the times was the obvious rejection of the Messiah by the Jews and the movement of the gospel to the Gentiles, all in fulfillment of prophecy. Yet in spite of this clear evidence, they had no sense of history being made or of prophecy being fulfilled.

> The sign of the prophet Jonah would be the resurrection of Christ on the third day.

In seeking for a sign when He Himself stood in their midst, the Pharisees and Sadducees exposed themselves as an evil and spiritually adulterous generation. No sign would now be given to them but the sign of the prophet Jonah. As explained in the notes on 12:39, this would be the resurrection of Christ on the third day. This generation would crucify its Messiah, but God would raise Him out from among the dead. This would be a sign of the doom of all who refuse to bow to Him as rightful Ruler.

The paragraph closes with the ominous words, "And He left them and departed." The spiritual implications of the words should be obvious to all.

Divine Mathematics (16:5-12)

When the disciples rejoined the Lord on the east side of the lake, they had forgotten to take food with them. Therefore when Jesus greeted them with a warning to beware of the leaven of the Pharisees and Sadducees, they thought He was saying, "Don't go to those Jewish leaders for food supplies!" Their preoccupation with food caused them to look for a literal, natural explanation where a spiritual lesson was intended.

They were still worrying about a food shortage in spite of the fact that He who fed the 5,000 and the 4,000 was with them. So He went over the details of the two miraculous feedings with them. It was a lesson in divine arithmetic and divine resourcefulness. The lesson that emerges from these figures is this: the less Jesus had to work with, the more He fed, and the more food there was left over. When there were only five loaves and two fish, He fed 5,000+ and had twelve baskets of food left. With more loaves and fish, He fed only 4,000+ and had left over only seven baskets. If we put our limited resources at His disposal, He can multiply them in inverse proportion to their amount. "Little is much if God is in it."

It should be mentioned that a different word is used for baskets here than in the feeding of the 5,000. Generally the seven baskets in this incident are considered to have been larger than the twelve on the previous occasion. But the underlying lesson abides: why worry about hunger and want when we are linked with One who has infinite power and resourcefulness?

When the Lord had spoken of the leaven of the Pharisees and Sadducees, He was not referring to bread but to evil doctrine and conduct. In Luke 12:1 the leaven of the Pharisees is defined as hypocrisy. They professed to obey the Scriptures in the smallest details, yet their obedience was external and shallow. Inwardly they were evil and corrupt. The leaven of the Sadducees was rationalism. They were the freethinkers of their day. Like the liberals of today, they had built up a system of doubts and denials. They denied the existence of angels and spirits. They denied the resurrection of the body. They denied the immortality of the soul. They denied eternal punishment. This leaven of skepticism, if tolerated, will spread and permeate like yeast in bread dough.

The "Watershed" of the Gospels (16:13-20)

Caesarea Philippi was about twenty-five miles north of the Sea of Galilee and five miles east of the Jordan. When Jesus came to the surrounding villages (Mark 8:27) an incident took place which is generally recognized as the climax of His teaching ministry. Up till this time He had been leading His disciples to a true understanding of His Person. Having succeeded in this mission, He now turns His face resolutely to go to the cross.

He began by asking His disciples what men were saying as to His identity. The replies He got were John the Baptist, Elijah, Jeremiah, or one of the other prophets. To the average person He was one among many. Good but not the Best. Great but not the Greatest. A prophet but not *the* Prophet. This view would never do. If He were only another man, then He was a fraud, because He claimed to be equal with God the Father. So He asked the disciples who *they* believed He was. This brought from Peter the historic confession, "You are the Christ, the Son of the living God." In other words, He was Israel's Messiah and God the Son.

Our Lord pronounced a blessing on Peter. The fisherman had not arrived at this new concept of the Lord Jesus as a result of his intellect or native wisdom; it had been supernaturally revealed to him by God the Father. The Father had spoken, but the Son had something important to say to Peter also. So Jesus added, "I also say to you that you are Peter, and on this rock I will build My church, and the gates of Hades shall not prevail against it." We all know that more controversy has swirled around this verse than almost any other verse in the gospel. The question, of course, is, "Who or what is 'the rock'?"

> The rock is Peter's confession that Christ is the Son of the living God.

Part of the problem arises from the fact that the Greek words for "Peter" and for "rock" are similar. The first is *petros,* and the second, *petra.* But the meanings are different. The first means "stone"; the second means "rock." So what Jesus really said was, ". . . you are Peter [stone], and on this rock I will build My church." He did not say He would build His church on a stone but on a rock.

If Peter is not the rock, then what is? From the context, the most obvious answer is that the rock is Peter's confession that Christ is the Son of the living God. The church is founded on the truth that Christ is none other than the Son of God. Ephesians 2:20 distinctly teaches that the church is built on Jesus Christ, the chief cornerstone. When it says that we are built upon the foundation of the apostles and prophets, it does not mean that they are the foundation; they laid the foundation in their teachings concerning the Lord Jesus Christ.

Christ is spoken of as a Rock in 1 Corinthians 10:4. In this connection, G. Campbell Morgan gives a helpful reminder:

> "Remember, He was talking to Jews. If we trace the figurative use of the word rock through Hebrew Scriptures, we find that it is never used symbolically of man, but always of God. So here at Caesarea Philippi, it is not upon Peter that the Church is built. Jesus did not trifle with figures of speech. He took up their old Hebrew illustration—rock, always the symbol of Deity—and said, 'Upon God Himself—Christ, the Son of the living God—I will build my church.'"

Peter never spoke of himself as the foundation of the church. Twice he referred to Christ as a Stone (Acts 4:11, 12; 1 Peter 2:4-8), but then the figure is different; the stone is the head of the corner, not the foundation.

> After Israel's rejection of Christ, a "gap" period, the church age, follows.

In verse 18 we have the first mention of the church in the Bible. The church did not exist in the Old Testament. In fact, it was obviously future when Jesus spoke these words. The church was formed on the day of Pentecost and is composed of all true believers in Christ, both Jew and Gentile. It is a distinct society known as the body and bride of Christ, and has a unique heavenly calling and destiny.

A question may arise, "Why is the church first mentioned in Matthew's gospel, a book in which Israel and the kingdom are the prominent themes?" The answer is that after Israel's rejection of Christ, a "gap" period, the church age, follows. This age will continue to the rapture. Then God will resume His dealings with Israel nationally. So it is fitting that God should introduce the church here as the next step in His dispensational program after Israel's rejection.

Christ's assurance that "the gates of Hades shall not prevail against it" may be understood in two ways. First, the gates of Hades are pictured in an unsuccessful offensive against the church—the church will survive any and all attacks upon it. Or the church itself may be pictured as taking the offensive and coming off victor. In either case, the powers of death will be defeated by the rapture of living believers and by the resurrection of the dead in Christ.

"I will give you the keys of the kingdom of heaven" (v. 19). As previously explained, the kingdom of heaven describes the sphere on earth containing all who claim allegiance to the King. "Keys" speak of access or entrance. The means by which men enter the kingdom are suggested in the Great Commission (Matt. 28:19)—discipling, baptizing, and teaching. These are the keys which open the door to the sphere of profession. Not that baptism is necessary for salvation; rather, it is the initiatory rite by which men publicly profess their allegiance to the King.

Peter first used the keys on the day of Pentecost when he preached to thousands of Jews in Jerusalem. This verse does not mean that Peter was given authority to admit men to heaven. This has to do with the kingdom of heaven on earth, not with heaven itself. And the keys were not given to Peter exclusively but to him as a representative of all the disciples (see Matthew 18:18, where the same promise is given to them all). Verse 19 and a companion passage in John 20:23 are sometimes used to teach that Peter and his successors were given the authority to forgive sins. We know that this cannot be so; only God can forgive sins.

_____ ❧ _____

The keys were not given to Peter exclusively, but to him as a representative of all the disciples.

_____ ❧ _____

We must remember that these words were spoken to Peter and the other apostles. It is undeniable that definite authority was given to them which was not handed down to others. An illustration of this is found in the case of Ananias and Sapphira. God ratified Peter's judgment, and both offenders were punished with instant death (Acts 5:1-10). In this instance, their sins were bound upon them. A case where sins were loosed is the incestuous man in Corinth. In 2 Corinthians 2:10 we see the apostle Paul loosing the guilty person from the consequences of his sin because he had repented. Paul loosed on earth, and his action was ratified in heaven.

The only way in which this is true today is in a *declarative* sense. In other words, when a sinner truly repents of his sins and receives Jesus Christ as Lord and Savior, a Christian can *declare* that person's sins to be forgiven. On the other hand, when a sinner rejects the Savior, a Christian worker can *declare* his sins to be retained. "Whenever the Church acts in the name of the Lord and really does His will, the stamp of God is upon their deeds" (William Kelly).

In verse 20, we again find the Lord Jesus charging the disciples to tell no one that He was the Messiah, for the same reasons explained already.

Peter's Protest Is Rebuked (16:21-23)

Now that the disciples had come to realize that Jesus is the Messiah, the Son of the living God, they were ready to hear His first direct prediction of His death and resurrection. The disciples now knew that His cause could never fail; that they were on the winning side; that no matter what happened, triumph was assured. So the Lord broke the news to prepared hearts. He must go to Jerusalem, must suffer many things from the religious leaders, must be slain, and must be raised on the third day. The news was enough to spell the doom of any movement—all except that last imperative, "must be raised on the third day." That is what made the difference.

Peter was indignant at the thought of His Master's enduring such treatment. Catching hold of Him as if to block His path, he protested, "Far be it from You, Lord; this shall not happen to You!" This drew a rebuke from the Lord Jesus (v. 23). In calling Peter "Satan," Jesus did not imply that the apostle was demon-possessed or Satan controlled. He simply meant that Peter's actions and words were what could be expected of Satan (whose name means "adversary"). By protesting against Calvary, Peter became a hindrance to Christ. His attitude was not in keeping with God's plan for the redemption of man; rather, he was thinking as a mere man.

Every Christian is called to take up his cross and follow the Lord Jesus. Whenever the cross looms up in the pathway ahead, a voice within says, "Be it far from you. Save yourself." Or perhaps it is the voice of loved ones seeking to deflect us from the path of obedience. In words of mock pity, the devil would spare us from the sharpness of the cross, the pain, the chill, the loneliness. At such times, we too must say, "Get behind me, Satan! You are a hindrance to me."

> "There are times when fond love seeks to deflect us from the perils of the path of God; but the real love is not the love which holds the knight at home, when he should go out to battle, but the love which sends him out to obey the commandments of the chivalry which is given, not to make life easy, but to make life great. It is quite possible for love to be so protecting that it seeks to protect those it loves from the adventure of the warfare of the soldier of Christ, and from the strenuousness of the pathway of the pilgrim

of God. That which really wounded Jesus' heart, and that which made Him speak as He did speak, was that the tempter spoke to Him that day through the fond but mistaken love of Peter's hot heart." (Unknown)

Suffering, Then Glory (16:24-28)

Now the Lord Jesus plainly states what is involved in being His disciples; it means denial of self, cross bearing, and following Him. To deny self is not the same as self-denial. It means to yield to His control so completely that self has no rights whatever. To take up the cross means the willingness to endure shame; suffering, and perhaps martyrdom for His sake; to die to sin, self, and the world. To follow Him means to live as He lived with all that involves of humility, poverty, compassion, love, grace, and every other godly virtue.

> To deny self is not the same as self-denial.

In verses 25 and 26, the Lord anticipates two hindrances to discipleship. The first is the natural temptation to save oneself from discomfort, pain, loneliness, or loss. The other is to become wealthy. As to the first, Jesus warned that those who hug their lives for selfish purposes would never find fulfillment; those who give up their lives to Him, not counting the cost, would find the reason for their existence.

The second temptation (of getting rich) is irrational. "Suppose," said Jesus, "that a man became so successful in business that he finally owned the whole world. This mad quest would absorb so much of his time and energy that he would miss the central purpose of his life. What good would it do to make all that money, then die and leave it all behind, then spend eternity empty-handed?" Man is here for bigger business than to make money. He is called to represent the interests of his King. If he misses that, he misses everything.

In verse 24, Jesus told them the worst. That is characteristic of Christianity—you are told the worst at the outset. But you never cease discovering the treasures and the blessings. "When one has seen all that is forbidding in the Scriptures, there is nothing left hidden that can come as a surprise. Every new thing which we shall ever learn in this life or the next will come as a delight" (Barnhouse).

In verses 27 and 28, the Lord reminds His own of the glory that follows the suffering. He points forward to His second advent when He will return to earth with His angels in the glory of His Father. Then He will reward those who live for Him devotedly, passionately, and sacrificially. The only way to have a successful life is to (1) project oneself forward to that glorious time; (2) decide what will really be important; and then (3) go after that with all one's strength.

In verse 28 Jesus made the startling statement that there were some standing there with Him who would not taste death before they saw Him coming in His kingdom. The problem, of course, is that those disciples have all died, yet Christ has not come in power and glory to set up His kingdom. The problem is solved if we disregard the chapter break and consider the first eight verses of the next chapter as an explanation of His statement. The next eight verses describe the incident when Peter, James, and John saw Christ transfigured. They were actually privileged to have a preview of Christ in the glory of His kingdom.

Are we justified in looking upon Christ's transfiguration as a pre-picture or miniature of His coming kingdom? Yes, we are. This is made very clear in 2 Peter 1:16-18. There Peter is describing his experience. There can be no doubt that he is referring to the mount of transfiguration. He says, for instance, "we were with Him on the holy mountain" (v. 18). And he speaks of the voice of God

> Peter, James, and John were actually privileged to have a preview of Christ in the glory of His kingdom.

from heaven, bearing witness to Jesus as His beloved Son (v. 17). That definitely restricts the event to the transfiguration. Now notice that in verse 16 Peter describes this event as "the power and coming of our Lord Jesus Christ." And he adds that they "were eyewitnesses of His majesty" (v. 16). The power and coming of the Lord Jesus refer to His second advent; His majesty describes the glory that will be publicly manifested when He comes again to reign.

Christ's first coming was in humiliation; His second coming will be in glory. And so the incident on the mount of transfiguration pictures His glorious appearing as King of kings and Lord of lords, and His subsequent glorious reign.

On the Mount of Transfiguration (17:1-8)

Six days after the incident at Caesarea Philippi, Jesus took Peter, James, and John up to a high mountain, somewhere in Galilee.

Peter, James, and John seem to have occupied a place of special nearness to Jesus. Now they were privileged to see Him transfigured. Up to now His glory had been veiled in a body of flesh; as far as outward appearance was concerned, He looked like an ordinary man. But now His face and clothing shone like the sun. This brightness was the visible manifestation of His deity, just as the glory cloud (or *Shekinah*) in the Old Testament symbolized God's presence.

The scene was a preview of what the Lord Jesus will be like when He comes back to set up His kingdom. He will no longer appear as the sacrificial Lamb but as the Lion of the tribe of Judah. No longer will His glory be veiled in human flesh; all who see Him will recognize Him immediately as God the Son.

Moses and Elijah appeared with Him on the mount and discussed His approaching death (exodus) at Jerusalem (Luke 9:30-31). If we take Moses as representing the law and Elijah the Prophets, then here we see both sections of the Old Testament pointing forward to the sufferings of Christ and to the glories that should follow. On the other hand, we may see Moses, Elijah, and the disciples as typifying three classes of people who will enjoy the blessings of Christ's earthly reign.

1. Moses, of course, went to heaven by way of death, and thus depicts all who will be raised from the dead to enter the millennium.

2. Elijah was translated to heaven, and thus suggests those who will reach the kingdom by the route of translation.

3. The disciples may suggest the faithful Jewish remnant who will be alive at the second advent, and who will enter the kingdom with Christ.

The multitude at the base of the mountain (v. 14, compare Luke 9:37) has been likened to the Gentile nations which will also share in the blessings of Christ's thousand-year reign.

Peter was deeply moved by the impressiveness of the occasion. He had a real sense of history, and he wanted to capture the splendor so that it would never vanish. Therefore he rashly suggested erecting three memorial tents—one for Jesus, one for Moses, and one for Elijah. He was right in putting Jesus first, but he was wrong in not giving Him the preeminence. Jesus is not one among equals, but Lord over all. In order to teach this lesson, God covered them all with a brightly glowing cloud, then announced, "This is my beloved Son, in whom I am well pleased. Hear Him" (v. 5). This is the way it will be in the kingdom; Christ will be the supreme Monarch whose word will be the final authority. And this is the way it should be in our hearts at the present time.

> **Jesus is not one among equals, but Lord over all.**

Stunned by the glory cloud and the voice of God, the disciples fell to the ground. But Jesus told them to get up and not to be afraid. As they rose, they saw no one else but Jesus. And so it will be in the kingdom.

What About the Forerunner? (17:9-13)

Descending from the mountain, Jesus commanded those three men to be silent about what they had seen until He had risen from the dead. The Jews were over-anxious for anyone who might liberate them from the Roman yoke. Already thousands had been killed in futile uprisings. Still, they would have welcomed Him to save them from Rome, but they did not want Him as a Savior from sin. For all practical purposes, Israel had rejected her Messiah and it was useless to tell the Jews of this vision of messianic glory. After the resurrection, the message would be proclaimed worldwide.

The disciples had now seen a preview of Christ's coming in power and glory. Malachi had prophesied that Elijah would appear before Messiah's advent (Mal. 4:5-6), so the disciples questioned Jesus about this. The Lord agreed that Elijah first had to come as a reformer, but He explained that Elijah *had* already come. Obviously He was referring to John the Baptist (see v. 13). John was not Elijah (John 1:21), but he had come "in the spirit and power of Elijah" (Luke 1:17). If Israel had accepted John and his message, he would have fulfilled the role prophesied of Elijah (Matt. 11:14). But the nation had not recognized the significance of John's mission, and they treated him as they pleased. And just as they had treated the forerunner, so they would subject the Messiah to suffering. When Jesus had explained this, the disciples realized that He was referring to John the Baptist.

There is every reason to believe that before Christ's return, a prophet will arise to prepare Israel for Him. Whether it will be Elijah personally or someone with a similar ministry, it is almost impossible to say.

The Valley of Human Need (17:14-21)

Life is not all a mountain-top experience. The time comes when we must leave the mountain to serve in the valley of human need. At the base of the mountain, a distraught father was waiting for Jesus. Kneeling before Him, he poured out a passionate plea that his demon-possessed son might be healed. The misery of the child's experiences was a classic example of the suffering caused by Satan, the most cruel of all taskmasters.

The father had gone to the disciples for help, but they had not been able to cure the boy. Verse 17 is addressed to the disciples who, in that respect, were a cross-section of the Jewish people of that day—faithless and perverse. As soon as the epileptic was brought to Him, Jesus rebuked the demon, and the sufferer was instantly healed.

> Nothing is impossible to true faith.

Puzzled by their powerlessness, the disciples privately asked the Lord for an explanation. His answer was straightforward: not enough faith. If they had faith the size of the mustard seed (the smallest of seeds), they could command a mountain to be cast into the sea and it would happen. Nothing is impossible to true faith. Of course, it should be understood that true faith must be based upon some command or promise of God. A Christian cannot expect to perform some spectacular stunt in order to gratify a personal whim. That is not faith, but presumption. But if God guides a believer in a certain direction or issues a command, then the Christian can have utmost confidence that mountainous difficulties will be miraculously removed. He can say to the mountain, "Move from here to there," and it will move (v. 20). Nothing is impossible to those who believe.

Second Passion Prediction (17:22-23)

Again, without drama or fanfare, the Lord Jesus forewarned His disciples that He would be put to death. But again there was that word of vindication and victory—He would be raised on the third day. If He had not told them of His death in advance, they would no doubt have been completely disillusioned when it happened. A death of shame and suffering was not consistent with their expectations of the Messiah. As it was, they were greatly distressed that He was going to leave them and that He would be slain. They heard His Passion prediction but seem to have missed His resurrection promise.

Who Pays Tribute? (17:24-27)

In Capernaum the collectors of the temple tribute asked Peter if his Teacher paid the half-shekel that was used for carrying on the costly temple service. Peter answered, yes. Perhaps the misguided disciple wanted to save Christ from embarrassment. The omniscience of the Lord is seen in what followed. When Peter came home, Jesus spoke to him first—before Peter had a chance to tell what had happened. "What do you think, Simon? From whom do the kings of the earth take customs or taxes, from their sons or from strangers?"

The question must be understood in the light of the days in which it was spoken. In those days a ruler taxed his subjects for the support of his kingdom and his family, but he didn't tax his own family. Under our form of government, everyone is taxed, including the ruler and his household. So Peter correctly answered that rulers collected tribute from strangers; that is, from those outside their own families.

Jesus then pointed out that the sons are free. The point, of course, was that the temple was God's house. Jesus is the Son of God. For Him to pay tribute for the support of this temple would be equivalent to paying tribute to Himself. However, rather than cause unnecessary offense, the Lord agreed to pay the tax. But what would He do for money? It is never recorded that Jesus personally carried money with Him. He sent Peter to the Sea of Galilee and told him to bring up the first fish he caught by hook and line. In the mouth of that fish was a shekel. Peter used that shekel to pay the tribute—one-half for the Lord Jesus and one-half for himself.

The miracle was astounding, yet it is narrated with utmost restraint. Christ's omniscience is seen in that (1) He knew which one of all the fish in the Sea of Galilee had a coin in its mouth; (2) He knew the location of that one fish; and (3) He knew that it would be the first fish that Peter would catch.

If any divine principle had been involved, Jesus would not have made the payment. It was a matter of moral indifference to Him, and He was willing to pay rather than offend. We as believers are free from the law. Yet in non-moral matters, we should respect the consciences of others and not do anything that might cause offense.

9

MATTHEW 18–20

Matthew chapter 18 has been called the discourse on greatness and forgiveness. It outlines principles of conduct that are suitable for those who claim to be subjects of Christ the King.

Humility (18:1-4)

The disciples had always thought of the kingdom of heaven as the golden age of peace and prosperity, and now they began to covet positions of power in it. Their ambitious, self-seeking spirit found expression in the question, "Who then is the greatest in the kingdom of heaven?" Jesus answered with a living object lesson. Placing a little child in the middle of the group, He said that people must be converted and become as little children to enter the kingdom of heaven. He was speaking here of the kingdom in its inward reality; in order to be a genuine believer, a person must be converted. He must give up thoughts of personal greatness and take the lowly position of a little child. This begins when he acknowledges his own sinfulness and unworthiness and receives Jesus Christ as his only hope. It is an attitude that should then continue throughout his Christian life.

> In order to be a genuine believer, a person must be converted.

Jesus was not implying that His disciples were not saved. They all had true faith in Him (except Judas), and they were therefore now right with God. But they had not as yet received the Holy Spirit as an indwelling Person; that did not take place till Pentecost. Therefore they lacked the power for true humility that we have today (but do not use as we should).

The greatest person in the kingdom of heaven is the one who humbles himself as a little child. Obviously the standards and values in the kingdom are the exact opposite of those in the natural world. Our whole mode of thinking must be reversed; we must think Christ's thoughts after Him (see Phil. 2:5-8).

Responsibility Towards His "Little Ones" (18:5-6)

In these verses the Lord Jesus glides almost imperceptibly from the subject of a natural child to a spiritual child. Whoever receives one of His humble followers in His name will be rewarded the same as if he had received the Lord Himself. By a process of divine transference, what is done for the disciple is reckoned as done for the Master.

> Anyone who seduces a believer to sin incures enormous condemnation.

On the other hand, anyone who seduces a believer to sin incurs enormous condemnation; it would be better for him to have a great millstone tied round his neck and be drowned in the deepest sea. It is bad enough to sin against oneself, but to cause another believer to sin is to destroy his innocence, corrupt his mind, and stain his reputation. Better to die a violent and tragic death than to trifle with another person's purity!

Self-Discipline (18:7-9)

Jesus went on to explain that the world being what it is, it is inevitable that temptations to sin should arise. The world, the flesh, and the devil are in league to seduce and pervert. But the guilt of the active human agent is great. So Jesus warned his listeners to take the most drastic action in disciplining themselves rather than to tempt a child of God to sin. Whether the sinning "member" is the hand, foot, or eye, it would be preferable to sacrifice it to the surgeon's knife rather than let it destroy the work of God in another person's life. It is better to enter into life without limbs or sight than to be consigned to hell with every member intact. (In verses 8 and 9, our Lord does not imply that some bodies will lack limbs in heaven. He is merely describing the physical condition at the time a believer leaves this life for the next. There can be no question that the resurrection body will be complete and perfect.)

The Sacredness of Life (18:10-14)

Next, Jesus warned against despising one of His "little ones." To emphasize their importance, He added that the humblest believer is continually represented in the divine presence by angelic beings (probably guardian angels, see Heb. 1:14). Not only so—these little ones are the object of the tender Shepherd's saving ministry. Even if one out of a hundred sheep goes astray, He leaves the ninety-nine and searches for the lost one till He finds it. The ninety-nine, of course, are self-righteous sinners who refuse to confess their guilt and unworthiness. The one sheep is a penitent sinner who confesses his sin and wants to be saved. The Shepherd gets more joy from the recovery of a single straying sheep than from all the rest who are too proud to repent.

These "little ones" are important not only to the angels, and to the Shepherd; they are also important to God the Father. It is not His will that one of them should perish. If they are important enough to engage angels, and the Lord Jesus, and God the Father, then clearly we should never despise them, no matter how unlovely or lowly they might appear.

Discipline of Offenders (18:15-20)

The rest of the chapter has to do with the settlement of differences among members of the church, and with the need for exercising unlimited forgiveness.

Explicit instructions are given concerning the responsibility of a Christian when he has been wronged by another believer. First, the matter should be handled privately between the two parties. If the offender acknowledges his guilt, reconciliation is achieved. The trouble is that we don't do this. We go to everyone else and gossip about it. Then the matter spreads like wildfire and strife is multiplied. Let us remember that step number one is, ". . . go and tell him his fault between you and him alone" (v. 15).

If the guilty brother does not listen, then the wronged one should take one or two others with him, seeking his restoration. This emphasizes the mounting seriousness of his continued hardness of heart. But in addition, it provides competent testimony, as required by the Scripture: "that by the mouth of two or three witnesses every word may be established" (v. 16; see Deut. 19:15). No one can measure the trouble that has plagued the church through failure to obey the simple rule that a charge against another person must be supported by the testimony of two or three others. In this respect, worldly courts often act more righteously than Christian churches or assemblies.

If the accused refuses to confess and apologize before the two or three brethren, then the matter should be taken before the local assembly. Notice here that the local assembly is the body which is responsible to hear the case, not a civil court. The Christian is forbidden to go to law against another believer (1 Cor. 6:1-8). If the defendant refuses to admit his wrong before the church, then he is to be considered as "a heathen and a tax collector" (v. 17).

> The local assembly is the body which is responsible to hear the case, not a civil court.

The most obvious meaning of this expression is that he should be looked upon as being outside the sphere of the church; that is, he should be excommunicated. Though he may be a true believer, he is not living as one. Therefore he should be taken at his profession and treated accordingly. Though still in the universal church, he should be barred from the privileges of the local church. Such discipline is a serious action; it temporarily delivers a believer to the power of Satan "for the destruction of the flesh, that his spirit may be saved in the day of the Lord Jesus" (1 Cor. 5:5). The purpose of this is to bring him to his senses and cause him to confess his sin. Until that point is reached, believers should treat him courteously but they should also show by their attitude that they do not condone his sin and cannot have fellowship with him as a fellow believer. The assembly should be prompt to receive him back again as soon as there is evidence of godly repentance.

Verse 18 is closely linked with what precedes. When an assembly, acting prayerfully and in obedience to the Word, excommunicates a person or takes other disciplinary action, that action is honored in heaven. On the other hand, when the disciplined person has repented and confessed his sin, and the assembly restores him to fellowship, that action too is ratified by God. In excommunication, the assembly binds disciplinary action on the offender. In forgiveness, he is loosed from that action (see John 20:23).

The question naturally arises, "How large does an assembly have to be before it can bind and loose, as described above?" The answer is that two believers may bring such matters to God in prayer with the assurance of being heard. While verse 19 may be used as a general promise of answers to prayer, in the context it refers to prayer concerning church discipline. When used in connection with collective prayer in general, it must be taken in the light of all other teaching on prayer.

Again, verse 20 should be interpreted in the light of its context. It does not refer primarily to the composition of a New Testament church in its simplest form. Neither does it refer to the general prayer meeting. It refers to a meeting where the church seeks to reconcile two Christians who have been separated by some sin. Of course, it may legitimately be applied to all meetings of believers where Christ is the reason for their gathering, but a specific type of meeting is in view here.

To meet "in His name" means by His authority, in acknowledgment of all that He is, and in obedience to His Word. No group of Christians can claim to be the only ones who meet in His name; if that were so, then His presence would be limited to a small segment of His body on earth. Wherever two or three are gathered in recognition of Him as Lord and Savior, He is there among them.

Unlimited Forgiveness (18:21-35)

At this point Peter raised the question as to how often he should forgive a brother who sinned against him. He probably thought he was showing unusual grace by suggesting seven as an outside limit. Jesus answered, "not up to seven times, but up to seventy times seven." In saying this, He did not intend us to understand a literal 490 times; this was a figurative way of saying "indefinitely."

> "Up to seventy times seven" was a figurative way of saying "indefinitely."

If this is so, then someone might ask, "Why bother to go through the various steps outlined above? Why go to an offender alone, then with one or two others, then take him to the church? Why not just forgive, and let that be the end of it?"

The answer is that there are stages in the administration of forgiveness, as follows:

1. When a brother wrongs me or sins against me in any way, I should forgive him immediately *in my heart* (Eph. 4:32). That frees me from a harsh, bitter, unforgiving spirit, and leaves the matter on his shoulders.

2. But while I have forgiven him in my heart, I do not tell him as yet that he is forgiven. It would not be righteous to administer forgiveness publicly to him until he has repented. So I am obligated to go to him and rebuke him in love, hoping to lead him to confession (Luke 17:3).

3. As soon as he apologizes and confesses his sin, then I tell him that he is forgiven (Luke 17:4).

In verses 23-35, the Lord Jesus gives a parable of the kingdom of heaven to warn against the consequences of an unforgiving spirit by subjects of the kingdom who have been freely forgiven. Specifically the parable shows how unreasonable it is for those who have been forgiven an enormous amount to refuse to forgive some trifling amount.

The story concerns a king who wanted to clear his bad debts off his books. One servant, who owed 10,000 talents ($10,000,000?) was bankrupt, so his lord ordered that he and his family be sold as slaves to pay the debt. (Notice that in God's governmental dealings, a man's family often suffers with him as a result of his sin.) The distraught servant begged for time, promising to pay all if given the chance. Like many debtors, he was incredibly optimistic about what he could do if only he had time (v. 26). Galilee's total revenue only amounted to 300 talents, and this man owed 10,000! The detail about the vast amount is intentional. It is to shock the listeners and so capture their attention, and also to emphasize an immense debt to God.

> *A man's family often suffers with him as a result of his sin.*

When the lord saw the servant's contrite attitude, he forgave him the entire debt. It was an epic display of grace, not justice.

Now, that servant had a fellow servant who owed him 100 denarii ($20?). Rather than forgive him, he grabbed him by the throat and demanded payment in full. The unfortunate debtor pled for an extension of the loan's due date, but no use. He was thrown into jail till he paid the debt—which was almost impossible to do, since his chance of earning money was gone as long as he was imprisoned.

The other servants, outraged by this inconsistent behavior, reported it to their lord. He was furious with the merciless lender. Having been forgiven a big debt, he was unwilling to forgive a pittance. Having been shown great

MATTHEW 18–20 ❖ 141

mercy, he was unwilling to show any mercy. So he was imprisoned till his debt was paid.

The application is clear. God is the King. All His servants had contracted a great debt of sin which they were unable to pay. In wonderful grace and compassion, the Lord paid the debt and granted full and free forgiveness. Now, suppose some Christian wrongs another. When he is rebuked, he apologizes and asks for forgiveness. But the offended believer refuses to forgive. He himself has been forgiven $10,000,000, but he won't forgive $20. Will the King allow such behavior to go unpunished? He certainly will not. The culprit will be chastened in this life and will suffer loss at the judgment seat of Christ.

From Galilee to Judea (19:1-2)

After completing His ministry in Galilee, the Lord turned southward for the trip to Jerusalem. Though His exact route is unknown, it seems clear that He traveled through Perea, on the east side of the Jordan. Matthew speaks of the area loosely as "the region of Judea beyond the Jordan." The Perean ministry extends from 19:1 to 20:16 or 20:28; it is not clearly stated when He crossed the Jordan into Judea.

Marriage and Divorce in the Kingdom (19:3-9)

The Pharisees probably learned of the Lord's whereabouts because of the multitudes that followed Him for healing. Like a pack of wild dogs, they began to close in on Him, hoping to trap Him by His words. They asked if divorce was legal on any and every ground. No matter how He answered, He would infuriate some segment of the Jews. One school took a very liberal attitude on the subject of divorce; another school was extremely strict.

Our Lord took them back to the creation and explained that God's original intention was that a man should have one—and only one—living wife. The same God who created male and female decreed that the marriage relationship should take priority over the parental relationship. He also said that in marriage, there is a union of persons. God's ideal is that this divinely ordained union should not be broken by human act or decree.

The Pharisees thought they had caught the Lord in a clear contradiction of the Old Testament, Hadn't Moses made provision for divorce? All a man had to do was give his wife a written statement, then he could put her out of his house (Deut. 24:1-4). Jesus agreed that Moses had permitted divorce, but not as God's best for mankind. He permitted it because of Israel's backslidden condition: "Moses, because of the hardness of your hearts, permitted you to divorce your wives, but from the beginning it was not so" (v. 8). God's original ideal was that there should be no divorce. But God often tolerates conditions that are not His directive will.

Then the Lord stated with absolute authority that the past leniency on divorce was, from that point on, discontinued. He was introducing a new dispensation. From now on, there would be only one valid ground for divorce—sexual immorality. If a person was divorced for any other reason and remarried, he was guilty of adultery. Although it is not directly stated, it seems obvious from the words of our Lord that where a divorce has been obtained on the grounds of adultery, the innocent party is free to remarry. Otherwise a divorce would serve no purpose that could not equally well be achieved by separation.

For a fuller discussion of divorce, refer to page 217 in the appendix.

Celibacy in the Kingdom (19:10-12)

When the disciples heard the Lord's teaching on divorce, they took an extreme and absurd position that if divorce is obtainable for only one reason, then it would be better not to marry at all. To avoid sinning in the married state, they proposed avoiding the married state altogether. But that would not save them from sinning in the single state, so Jesus reminded them that the ability to remain celibate was not the general rule; only those to whom special grace was given could forego marriage. The dictum, "All cannot accept this saying, but only those to whom it has been given," does not mean that no one can understand the meaning of what follows, but rather that they cannot live a celibate life unless they are called to it.

The Lord Jesus went on to explain that there are three types of eunuchs, two involuntary and one voluntary. (1) Some men are eunuchs because they were born without the power of reproduction. (2) Others have this disability because they were castrated by men; oriental rulers often subjected the harem attendants to surgery to make them eunuchs. (3) But the ones whom Jesus had in mind were those who made themselves eunuchs for the sake of the kingdom of heaven. These are men who *could* be married.

They have no physical impairment. Yet in dedication to the King and His kingdom, they willingly forego the marriage relationship in order to give themselves to the cause of Christ without distraction. As Paul wrote later, "He who is unmarried cares for the things of the Lord—how he may please the Lord" (1 Cor. 7:32). Their celibacy is not physical but a matter of voluntary abstinence. Not all men can live such a life; only those divinely empowered (1 Cor. 7:7).

"Let the children come . . ." (19:13-15)

It is interesting that children are introduced shortly after the discourse on divorce (see also Mark 10:1-16); often they are the ones who suffer most severely from broken homes.

Parents brought their children to Jesus that He might lay His hands on them and pray. Someone has said, "No wonder. . . . They had seen what these hands could do, they had seen them touch disease and pain away. They had seen them bring sight to the blind eyes, and peace to the distracted mind; and they wanted hands like that to touch their children." The disciples looked upon the arrival of the children as an intrusion and unnecessary annoyance. When they began to rebuke the parents, Jesus intervened with those words that have endeared Him to children of every age since then: "Let the little children come to Me, and do not forbid them; for of such is the kingdom of heaven."

Several important lessons emerge from those words. First, children who wish to confess their faith in the Lord Jesus should be encouraged, not held back. No one knows the age of the youngest person in hell. So if a child truly wishes to be saved, he should not be told that he is too young. (At the same time, children should not be pressured into making a false profession. Susceptible as they are to emotional appeals, they should be protected from high-pressure methods of evangelism.)

> To be saved, adults have to become like children.

Then secondly, these words of our Lord answer the question, "What happens to children who die before they reach the age of accountability?" Jesus said, ". . . of such is the kingdom of heaven." That should be adequate assurance to parents who have suffered the loss of little ones.

Children do not have to become adults to be saved, but adults do have to become like children (18:3-4). Sometimes this passage is used to support the baptism of children in order to make them members of Christ and inheritors of the kingdom. Closer reading will show that the parents brought the children to Jesus, not to the baptistry. It will show that the children were already possessors of the kingdom. And it will show that there is not a drop of water in the passage.

Can a Rich Man Be Saved? (19:16-26)

This next incident provides a study in contrasts. We have just seen that the kingdom of heaven belongs to little children. Now we will see how difficult it is for rich adults to enter.

A rich man asked Jesus, "Good Teacher, what good thing must I do that I may have eternal life?" The question revealed his ignorance of who Jesus was, and of the way of salvation. He called Jesus "Good Teacher," putting Him on the same level as other great men of His day. And he spoke of gaining eternal life as a debt rather than as a gift.

The answer of our Lord probed the questioner on these two points. First, He gave him the opportunity to acknowledge His deity. "Why do you call Me good? No one is good but One, that is, God." In other words, "If you want to know anything about matters of absolute goodness, you should go to One who is absolutely good, and that one is God." This provided the rich man with a perfect opportunity to say, "That's why I've come to You—You are God." In asking this question, the Lord was not denying His own deity, but was simply seeking to lead the man to acknowledge it.

> ── ❧ ──
>
> **The law was never intended as a means of salvation, but as a revealer of sin.**
>
> ── ❧ ──

Then to test him on the way of salvation Jesus said, "If you want to enter into life, keep the commandments." At first glance, it appears that the Lord was implying that man can be saved by keeping the Ten Commandments. But we know from the rest of Scripture that He could not have meant this. The law was never intended as the means of salvation, but as the revealer of sin (Rom. 3:20). The Lord was using the law to produce conviction of sin in the man's heart. The proper response would have been this: "The law demands absolute perfection. I cannot produce it and therefore I am lost. But

I cast myself on your mercy, love, and grace. Please save me!" But the man had no real sense of his own sin, so he replied, "Which commandment?"

Jesus listed five commandments which deal with relations with our fellow man, then climaxed them by saying, "You shall love your neighbor as yourself." The man was blind to his own selfishness and greed; he boasted that he had always kept these commandments. Wasn't there something else he could do? Our Lord then exposed his utter failure to love his neighbor as himself by telling him to sell all his possessions and give the money to the poor. If he really loved his neighbor as himself, would he hold on to wealth while people were dying of starvation? His hoarded treasures condemned him as a sinner. If he would be perfect (that is, complete and lacking nothing), he should first prove the reality of his love to his neighbor by selling his possessions and giving to the poor. This would not save him, but it would show the reality of his repentance. Then he should come to Jesus and follow Him.

—————— ❧ ——————
**Riches tend to
become an idol.**
—————— ❧ ——————

This is the gospel invitation. Having confessed himself a sinner, he should put his faith in Christ as Savior, then follow Him in a life of love and godliness. However, the man went away sorrowful because he was very rich. He loved his wealth more than his neighbor, more than Christ Jesus, and more than eternal life.

This prompted Jesus to observe that it is hard for a rich man to enter the kingdom of heaven. The reason is that riches tend to become an idol. They become the reason for existence. And it is hard to have them without trusting in them.

Then our Lord declared that it is easier for a camel to go through the eye of a needle than for a rich man to enter the kingdom of God. Here He was using hyperbole again, the figure of speech in which a statement is made in intensified form to produce a vivid effect. Hyperbole is not a form of deception because it is so obviously an exaggeration.

It is quite clearly impossible for a camel to go through the eye of a needle. Some have tried to explain the Lord's reference to the needle as the smaller opening of a gate in the city wall. A camel could get through by kneeling down, but only with great difficulty. The explanation is doubtful, as the word used for needle is the same word used to describe the needle used by surgeons.

The disciples, following His line of thought, asked, "Who then can be saved?" Why did they ask that? Their question seems to imply that everyone is either rich or wishes he were. Whatever their thinking was, the Lord replied, "With men this is impossible, but with God all things are possible." What are we to conclude here on the salvation of the rich?

Humanly speaking it is impossible for anyone to be saved, rich or poor; only God can save a soul. But there is a special difficulty in connection with rich people. It is far more difficult for a wealthy man to surrender his will to Christ than for a poor man. This is seen in the fact that so few rich men are converted. They find it almost impossible to replace their trust in visible means of support for faith in an unseen Savior.

> **Hoarded wealth condemns us as not loving our neighbors as ourselves.**

Commentators and preachers invariably inject here that it is perfectly all right for Christians to be rich. It is strange that they should use a passage in which the Lord denounces wealth as a hindrance to man's eternal welfare, to justify gathering earthly treasures. Certainly these verses do not endorse materialism. And anyway, it is difficult to see how a Christian can cling to riches in view of the appalling need everywhere, in view of how soon Christ may return, and in view of the Lord's clear command against laying up treasures on earth. Hoarded wealth condemns us as not loving our neighbors as ourselves.

Before leaving this section we should notice that the expressions "kingdom of heaven" and "kingdom of God" are used interchangeably in verses 23 and 24. Things equal to the same thing are equal to each other. Therefore the two terms are synonymous.

Rewards for Sacrificial Living (19:27-29)

Remembering what Jesus had said to the rich man about forsaking all, Peter boasted that he and the other disciples had done exactly that. Then he spoiled it all by asking, "What shall we have?" (v. 27). Peter's self-life was showing; his old nature was reasserting itself. It was a spirit that each of us has to guard against.

The Lord's reply had two parts. First He assured Peter that everything done for Him would be well rewarded (vv. 28-29). But then He warned that a selfish spirit might place a man last in the scale of rewards (v. 30).

As to the Twelve specifically, they would have places of authority in the millennium. The regeneration (v. 28) refers to Christ's future glorious reign on earth; it is explained by the expression "when the Son of Man sits on the throne of His glory." We have previously referred to this phase of the kingdom as the kingdom in *manifestation*. At that time the Twelve will sit on thrones, judging the twelve tribes of Israel. Rewards in the New Testament are closely linked with positions of administration in the millennium (see Luke 19:17-19). They are *awarded* at the judgment seat of Christ but *manifested* when the Lord returns to earth to reign.

Then, as to all other believers, Jesus added that all who have left homes, families, and lands for His sake will receive a hundredfold, *and* inherit eternal life. In this life, they enjoy a world-wide fellowship of believers which more than compensates for broken earthly ties. For the one house they leave, they receive a hundred Christian homes where they are warmly welcomed. For lands or other forms of wealth forsaken, they receive spiritual riches that can't be counted.

And then they will also inherit eternal life. Again we must explain that eternal life is not presented here as a reward for sacrifice, although it appears that way on the surface. Eternal life is a gift from God and cannot be earned or merited. But there will be varying capacities for enjoying eternal life in heaven, and that is what is referred to here. All believers are assured of heaven, but some will have greater capacity for enjoying heaven than others. Everyone's cup will be full, but some will have bigger cups than others. Capacity for enjoying heaven will be proportionate to faithfulness and devotion on earth. And so when Jesus spoke of inheriting eternal life, He was referring to the earned capacity for enjoying that life in its fullness in eternity.

The Lord closed His remarks with a warning against a selfish spirit. He was saying to Peter, in effect, "Anything you do for my sake will be rewarded, Peter, but be careful that you are not guided by selfish considerations, because in that case, many that are first will be last and the last first." This is illustrated by a parable recorded in chapter 20.

The Parable of the Landowner (20:1-16)

This parable is a continuation of the discourse on rewards at the end of chapter 19. The chapter break unfortunately obscures the flow of thought. The parable illustrates the truth that while all true disciples will be rewarded, the order of rewards will be determined by the spirit in which the disciple served.

The parable describes a farmer who went out early in the morning to hire laborers to work in his vineyard. These men contracted with him to work for one denarius a day, which was a reasonable wage at that time. Let us say that they began to work at 6 a.m. At 9 a.m. the farmer found some other unemployed laborers in the market place. In this case there was no labor-management agreement. They went to work with nothing but his word that he would give them what was right.

At noon and at 3 p.m. the farmer hired more men on the basis that he would give them a fair wage. At 5 p.m. he found some more men who were unemployed. They were not lazy; they wanted work but hadn't been able to find it. So he sent them to work in the vineyard without discussing pay. It is important to notice that the first men were hired as a result of a bargaining agreement; all the others left the matter of pay to the farmer.

At the end of the day, the farmer instructed his paymaster to pay the men off, beginning with the last hired and working back to the first. (In this way the earliest men hired saw what the others received.) It was the same pay for all—one denarius. The 6 a.m. men thought that they would receive more, but no—they too got one denarius. They were bitterly resentful; after all, they had worked longer and through the hottest part of the day.

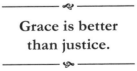

Grace is better than justice.

In the farmer's reply to one of them, we find the abiding lessons from the parable. First he said, "Friend, I am doing you no wrong; did you not agree with me for a denarius? Take what is yours and go your way. I wish to give to this last man the same as to you." The first had bargained with him for a denarius a day, and they got the wage agreed on. The others cast themselves on the farmer's grace, and they got grace. Grace is better than justice. It is better to leave our rewards up to the Lord than to strike a bargain with Him.

Then the farmer said, "Is it not lawful for me to do what I wish with my own things?" The lesson here, of course, is that God is sovereign. He can do as He pleases. And what He pleases will always be right, just, and fair. The farmer added, "Or is your eye evil because I am good?" This question exposes the selfish streak in human nature. The 6 a.m. men got exactly what they deserved, yet they were jealous because the others got the same pay for working less hours. Many of us have to admit that it seems a bit unfair to us too. But this only proves that in the kingdom of heaven we have to adopt an entirely new kind of thinking. We must abandon our greedy, competitive spirit, and think like the Lord.

The farmer knew that all these men needed the money. No doubt they had families who were waiting for food. So the farmer paid them according to need rather than greed. No one received less than he deserved, but all received what they needed for themselves and their families. The more we study the parable in this light, the more we realize that it is not only fair but eminently beautiful. Those who were hired at 6 a.m. should have counted it an added benefit to serve such a wonderful master all day long.

Jesus closed the parable with the words, "But many who are first will be last, and the last first" (v. 16; see 19:30). There will be surprises in the matter of rewards. Some who think they will "be first" will be last because their service was motivated mainly by self-interest. Others who serve out of gratitude will be highly honored.

Third Passion Prediction (20:17-19)

It is clear that the Lord was now leaving Perea for the trip to Jerusalem via Jericho (see v. 29). Once again He took His disciples aside to explain what would happen to Him after they reached the Holy City. He would be betrayed to the chief priests and scribes—an obvious reference to what Judas Iscariot would do. He would be condemned to death by the Jewish leaders. Since the Jews did not have authority to inflict capital punishment, they would turn Him over to the Gentiles (the Romans) to be crucified. But death would not hold Him—He would be raised on the third day.

Places of Honor in the Kingdom (20:20-28)

It is a sad commentary on human nature that immediately after the third prediction of His passion, His followers were thinking more of their own glory than of His sufferings.

Christ's first prediction of suffering gave rise to Peter's objection (16:22), and the second was soon followed by the disciples' questions, "Who is the greatest . . .?" So here, we find the third capped with the ambitious request of James and John. They persistently closed their eyes to warnings of trouble, and opened them only to the promise of glory—so getting a wrong, materialistic view of the kingdom.

The mother of James and John came to Jesus asking that her boys might sit on either side of Him in His kingdom. It is to her credit that she believed in His coming reign. But she did not understand the principles upon which honors would be bestowed in the kingdom. Mark says that the sons made the request themselves (Mark 10:35); perhaps the sons did it at her direction, or perhaps the three of them approached the Lord together.

Jesus said frankly that they did not understand what they were asking. They wanted a crown without a cross. They wanted the glory but they didn't want the suffering that leads to it. And so He asked them pointedly, "Are you able to drink the cup that I am about to drink?" We are not left to wonder what He meant by "the cup"; He had just described it in verses 18 and 19. He must suffer and He must die.

James and John's "yes" response was based more on zeal than on knowledge. Jesus assured them that they would indeed drink of the cup. James would be martyred for Him and John would be persecuted and exiled to the Isle of Patmos. As Robert Little has said, "James died a martyr's death; John lived a martyr's life."

Then Jesus patiently explained that it was *the Father* who had determined the special basis on which these positions would be assigned. They thought that because they were so close to Christ, they had a special claim to places of preference. But in the counsels of God, the places on His right hand and left hand would be given out on the basis of suffering for Him. This means, of course, that the chief honors in the kingdom are not limited to first century Christians, but that some living today might eventually win them—by suffering.

The other ten disciples expressed indignation that the sons of Zebedee should have made such a request. But why were they indignant? Probably because they themselves wanted to be greatest and resented any prior claims being made by James and John. This gave our Lord the chance to make a revolutionary statement concerning greatness in His kingdom, as contrasted with the world. The Gentiles think of greatness in terms of mastery and rule.

In Christ's kingdom, greatness shows itself by service. Whoever aspires to greatness, therefore, must become a servant, and whoever wants first place must become a bond slave.

The Lord Himself is the perfect example of lowly service. He came into the world not to be served but to serve and to give His life as a ransom for many (Mark 10:45). The whole purpose of the Incarnation can be summed up in two words—"serve" and "give." It is amazing to think that the exalted Lord humbled Himself to the manger and to the cross. His greatness was demonstrated in the depth of His humiliation. And so it must be for us.

> Christ's death satisfied all God's righteous demands.

Jesus Christ gave His life a ransom for many. His death satisfied all God's righteous demands against sin. It was sufficient in its value to put away the sins of all the world. But, of course, it is effective only for those who accept Him as Lord and Savior. Have you ever done this?

Jesus Heals Two Blind Jews (20:29-34)

By now Jesus had crossed the Jordan from Perea and had reached Jericho. As He was leaving the city, two blind men cried out to Him, "Have mercy on us, O Lord, Son of David." Their use of the title "Son of David" means that although they were physically blind, their spiritual vision was so acute as to recognize Jesus as the Messiah of Israel. They may very well represent the believing remnant of blinded Israel who will acknowledge Him as the Christ when He returns to reign (Isa. 35:5; 42:7; Rom. 11:25, 26; 2 Cor. 3:16; Rev. 1:7).

The crowd tried to hush them, but they cried after Him all the more. When Jesus asked them what they wanted, they didn't speak in generalities, as we so often do when we pray. They came right to the point: "Lord, that our eyes may be opened." Their specific request received a specific response. In pity Jesus touched their eyes, and immediately they received their sight and followed Him.

It should be mentioned that there are difficulties in reconciling Matthew's account of this incident with the narrative in Mark 10:46-52 and Luke 18:35-43; 19:1. Here there are two blind men; in Mark and Luke only one is mentioned (although, of course, there could have been another).

In Matthew and Mark, the incident is said to have occurred as Jesus left Jericho; in Luke, it is said to have happened as He drew near to the city. The simplest explanation is that there actually were two towns called Jericho, and. the miracle of healing took place as Jesus was leaving one and entering the other.

10

MATTHEW 21–23

Jesus Enters Jerusalem (21:1-11)

On the way up from Jericho, Jesus came to the east side of the Mount of Olives where Bethany and Bethphage (pronounced Beth-fa-jay) were located. From there the road skirted the south end of Olivet, then dipped into the Valley of Jehoshaphat, crossed the Brook Kidron and climbed up to Jerusalem.

When Jesus came to Bethphage He sent two of His disciples to Bethany, already knowing that they would find a tethered donkey, and a colt with her. They were to untie the animals and bring them to Jesus. If any challenged their right to do this, they were to explain simply that the Lord needed them. Then the owner would consent. It is possible that the owner knew Jesus and had previously offered to help Him in any way possible. Or this incident may simply demonstrate the omniscience and supreme authority of the Lord.

The requisitioning of the animals fulfilled predictions in Isaiah 62:11 and Zechariah 9:9.

After the disciples had spread their garments on the animals, Jesus mounted the colt (Mark 11:7) and rode onward to Jerusalem. It was a historic moment in God's great program. Sixty-nine weeks of Daniel's prophecy had now run out, according to Sir Robert Anderson (see his computations in the book *The Coming Prince*). Next, the Messiah would be cut off (Dan. 9:26). In riding into Jerusalem in this manner, the Lord Jesus was making a deliberate, unveiled claim to being the Messiah.

"Once in His life He grants to His own publicly to proclaim what lies so deeply at their heart, and He fulfills intentionally a prophecy which at His time was unanimously interpreted of the Messiah. If He has previously considered the declaration of His dignity as dangerous, He now counts silence inconceivable. . . . It was hereafter never possible to say that He had never declared Himself in a wholly unequivocal manner. When Jerusalem was afterwards accused of the murder of the Messiah, it should not be able to say that the Messiah had omitted to give a sign intelligible for all alike. Our Lord will prove that He is more than a prophet, mighty in word and deed; that He is King in the full force of the word." (Lange's Commentary)

Most of the crowd welcomed Him as their king, spreading their garments as a carpet on the road. Others paved the way with branches cut from the trees. People marching in front of Him and behind Him shouted, "Hosanna to the Son of David! Blessed is He who comes in the name of the Lord! Hosanna in the highest!" This was a quotation from Psalm 118:25-6, applying obviously to the Messiah's coming. *Hosanna* means "save now"; as used here it was a salute or a cheer. The Son of David, as already mentioned, was a title of the Messiah. He was the blessed One who had come by the authority of Jehovah and to do His will. "Hosanna in the highest" called on the heavens to join the earth in acclaiming Him with praise.

Inside the city, people were questioning who He was. Those who asked were told no more than that He was the prophet Jesus from Nazareth of Galilee. From this it is clear that very few really understood that He was God's Anointed One. In less than a week, the fickle crowd would be crying "Crucify Him! Crucify Him!"

Jesus Cleanses the Temple (21:12-13)

This is the second cleansing of the temple recorded in the Gospels. The first, described in John 2:13-16, took place at the beginning of Christ's public ministry. This one occurred as His ministry was drawing to a close.

A brisk business had once again sprung up in the outer court of the temple. Sacrificial animals and birds were being bought and sold. Money changers were converting other currencies into the half-shekel which Jewish men had to pay as tribute for the upkeep of the temple and its services. Profiteering abounded. In righteous indignation the Lord Jesus quoted from Isaiah 56:7 to remind them that God intended the temple to be a house of prayer. By their commercialism, they had made it a den of thieves. (Isaiah spoke of the temple as "a house of prayer for all nations"; Jesus omitted the words "for all nations." In His day, the temple was for Israel; when He comes the second time, it will be for all nations.) This cleansing of the temple precincts was His first official act after entering Jerusalem. By it He was clearly asserting His lordship over the temple.

The incident has a two-fold message for us today. In our church life we need His cleansing power to drive out fund-raisers, fairs, suppers, and a host of other money-making gimmicks. In our personal lives also, there is constant need for the purging ministry of the Lord in our bodies, which are the temples of the Holy Spirit.

The Indignant Priests and Scribes (21:14-17)

The next scene finds our Lord healing the blind and the lame in the temple yard. He attracted the needy wherever He went, and never sent them away without meeting their need. It seems so "in character" for Jesus to be helping others.

> It seems so "in character" for Jesus to be helping others.

But hostile eyes were watching; they could see nothing good in His actions. And when these chief priests and scribes heard children calling Jesus "Son of David," they got angry. They said, "Do you hear what these are saying?"—as if they expected Him to forbid the children from addressing Him as the Messiah of Israel! Indeed, if Jesus had not been the Messiah, this would have been an appropriate time to say so once for all. But His answer indicated that the children were right. He quoted Psalm 8:2 from the Septuagint (Greek translation of the Old Testament): "Out of the mouths of babes and nursing infants You have perfected praise." In other words, if the supposedly knowledgeable priests and scribes would not praise Him as the Anointed, then the Lord would be worshiped by little children. Children often have spiritual insight beyond their years, and their words of faith and love bring unusual glory to the name of the Lord.

> Children often have spiritual insight beyond their years.

Leaving the religious leaders to think about this truism, Jesus returned to Bethany and spent the night there.

The Barren Fig Tree (21:18-22)

As He was returning to Jerusalem in the morning, the Lord came to a fig tree, hoping to find fruit on it to satisfy His hunger. But when He found nothing but leaves He said, "Let no fruit grow on you ever again." Immediately the tree withered.

In Mark's account (11:12-14), the comment is made that "he found nothing but leaves, for it was not the season for figs." The International Standard Bible Encyclopedia explains the difficulty as follows:

"In Palestine and other warm climates the fig yields two crops annually—an earlier one, ripe about June, growing from the 'old wood,' i.e., from the midsummer sprouts of the previous year, and a second, more important one, ripe about August, which grows upon the 'new wood,' i.e., upon the spring shoots.

The miracle of our Lord . . . occurred in the Passover season, about April. . . . When the young leaves are newly appearing, in April, every fig-tree which is going to bear fruit at all will have some *taksh* ('immature figs') upon it, even though 'the time of figs' i.e., of ordinary edible figs—either early or late crop—'was not yet.' This *taksh* is not only eaten today, but it is sure evidence, even when it falls, that the tree bearing it is not barren."

Jesus is often accused of acting like a spoiled child here, of venting frustration on a living tree because it yielded no fruit. Such criticisms betray an ignorance of the Person of Christ. He is God, the Sovereign of the universe, and therefore He can do as He

———— ❧ ————
The fig tree represents the nation of Israel.
———— ❧ ————

pleases. Man's mind is not big enough to understand the implications of all He does. If we knew as much as He knows, we would do things exactly the way He does them. Some of His dealings are mysterious to us, but we must begin with the premise that they are always right. In this particular case, the Lord knew that the fig tree would never bear figs and what He did was no different than a farmer removing a barren tree from his orchard.

Even those who criticize our Lord for cursing the fig tree admit that it was a symbolic action. Like the vine and the olive tree, the fig tree represents the nation of Israel. When Jesus came to Israel, He hoped to find some fruit, but there was nothing but leaves. Leaves, of course, speak of profession. There were leaves with no fruit, just as there are lives with no reality. The

Lord pronounced a judgment on the nation: "Let no fruit ever grow from you ever again." When we apply this curse to Israel, we must remember that while unbelieving, apostate Israel will be fruitless forever, yet a remnant of the nation will turn to the Messiah after the church is taken out of the world. They will bring forth fruit for Him during the tribulation and during His millennial reign.

When the disciples expressed amazement at the sudden withering of the tree, the Lord told them that they themselves could do greater miracles than this if they had faith. For instance, they could say to a mountain, "Be removed and be cast in a sea," and it would happen. "And whatever things you ask in prayer, believing, you will receive."

—————— ❧ ——————

Faith must have some word of God to rest on.

—————— ❧ ——————

Again, we must explain that these seemingly unqualified promises concerning prayer must be understood in the light of all that the Bible teaches on the subject. Verse 22 does not mean that any Christian can ask anything he wants and expect to get it. He must pray in faith, and faith must have some word of God to rest on. He must pray in accordance with the conditions laid down in the Bible.

J. R. Miller summarizes some of the scriptural qualifications for answered prayer:

> "In the first place, it is not all asking that is really praying, and therefore not all asking that receives. James says, 'Ye ask, and receive not, because ye ask amiss, that ye may spend it in your pleasures.' A man asks for money, not to use it for the glory of God and the good of others, but for his own glory and pleasure. Again, the Psalmist says, 'If I regard iniquity in my heart, the Lord will not hear me.' That is, if one is cherishing a secret sin in his heart while he is trying to serve God, no prayers that he offers will be heard or answered. So here are at least two kinds of asking that will not bring an answer.

> "Then there are conditions. One is that we must ask in Christ's name. That implies that we believe in Christ as our Saviour, and are his faithful friends, and therefore have a right to use his name. This condition narrows down the promise to the true followers of Christ. Another condition is that we are abiding in Christ, and his words are abiding in us. So there is a double 'if.' Even a Christian

who is following afar off does not come within the circle of this promise.

"Then there is another qualification which belongs to all promises to prayer. God himself must be the judge as to the things we ask, whether they would really be blessings to us or not. There may be things we desire very earnestly that it would be the greatest unkindness to grant us. Is God then bound by this promise to give us what we crave? By no means. 'What is *good* the Lord will give.' 'No *good thing* will he withhold from them that walk uprightly.' But he will withhold from them which walk the most uprightly the things which in his Divine wisdom he sees would not be good things. This is implied in every such promise as this."

The Question of Authority (21:23-27)

When Jesus entered the temple (that is, the temple court), the chief priests and elders interrupted His teaching by asking Him what authority He had to teach, to perform miracles, and to cleanse the temple. These leaders considered themselves to be the duly authorized guardians of the Jewish faith. They were the professionals who by formal training and human appointment were authorized to direct the religious life of the people. They knew that Jesus had no formal schooling, and He certainly had no credentials from Israel's rulers. Their challenge reflected the age-old resentment felt by professional religionists against men with the power of a divine anointing.

The Lord offered to explain His authority if they would answer a question: "The baptism of John—where was it from? From heaven or from men?" John's baptism should be understood as meaning John's ministry. Therefore the question was, "Who authorized John to carry on his ministry? Was his ordination human or divine? What credentials did he hold from Israel's leaders?" The answer was obvious: John was a man sent from God. His power came from God, not from human endorsement.

The priests and elders were in a dilemma. If they admitted for a moment that John was sent by God, then they were trapped. John had pointed men to Jesus as the Messiah. If John's authority was divine, why hadn't they repented and believed on Christ? On the other hand, if they said that John was not commissioned by God, then they were adopting a position that would be ridiculed by the people in general. Most of the people agreed that John had been a prophet from God.

If they had answered Jesus' question correctly—that John was divinely sent—then they would have had the answer to their own question—Jesus was the divinely sent Messiah of whom John had been the forerunner. But they refused to face the facts, so they pleaded ignorance. Then Jesus said, "Neither will I tell you by what authority I do these things." Why should He tell them what they already knew but were unwilling to admit?

The Parable of the Two Sons (21:28-32)

In this parable, Jesus delivers a stinging rebuke to the chief priests and elders for their failure to obey John's call to repentance and faith. The parable concerns a man who had two sons, both of whom were asked to work in the vineyard. One refused, then repented and went. The other agreed to go, but never did. When the Lord asked the religious leaders which son did the will of his father, they unwittingly condemned themselves by saying, "The first."

> Those who are avowed sinners receive the gospel more readily than those who pretend to be pious.

The Lord interpreted the parable. The tax collectors and harlots were like the first son. They did not make an immediate pretense of obeying John the Baptist, but eventually many of them did repent and believe in Jesus. The chief priests and elders were like the second son. They professed to approve the preaching of John, but they never confessed their sins or trusted the Savior. Therefore the out-and-out sinners entered the kingdom of God while the self-satisfied religious leaders remained outside. And it is still the same today. Those who are avowed sinners receive the gospel more readily than those who pretend to be pious.

The expression "John came to you in the way of righteousness" (v. 32) means that he came preaching the necessity of righteousness through repentance and faith.

The Parable of the Vineyard (21:33-46)

In further answer to the question about authority, Jesus told the parable of a farmer who planted a vineyard, put a hedge around it, installed a wine press in it, built a tower, rented it out to tenants, and went away to a distant country. At harvest time he sent servants to get his share of the crop, but the tenants beat one, killed one, and stoned another. When he sent other servants, they received the same treatment. The third time he sent his son, thinking that they would respect him. Knowing full well that he was the son, they killed him with the idea of seizing his inheritance.

At this point the Lord paused to ask the priests and elders, "What do you think the owner will do to those tenants?" They answered, "He will destroy those wicked men miserably, and leave his vineyard to other vinedressers who will render to him the fruits in their seasons."

The interpretation of the parable is not difficult to find. God is the householder. Israel is the vineyard (Ps. 80:8; Isa. 5:1-7; Jer. 2:21). The hedge speaks of the dividing wall (Eph. 2:14) which separated Israel from the nations. The wine press, by implication, signifies the fruit which Israel should have brought forth for God. The tower suggests Jehovah's watchful care for His people. The tenants, of course, are the chief priests and scribes.

Time after time God sent His servants, the prophets, to see if there was any fruit from the vineyard. Some of the prophets were beaten, some killed, and others stoned. Finally, God sent His Son, saying, "They will respect my son" (v. 37). The chief priests and scribes said, "This is the heir"—a fatal admission. Among themselves they agreed that Jesus was the Son of God (though publicly they denied it) and thus answered their own question concerning His authority. His authority came from the fact the He was God the Son.

In the parable they are quoted as saying, "This is the heir. Come, let us kill him and seize his inheritance" (v. 38). In real life they said, "If we let Him alone like this, everyone will believe in Him, and the Romans will come and take away both our place and our nation" (John 11:48). And so they rejected Him, cast Him forth, and crucified Him at Calvary.

When Jesus asked them what the owner of the vineyard would do, they condemned themselves by their answer, as He goes on to show in verses 42 and 43. He reminded them of the words of Psalm 118:22. Jesus Himself is the stone, and the chief priests and scribes were the builders. When Christ presented Himself to the leaders of Israel, they had no place for Him in their "building plans." They threw Him aside as useless. But the rejected stone has become the head of the corner, that is, the stone with the preeminent place in the building: "God has highly exalted Him and given Him the name which is above every name . . ." (Phil. 2:9).

Jesus then bluntly announced that the kingdom of God would be taken away from the nation of Israel and given to a nation producing the fruits of it. And so it happened. Israel has been set aside as God's chosen people. The nation has been judicially blinded. A hardening has come upon the race that rejected its Messiah. The prophecy that the kingdom of God would be given to a nation producing the fruits of it has been understood as referring to:

1. The church of God, composed of believing Jews and Gentiles— "a holy nation, God's own people" (1 Peter 2:9), or

2. The believing portion of the nation of Israel that will be living at the time of Christ's second advent. Redeemed Israel will bring forth fruit for God.

Verse 44 suggests the two advents of Christ. When He came the first time, the Jewish leaders stumbled over Him and were broken to pieces. When He comes again, He will descend in judgment, scattering His enemies as dust.

The Jewish leaders realized that these parables were aimed directly at them in answer to their question concerning Christ's authority. They would like to have seized Him then and there, but they feared the crowd, who still thought of Jesus as a prophet.

The Parable of the Marriage Feast (22:1-14)

The Lord Jesus was not through with the chief priests and elders. Now in a parable about a marriage feast He again pictured favored Israel as being set aside, and the despised Gentiles sitting as guests at the table.

Jesus likened the kingdom of heaven to a king who arranged a marriage feast for his son. The invitation went out in two stages. First, there was a preliminary, advance invitation, personally conveyed by servants; it met with a flat refusal. The second invitation announced that the feast was spread. It was treated with disdain by some; they were too busy with their farms and businesses. It was treated violently by others; they seized the servants, abused them, and killed them.

The king was so angry he destroyed the murderers and burned their city. Then, scrapping the first guest list, he sent out a general invitation to everyone. This time there wasn't an empty seat in the banquet hall. Among the guests, however, was one who didn't have a wedding garment. When challenged on his unfitness to attend, he was speechless. Then the king ordered him to be cast out into the night, where he would weep and gnash his teeth. The attendants in verse 13 are not the same as the servants in verse 3.

Our Lord concluded the parable with the words, "For many are called, but few are chosen" (v. 14).

As to the meaning of the parable, the king is God and his son is the Lord Jesus. The marriage feast is an appropriate description of the festive joy which characterizes the kingdom of heaven. It is better not to introduce the church as the bride of Christ in this parable; that unnecessarily complicates the picture. The main thought is the setting aside of Israel rather than the distinctive call and destiny of the church.

The first stage of the invitation pictures John the Baptist and the twelve disciples inviting Israel to the marriage feast. But the nation obstinately refused to accept this gracious invitation. The words, "they were not willing to come" (v. 3), were climactically dramatized in the crucifixion of the Lord Jesus. The second stage of the invitation suggests the proclamation of the gospel to the Jews in the book of Acts. Some treated the message with contempt; they were too busy making money. Some treated the messengers with violence; most of the apostles were martyred.

The King was justifiably angry with Israel. He sent "his armies," that is, He permitted Titus and his Roman legions to destroy Jerusalem and most of its people in AD 70. They were "his armies" in the sense that He used them as His instruments to punish Israel. They were His officially even if they did not know Him personally.

Now Israel is set aside nationally and the gospel goes out to the Gentiles, both bad and good, that is, to Gentiles of all degrees of respectability (Acts 13:45, 46; 28:28). But the reality of each individual who comes is tested. The man without a wedding garment is one who professes to be ready for the kingdom but who has never been clothed in the righteousness of God through the Lord Jesus Christ (2 Cor. 5:21). Without Christ he is speechless when challenged as to his right to enter the kingdom (Rom. 3:19). His doom is being cast into the outer darkness. The weeping suggests the suffering and remorse of hell. Some suggest that the gnashing of teeth signifies continued hatred of God and rebellion against Him. If so, it disproves the idea that the fires of hell exert a purifying effect on those who are there.

Verse 14 refers to the whole parable and not just to the incident of the man without the wedding garment. Many are called, that is, the gospel invitation goes out to many. But few are chosen. Some refuse the invitation, and even of those who respond favorably, some are exposed as false professors. The expression "few are chosen" does not mean that God is arbitrary in selecting only a few for salvation. All who respond to the good news are chosen. The only way a person can tell whether he is chosen is by what He does with the Lord Jesus Christ.

—————— ❧ ——————

All who respond to the good news are chosen.

—————— ❧ ——————

Caesar or God? (22:15-22)

This is the second of four deputations which sought to trap Jesus. We have already studied the efforts of the chief priests and elders (21:23-22:14). Here we have an attempt by the Pharisees and Herodians. The Sadducees come forward in 22:23-33. And the Pharisees try again in 22:34-46.

The goal of the Pharisees was to lure Christ into making a political statement with dangerous implications. They took advantage of the fact that the Jewish people were divided on the subject of allegiance to Caesar. Some were passionately opposed to submitting to the Gentile emperor. Others, like the Herodians, were willing to compromise in order to make the best of a bad bargain.

Notice, first, their flattery. They insincerely complimented Him for His purity of character, His truthfulness, and His fearlessness. Then they dropped the loaded question, "Is it lawful to pay taxes to Caesar, or not?" If Jesus answered no, He would not only antagonize the Herodians, but He would be accused of rebellion against the Roman government. The Pharisees would have hustled Him off and would have pressed the charge against Him.

If He said yes, then He would run afoul of the intense nationalistic spirit among the Jews. He would lose much support among the common people—support which so far hindered the leaders in their efforts to get rid of Him. Jesus bluntly denounced them as hypocrites trying to snare Him. Then He asked them to show Him a denarius, the coin which was used to pay taxes to the Roman government.

This request for the coin was full of meaning. Every time the Jews looked at the coin, they saw a likeness of Caesar, and his title. The coin was an annoying reminder that the Jews were under Gentile authority, paying reluctant taxes to a Gentile king. The fact that they used the denarius should have reminded them that their bondage to Rome was a result of their sin. Had they been true to Jehovah, the question of paying taxes to Caesar would never have arisen.

Jesus asked, "Whose likeness and inscription is this?" They were forced to answer, "Caesar's." Then the Lord told them to give to Caesar the things that are Caesar's, and to God the things that are God's. Their question had boomeranged on them. The fact was, they did give Caesar his due. But One stood before them who is the express image of God's Person (Heb. 1:3) and they failed to give *Him* the place He deserved.

> One stood before them who is the express image of God, and they failed to give Him the place He deserved.

The reply of Jesus shows that the believer has dual citizenship. He is responsible to obey human government and to support it financially (Rom. 13:1-7). As a citizen of heaven, He is responsible to obey God. If there is ever a conflict between the two, his first loyalty is to God (Acts 5:29).

In quoting verse 21, most of us emphasize the part about Caesar and skip lightly over the part about God. That was exactly the fault for which Jesus rebuked the Pharisees. When the Pharisees heard His answer, they knew they were outdone. All they could do was marvel, then leave.

The Sadducees and their Resurrection Riddle (22:23-33)

As mentioned previously, the Sadducees were the liberal theologians of that day. They denied the resurrection of the body. They denied the existence of angels. They denied miracles. In fact, their denials were more numerous than their affirmations.

A group of them came to Jesus with a story that was designed to make the whole idea of resurrection look ridiculous. They reminded the Lord of the law of Moses concerning levirate marriage, as found in Deuteronomy 25:5. Under that law, if an Israelite died without leaving children, his brother was supposed to marry the widow. This would preserve the family name in Israel and keep the inheritance within the family.

In their riddle, they supposed that a woman lost her husband, then married one of his brothers. The second brother died, so she married the third—and so on, down to the seventh. Finally the woman died. Then came the question designed to humiliate Him who is the resurrection (John 11:25): "In the resurrection, whose wife will she be? For they all had her" (v. 28).

Basically their argument was that the idea of resurrection posed insuperable difficulties, therefore it was not reasonable, therefore it was not true. Jesus answered that the difficulty was not in the doctrine but in their minds; they were ignorant of the Scriptures and the power of God. First, they were ignorant of the Scriptures. The Bible never says that the husband-wife relationship will be continued in heaven. While men will be recognizable as men, and women as women, they will all be like the angels in the sense that they neither marry nor are given in marriage.

> *The Bible never says that the husband-wife relationship will be continued in heaven.*

Second, they were ignorant of God's power. If He could create men from dust in the first place, could He not as easily raise the dust of those who had died and refashion it into bodies of glory? Then the Lord Jesus brought forth a very effective argument from the Scriptures to prove resurrection. In Exodus 3:6 God spoke of Himself as the God of Abraham, Isaac, and Jacob. And yet, as Jesus pointed out, God is not the God of the dead but of the living. How then can God speak of Himself as the God of three men whose bodies are in the grave? There is only one answer— resurrection. Before their death, God had made covenants with these men. However, they died before the covenants were completely fulfilled. Now God cannot fail to fulfill His promises. Yet how can He when these men have already died? There is only one answer—resurrection.

In interpreting the Lord's words, it is not enough to say that Abraham, Isaac, and Jacob are now alive in heaven, as to spirit, and that therefore God is the God of the living. The subject here is resurrection, and resurrection is concerned with the body. Jesus argued the necessity of the resurrection from what God said and from what God is.

No wonder the multitudes were amazed at His teaching; we are too.

The Great Commandment (22:34-40)

When the Pharisees heard that Jesus had silenced their antagonists, the Sadducees, they came to Him for an interview. Their spokesman, a lawyer, asked Jesus to single out the great commandment in the law.

In a masterful way the Lord Jesus summarized man's obligation to his God as the great and first commandment: "You shall love the Lord your God with all your heart, and with all your soul, and with all your mind." In Mark's account, there is the added phrase, "and with all your strength" (Mark 12:30). This means that man's first obligation is to love God with the totality of his being. As has often been pointed out, "the heart speaks of the emotional nature; the soul speaks of the volitional nature; the mind speaks of the intellectual nature; the strength speaks of the physical nature."

Then Jesus added that man's next responsibility is to love his neighbor as himself. We should frequently ponder the words, "Love your neighbor as yourself." We should think of how very much we do love ourselves, of how much of our activity centers around the care and comfort of self. Then we should try to imagine what it would be like if we showered that care and concern on our neighbors. Then we should do it.

> *Man's first obligation is to love God with the totality of his being.*

Of course, such behavior is not natural; it is supernatural. It cannot be done by our own strength but only by divine power. Only those of us who have been born again can do it, and then only by allowing Christ to do it through us.

David's Son Is David's Lord (22:41-46)

While the Pharisees were still awed by Jesus' answer to the lawyer, He faced them with a most provocative problem. What did they think of the Christ? Whose Son was He?

Remember, the Pharisees did not believe that Jesus was the Christ; they were still waiting for the Christ to come. So Jesus was not asking them, "What do you think of Me?" (though that, of course, was involved). He was asking in a general way whose son the Messiah would be when He appeared. They answered correctly that the Messiah would be a descendant of David.

Then the Lord Jesus quoted Psalm 110:1 where David said, "The Lord said to My Lord, sit at My right hand, till I make Your enemies Your footstall." The first use of the word "Lord" refers to God the Father. The second refers to the Messiah. And so David spoke of the Messiah as his Lord.

Now Jesus posed the question, "If David then calls him 'Lord,' how is He his son?" The answer, of course, is that the Messiah is both David's Lord and David's son. In other words, the Messiah is both God and Man. As God, He is David's Lord; as Man, He is David's son.

If the Pharisees had only been teachable, they would have realized that Jesus was the Messiah. He was the Son of David through the line of Mary. He was the Son of God, as shown by His words, works, and ways. But they refused to see. Completely baffled by His wisdom, they ceased trying to trick Him with questions. After this they would use another method—violence.

> The Messiah is both God and man.

Warning Against High Talk, Low Walk (23:1-12)

In the opening verses of this chapter, Jesus warns the crowds and the disciples against the scribes and Pharisees. He says that these leaders sat on Moses' seat; that is, they taught the law of Moses. In general, their teachings were dependable, but their practice was something else. Their creed was better than their conduct. It was a case of high talk and low walk. They made heavy demands on the people—probably this means extreme interpretations of the letter of the law—but they would not help anyone in lifting these intolerable loads.

Theirs was a religion of outward show instead of inward sincerity. They went through religious observances in order to be seen of men. Their use of phylacteries is an example. God had commanded Israel to bind His words as a sign upon their hands and as frontlets between their eyes (Ex. 13:9, 16; Deut. 6:8; 11:18). He obviously meant that the law should be continually guiding all their activities. But they took what was intended as a spiritual command and reduced it to a physical, literal sense. They enclosed short portions of the Scriptures in leather capsules and bound them to their forehead or arms. By wearing ridiculously large phylacteries, they gave the appearance of being super-spiritual. They weren't concerned about obeying the law as long as they appeared to be pious by carrying the law in these leather containers.

The law of Moses also commanded the Jews to make tassels on the corners of their garments, and to put a cord of blue on the tassels (Num. 15:37-41; Deut. 22:12). These distinctive trimmings were intended to remind the Jews that they were a distinct people, and that they should walk in separation from the nations. The Pharisees overlooked the spiritual lesson and satisfied themselves with making longer fringes. They showed their self-importance by scrambling for the places of honor at feasts and in the synagogues. They nourished their ego on greetings in the market places and especially enjoyed being called rabbi (meaning "teacher").

Here the Lord paused to warn His disciples against the use of special titles. They were not to be called rabbi or master and should call no man father. It should be clear that this warning applies only to spiritual relationships, not to natural or professional relationships; it does not forbid a child's calling his father by that name. Neither does it forbid a patient addressing his doctor by that title. As far as earthly relationships are concerned the rule is ". . . fear to whom fear [is due], honor to whom honor [is due]" (Rom. 13:7). But in the spiritual realm these titles are to be reserved for the Godhead. We should not be called Teacher, as a distinctive title, because there is one Teacher (the Holy Spirit, John 14:26, 1 John 2:27). We should not call any man father because God is our Father. We should not be called master, because Christ is our Master.

> *True greatness stoops to serve.*

The obvious meaning of Christ's words is that in the kingdom of heaven, all believers form an equal brotherhood and that there is no place for titles that set one above another. Yet think for a moment of the pompous titles that are found in Christendom today: Reverend, Very Reverend, Right Reverend, Most Reverend, Father, Padre, Doctor, and many others. The seemingly harmless word "doctor" means teacher; it comes from the Latin word *docere,* to teach. Jesus said, "Do not be called 'Rabbi' [teacher], for One is your Teacher, the Christ . . ." (v. 8).

Once again the revolutionary character of the kingdom of heaven is seen in the fact that true greatness is the exact opposite of what men would suppose. Jesus said, "But he who is greatest among you shall be your servant. And whoever exalts himself will be humbled, and he who humbles himself will be exalted." True greatness stoops to serve. Pharisees who exalt themselves will be brought low. True disciples who humble themselves will be exalted in due time.

Seven Woes Against the Scribes and Pharisees (23:13-36)

The Lord Jesus next delivered a sevenfold indictment against the proud religious hypocrites of His day. Since seven is the number of completion or fulfillment, this seems to suggest that the measure of their condemnation was full.

The first woe is directed against their stubbornness and obstructionism. They defiantly refused to enter the kingdom themselves, and aggressively hindered others from entering. It is strange that religious leaders are often the most active opponents of the gospel of grace. They can be sweetly tolerant of everything but the good news of salvation. The natural man doesn't want to be the object of God's grace and he doesn't want God to show grace to others.

> Religious leaders are often the most active opponents of the gospel of grace.

The second charge against them is misdirected zeal. They went to great lengths to make one convert, but after he was won they made him twice as wicked as themselves. A modern illustration of this is the zeal of the false cults. One group is willing to knock on 700 doors to reach one person for their cause; but the final result is evil. Third, the Lord denounced the scribes and Pharisees for the false system of reasoning they had designed to evade the payment of vows. For instance, they taught that if you swore by the temple, you were not obligated to pay, but if you swore by the gold of the temple, then you must perform the vow. Also they said that swearing by the gift on the altar was binding, whereas swearing by the empty altar was not. What it means is that they valued gold above God (the temple was the house of God), and they valued the gift on the altar (wealth of some form) above the altar itself. They were more interested in the material than the spiritual. They were more interested in getting (the gift) than in giving (the altar was the place of giving).

Addressing them as blind fools, Jesus exposed the evil of their deceptively subtle reasoning. The temple was of value because it was God's abode; the gold took on special value only because it was associated with the temple. And so with the gift on the altar; it was the altar that gave value to the gift. People who think that gold has intrinsic value are blind; it is only as it is used for the glory of God that it becomes valuable. And gifts given for carnal motives are valueless; but those that are given to the Lord or in the Lord's name—these have eternal value. The fact is that no matter what these Pharisees swore by, God was involved and they were obligated to fulfill the vow. The altar is the altar of God. The gift on the altar is made sacred by it. The temple is the house of God. The gold of the temple is made sacred by it. Heaven is the throne of God, so to swear by heaven was to swear by Him who sits upon it.

Vows are binding and promises must be kept. It is useless to appeal to technicalities to evade obligations.

The fourth woe is against ritualism without reality. The scribes and Pharisees were very particular in giving the Lord a tenth of the most insignificant herbs they raised. But they were completely without principle when it came to showing justice, mercy, and faithfulness to others. Jesus did not condemn them for being careful about the small details of obedience, but He rebuked them for being ruthless, mean, and crooked in important matters. Then, using a figure of speech unsurpassed for expressiveness, Jesus described them as straining out a gnat and swallowing a camel. The gnat was a tiny insect that often fell into a cup of sweet wine; it was strained out by sucking the wine through the teeth. How ludicrous to take such care with what is insignificant, then gulp down the largest unclean animal in Palestine! So the Pharisees were infinitely concerned with miniscule matters but grossly blind to enormous sins like hypocrisy, dishonesty, cruelty, and greed.

The fifth woe concerned externalism. The Pharisees were careful to maintain an outward show of religiousness and morality, but their hearts were filled with extortion and covetousness. They should first cleanse the inside of the cup and plate—that is, they should make sure that their hearts were cleansed through repentance and faith. Then, and only then, would their outward behavior be acceptable. There is a difference between our person and our personality. Our person is what we are; our personality is what we want other people to think we are. We tend to emphasize the personality; God emphasizes the person. He desires truth in the inward being (Ps. 51:6).

The sixth woe resembles the previous one in that it strikes out against externalism. The difference is that the fifth woe reproves an outward respectability that conceals greed, whereas the sixth condemns the concealment of hypocrisy and iniquity. Tombs were whitewashed so that Jewish people would not touch them by mistake and thus be ceremonially defiled. Jesus likened the scribes and Pharisees to whitewashed tombs, which looked clean on the outside but were full of corruption inside. Men thought that contact with these religious leaders would be sanctifying, but actually it was a defiling experience because they were full of hypocrisy and iniquity.

The final woe was launched against what we might label outward homage (worship), inward homicide. The scribes and Pharisees pretended to honor the Old Testament prophets by building and/or repairing their tombs and by putting wreaths on their monuments. In their memorial speeches, they said that they would not have joined with their ancestors in killing the prophets.

Jesus said to them, "Therefore you are witnesses against yourselves that you are sons of those who murdered the prophets" (v. 31). But how did they witness this? It almost seems from the preceding verse that they disassociated themselves from their fathers who killed the prophets.

1. They admitted that their fathers shed the blood of the prophets. They were sons of the fathers in a physical sense. But Jesus used the word sons in another sense, i.e., as meaning people with the same characteristics. The Lord knew that at the very time they were decorating the graves of the prophets, they were plotting His death.

2. In showing such respect for the dead prophets, they were saying, "The only kind of prophets we like are dead ones." In this sense also they were sons of their fathers.

Then our Lord added, "Fill up, then, the measure of your fathers' guilt" (v. 32). The fathers had filled the cup of murder part way by killing the prophets. The scribes and Pharisees would soon fill it to the brim by killing the Lord Jesus and His followers. Thus they would bring to a terrible climax what their fathers had begun.

It is at this point that we hear the Christ of God utter those thunderous words, "Serpents, brood of vipers! How can you escape the condemnation of hell?" Is it possible that Incarnate Love can speak such severe, stinging words? Yes, because true love must also be righteous and holy. The popular conception of Jesus as an inoffensive reformer, capable of no emotion but love, is thoroughly unbiblical. Love can be firm at times, and it must always be just.

It is solemn to remember that these severe words of condemnation were hurled at religious leaders, not at drunkards and reprobates. In an ecumenical age when evangelical Christians are joining forces with avowed enemies of the cross of Christ, it is good for us to ponder the example of Jesus, and also to remember the words of Jehu to Jehoshaphat, "Should you help the wicked and love those who hate the Lord?" (2 Chron. 19:2).

> "Should you help the wicked and love those who hate the Lord?"

Not only did Jesus foresee His own death; He plainly told the scribes and Pharisees that they would also murder some of the messengers whom He would send. Some who escaped martyrdom would be attacked and persecuted from town to town. In this way the religious leaders of Israel would heap to themselves the accumulated guilt of the history of martyrdom. Upon them would come all the righteous blood shed on earth, from Abel to Zechariah. Abel, of course, was the first martyr, and Zechariah (not the post-exilic prophet of the same name) was the last martyr recorded in the Old Testament (read 2 Chronicles 24:20-21, the last book in the Hebrew Bible).

The guilt of all the past would come on the generation or race to which Christ was speaking. It is as if all previous shedding of innocent blood was somehow combined and climaxed in the death of the sinless Savior. A torrent of punishment would be poured out on the nation that hated its Messiah without a cause and nailed Him to a criminal's cross.

Jesus Laments Over Jerusalem (23:37-39)

It is highly significant that the chapter which, more than almost any other, contains the woes of the Lord Jesus should close with His tears! After His bitter denunciation of the Pharisees, He utters a poignant lament over the city of lost opportunity. Even the repetition of the name—"O Jerusalem, Jerusalem"—is charged with unutterable emotion. Though she had killed the prophets and stoned God's messengers, yet the Lord loved her, and would often have protectively and lovingly gathered her children to Himself—like a hen gathers her brood—but she was not willing.

In closing His lament, the Lord Jesus said, "See! Your house is left to you desolate." Primarily the "house" here is the temple, but it may also include the city of Jerusalem and the nation itself.

There would be an interval between His death and His second coming during which unbelieving Israel would not see Him (after His resurrection He was seen only by believers). Verse 39 looks forward to the second advent when a believing portion of the nation of Israel will accept Him as their Messiah-King. This acceptance is implicit in the words, "Blessed is He who comes in the name of the Lord!" (v. 39).

There is no suggestion that the Jews who murdered Christ will have a second chance. He was speaking of Jerusalem and thus, by implication, of its inhabitants and of Israel in general. The next time the inhabitants of Jerusalem would see Him after His death would be when they would look on Him whom they pierced and mourn for Him as one mourns for an only son (Zech. 12:10). In Jewish reckoning there is no mourning as bitter as that for an only son.

11

MATTHEW 24–25

The Olivet Discourse (24:1-2)

Chapters 24 and 25 form what is known as the Olivet Discourse, the name arising from the fact that this important pronouncement was given on the Mount of Olives. The discourse is entirely prophetic in nature: it points forward to the tribulation period and to the second coming of the Lord Jesus Christ. It is concerned primarily, though not exclusively, with the nation of Israel. Its locale is obviously Palestine; for example, "Let those who are in Judea flee to the mountains" (v. 16). Its setting is distinctly Jewish; for example, "Pray that your flight may not be . . . on the Sabbath" (v. 20). When reference is made to the elect (v. 22), it should be understood as God's Jewish elect and not the church. Actually the church is not found anywhere in the discourse, either in the prophecies or parables. We shall seek to demonstrate this as we proceed.

> The discourse is entirely prophetic.

The discourse is introduced by a statement that is full of meaning: "Jesus left the temple and was going away. . . ." This movement is especially significant in view of the words He had just spoken, ". . . your house is left to you desolate" (23:38). It reminds us of Ezekiel's description of the glory of God departing from the temple (Ezek. 9:3; 10:4; 11:23).

The disciples wanted to delay Him so He could admire the architectural beauty of the temple with them. They were caught up in a world of passing things; occupied with the transient instead of the eternal. Jesus warned them that the building would be so completely destroyed that not one stone would be left on top of another. This judgment was executed in AD 70 when the Romans under Titus sacked Jerusalem.

The First Half of the Tribulation (24:3-14)

After Jesus had crossed over to the Mount of Olives, the disciples came to Him privately and asked three questions:

1. When would these things happen; that is, when would the temple be destroyed?

2. What would be the sign of His coming; that is, what supernatural event would precede His return to the earth to set up His kingdom?

3. What would be the sign of the end of the age; that is, what would announce the end of the age immediately prior to His glorious reign?

The second and third questions were essentially the same.

We must remember that these were Jewish disciples whose thinking largely revolved around the glorious age of the Messiah's rule on earth. When they asked these questions, they were not thinking about Christ's coming for the church; they knew little if anything about this phase of His coming. Their expectation was His coming in power and glory to destroy His enemies and rule over the world. Also we should be clear that they were not talking about the end of the *world*, but the end of the age (v. 3).

Their first question is not answered directly in Matthew's account. Rather, the Lord seems to merge the siege of Jerusalem in AD 70 (see Luke 21:20-24) with a similar siege that will occur in the latter days. In the study of prophecy, we often see the Lord moving almost imperceptibly from an early, partial fulfillment to a later, final fulfillment. The answers to the second and third questions are given in verses 4 to 44 of this chapter. These verses describe the seven year tribulation period which will precede Christ's glorious advent.

The first 3½ years are described in verses 4-14. The final 3½ years are known as the great tribulation and the "time of Jacob's trouble" (Jer. 30:7). It will be a time of unprecedented suffering for those who dwell on the earth. Many of the conditions which will characterize the first half of the tribulation period have existed to a certain extent throughout human history (like famines and earthquakes), but they will appear in a greatly intensified form during the tribulation. Even those of us in the church have been promised tribulation (John 16:33), but this is far different from *the* tribulation which will be poured out on a world that has rejected God's Son.

We believe that the church will be taken out of the world (1 Thess. 4:13-18) before the day of God's wrath begins (1 Thess. 1:10; 5:9; 2 Thess. 2:1-12; Rev. 3:10). But what will be the conditions prevailing during the first half of the tribulation period?

First of all, there will be the appearance of many false messiahs who will succeed in deceiving multitudes (vv. 4-5). The rise of many false cults in our day may be a prelude to this, but it is not a fulfillment. These false religious leaders will be Jews who will claim to be the Christ, the King of Israel. Second, there will be wars and rumors of wars (vv. 6-7). Nation will rise against nation. The wars that we see happening today are mild compared to what will be. Actually the next event in God's time schedule is the rapture of the church (John 14:1-6; 1 Cor. 15:51-57). There is no prophecy to be fulfilled before then. After the church is removed, God's prophetic clock will begin and these conditions will quickly manifest themselves.

Verse 8 clearly identifies this period as the beginning of the sufferings; it is the onset of birth-pangs which will finally result in the bringing forth of a new order under Israel's Messiah-King. For Christ's faithful Jewish followers, it will be a time of severe persecution. The nations will conduct a bitter hate campaign against all who are true to Him. Many will be martyred because they refuse to recant. The pressure will be so great that many will fall away from Christ rather than suffer and die. Family members will inform against their own relatives and betray them into the hands of cruel persecutors. Disciples of the Lord Jesus will be hated in proportion to the intensity of the persecution.

> *There will be the appearance of many false messiahs.*

Many false prophets will appear (v. 11), deceiving many. These are not to be confused with the false messiahs of verse 5. False prophets are men who claim to be spokesmen for God. They can be detected in two ways: their prophecies do not always come to pass, and their teachings always lead men away from the true God. The mention of false *prophets* adds confirmation to our previous statement that the tribulation is primarily Jewish in character. *False prophets* are associated with the nation of Israel; in the church the danger comes from *false teachers* (2 Peter 2:1).

With wickedness rampaging, human affections will be less and less evident. "But he who endures to the end will be saved" (v. 13). This obviously does not mean that men's souls will be saved at that time by their enduring;

salvation is always presented in the Bible as being a gift of God's grace, received by faith in Christ, and based upon His substitutionary death and resurrection. Neither can it mean that all who endure will be saved from physical harm, because we have already learned that many true believers will be martyred (v. 9). It is a general statement that those who stand fast in their confession of Christ, enduring persecution, will be delivered at Christ's second advent.

> *Salvation is always presented in the Bible as being a gift of God's grace.*

During this period, there will be a world-wide proclamation of the gospel of the kingdom as a testimony to all nations. As explained in the notes on the gospel of the kingdom (see pages 18-19), one aspect of the gospel is the fact that Christ is coming to set up His kingdom on earth, and that those who receive Him by faith during the tribulation will enjoy the blessings of His millennial reign.

Verse 14 is often used to show that Christ could not return for His church at any moment because there are so many tribes that have not been reached with the gospel. The difficulty is removed when we realize that this refers to His coming *with* His saints, not His coming *for* His saints. And this refers to the gospel of the kingdom, not to the gospel of the grace of God (see notes on 4:23).

There is a striking parallel between the events listed in verses 3-14 and those of Revelation 6:1-11. The rider on the white horse—false messiah; the rider of the red horse—war; the rider of the black horse—famine; the rider on the pale horse—pestilence or death; the souls under the altar—martyrs. The events described in Revelation 6:12-17 are linked with those in Matthew 24:19-31.

The Great Tribulation (24:15-28)

At this point we have come to the middle of the tribulation. We know this by comparing verse 15 with Daniel 9:27. Daniel predicted that in the middle of the seventieth week, that is, at the end of 3½ years, a great idolatrous image would be set up in the temple in Jerusalem. Everyone will be ordered to worship this abominable idol. Failure to comply will be punishable by death (Rev. 13:15).

The erection of the idol will be the signal for those who know the Scriptures to understand that the great tribulation has begun (v. 15). Those who are in Judea should flee to the mountains; as long as they are in the vicinity of Jerusalem, their refusal to bow to the image would be quickly detected.

Utmost haste will be necessary. If a man is sitting on the housetop, visiting with friends, he should leave all his possessions behind. The time spent in going inside to gather his belongings might mean the difference between life and death. The man working in the field should not return for his coat, wherever he may have left it. Pregnant women and nursing mothers will be at a distinct disadvantage—it will be so hard for them to make a speedy escape.

Believers should pray that the crisis moment will not come in the winter; then they would have added travel hazards. And they should pray that it will not come on a Sabbath; in that case the distance they could travel would be limited by law (Ex. 16:29). A Sabbath day's journey would not be long enough to take them out of the danger area.

The description in verse 21 isolates the period under discussion from all the inquisitions, pogroms, purges, massacres, and genocides of history. This prophecy could not have been fulfilled by any previous times of persecution because it is clearly stated that it will be ended by the second advent of Christ.

---------- ✍ ----------

Miracles can be satanic in origin.

---------- ✍ ----------

The tribulation will be so intense that unless the days were shortened, nobody would survive. This cannot mean that the great tribulation itself will be shortened, because the time is so often specified as three and a half years. It probably means that God will miraculously shorten the hours of daylight—during which most fighting and slaughter occur. For the elect's sake, that is, for those who have received the Lord Jesus as Lord and Savior, the Lord will grant the respite of earlier darkness.

In verses 23 and 24 there are renewed warnings against false messiahs and false prophets. In an atmosphere of impending crisis, reports will circulate as to the messiah's whereabouts. Such reports could be used to trap those who were sincerely looking for Christ. So the Lord warns all disciples not to believe reports of a local, secret, private advent. Even if men arise performing miracles, that does not prove they are from God. Miracles can be satanic in origin.

There will be no mistaking His coming; it will be sudden, public, universal, and glorious. Like the lightning that streaks across the sky from east to west, it will be instantly and clearly visible to all.

And no moral corruption will escape its fury and judgment. For "wherever the carcass is, there the eagles will be gathered together" (v. 28). The body or carcass here pictures apostate Judaism and apostate Christendom; in fact, it includes the whole world system that is leagued against God and against His Christ. The eagles or vultures typify the judgments of God which will be unleashed at the Messiah's appearing.

The Second Advent (24:29-31)

At the close of the great tribulation there will be terrifying disturbances in the heavens. The sun will be darkened and since the moon's light is only a reflection of the sun's, the moon will also withhold its light. The stars will plunge from heaven and planets will be moved out of their orbits. It goes without saying that such vast cosmic upheavals will affect the weather, the tides, and the seasons here on the earth. A faint idea of what it will be like can be gathered from the following description of what would happen if a heavenly body came close to the earth and caused it to tilt on its axis:

> "At that moment an earthquake would make the earth shudder. Air and water would continue to move through inertia; hurricanes would sweep the earth and the seas would rush over continents, carrying gravel and sand and marine animals, and casting them on the land. Heat would be developed, rocks would melt, volcanoes would erupt, lava would flow from fissures in the ruptured ground and cover vast areas. Mountains would spring up from the plains and would travel and climb on the shoulders of other mountains, causing faults and rifts. Lakes would be tilted and emptied, rivers would change their beds; large land areas with all their inhabitants would slip under the sea. Forests would burn and the hurricane and wild seas would wrest them from the ground on which they grew and pile them, branch and root, in huge heaps. Seas would turn into deserts, their waters flowing away." (Velikovsky)

"Then the sign of the Son of Man will appear in heaven." We are not told what this sign will be. His first advent was accompanied by a sign in heaven—the star. It is not unreasonable to suppose that a miracle star will also announce His second coming. Some believe that the Son of Man is

Himself the sign. Whatever is meant, it will be clear to all when it appears. All the tribes of the earth will mourn—no doubt because of their rejection of Him. But primarily the tribes of the *land* will mourn—that is, the twelve tribes of the land of Israel. "Then they will look on Me whom they pierced. Yes they will mourn for Him as one who mourns for his only son, and grieve for Him as one grieves for a firstborn" (Zech. 12:10).

Then they will see the blessed Lord Jesus coming on the clouds of heaven with power and great glory. What a wonderful moment that will be! The One who was spit upon and crucified will be vindicated as the Lord of life and glory. The sacrificial Lamb will descend as the conquering Lion. His chariots will be the clouds of heaven. He will come in regal power and splendor. It is the moment for which creation has groaned for thousands of years.

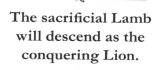

The sacrificial Lamb will descend as the conquering Lion.

At the time of His descent, He will send His angels throughout the earth to gather His elect people, believing Israel, to the land of Palestine. From all parts of the earth they will gather to greet their Messiah and to enjoy His glorious reign.

Lesson of the Fig Tree (24:32-35)

"Let the fig tree teach you a lesson" (TEV). Once again our Lord draws a spiritual lesson from the world of nature. When the branches of the fig tree become green and tender, farmers know that summer is near. We have already seen that the fig tree pictures the nation of Israel (21:18-22). For hundreds of years Israel has been dormant, as if in the clutch of winter. It has had no government of its own, no land, no temple, no priesthood. There has been no sign of national life. The people have been scattered throughout the world.

In 1948, however, Israel became a nation with its own land, government, currency, stamps, etc. Spiritually, the nation is still barren and cold; there is no fruit for God. But nationally, we might say that its branches are green and tender. "In the same way, when you see all these things, you will know that the time is near, ready to begin" (v. 33, TEV). The emergence of Israel as a nation means not only that the beginning of the tribulation is near, but that the Lord Himself is near.

If Christ's coming to reign is so near, how much more imminent is the rapture of the church? If we already see shadows of events that must precede His appearing in glory, how much closer are we to the first phase of His coming (1 Thess. 4:13-18). Following His reference to the fig tree, Jesus added, "Assuredly I say to you, this generation will by no means pass away till all these things take place" (v. 34). Now the phrase "this generation" could not possibly mean the people who were living when Christ was on earth, because they have all passed away, and yet the events of chapter 24 have not taken place. What then did Jesus mean by "this generation"? There are two possible explanations.

F. W. Grant and others believe that the very generation that sees the beginning of these things will see the end. The same people who see the rise of Israel as a nation (or who see the beginning of the tribulation), will see the Lord Jesus coming in the clouds of heaven to reign. The other explanation is that generation should be understood as meaning "race." This is a legitimate translation of the Greek word; it means men of the same stock, breed, or family (Matt. 12:45; 23:35-36). So Jesus was predicting that the Jewish race would survive to see all these things accomplished. Their continued survival, in spite of the most atrocious persecution, is one of the miracles of history.

—————— ❧ ——————

Only those who willingly submit to Christ's rule will be spared to enter the millennium.

—————— ❧ ——————

There is another aspect worth considering. In Jesus' day, "this generation" was a race that steadfastly refused to acknowledge Him as Messiah. Maybe He was predicting that national Israel would continue in its Christ-rejecting condition till His second coming. Then all rebellion will be crushed, and only those who willingly submit to His rule will be spared to enter the millennium.

To emphasize the unfailing character of His predictions, Jesus added that heaven and earth would pass away but His words would not pass away. In speaking of heaven passing away, He was referring to the stellar heaven and the atmospheric heaven—the blue firmament above us—not the heaven which is God's dwelling place (2 Cor. 12:2-3). The dissolution of the heaven and the earth is described in 2 Peter 3:10-13 and again in Revelation 20:11.

The Day and Hour Are Unknown (24:36-44)

As to the exact day and hour of His second advent, "no one knows, not even the angels of heaven, but the Father only" (v. 36). The fact that no man knows should warn us against the temptation to set dates or to believe those who do. We are not surprised that angels do not know; they are finite creatures with limited knowledge. But a definite difficulty presents itself in the statement that the Son does not know the time of His own second coming to earth. (The words "nor the Son" are omitted here in many ancient manuscripts, but they are definitely included in Mark 13:32.) Since Jesus is God, and since God knows everything, how can He fail to know the time?

We shall seek to answer the question by a series of clarifying statements.

1. Jesus is the Son of God, and God is omniscient. Therefore Jesus is omniscient.

2. In coming into the world, God the Son did not lay aside any of the attributes of deity. He was still omnipotent, omniscient, and omnipresent. He is perfect God as well as perfect Man. He could not be God without the attributes of God.

3. Although He still possessed the attributes of deity, they were veiled in His body of flesh. At times the glory of His deity shone forth, as on the Mount of Transfiguration. But at other times, His deity was not evident to the human eye.

4. As the Servant of Jehovah it was not given to the Lord Jesus to know the time of His Advent. ". . . a servant does not know what his master is doing . . ." (John 15:15). As God He, of course, knows, but as Servant, it was not given to Him to know or to reveal it to others. James H. Brookes says, "It is not a denial of our Lord's divine omniscience, but simply an assertion that in the economy of human redemption it was not for Him 'to know times or seasons which the Father has fixed by his own authority' (Acts 1:7). Jesus knew that He will come again, and often spoke of His second advent, but it did not fall to His office as Son to determine the date of His return, and hence He could hold it up before His followers as the object of constant expectation and desire."

"Christ was here as Man. In human condition, He learned by revelation. Think of Him as a student of the Scriptures. He could not find any word there to tell the day or the hour of His second coming. He would not draw on His essential knowledge as God to communicate what was not a subject of divine revelation. He did not have that knowledge as a deposit" (C. Grain).

While those living prior to Christ's return to reign will not know its *day* or *hour,* it seems clear that those who are familiar with the prophetic Word will be able to know the *year.* They will know, for instance, that it will be approximately 3½ years after the idol image is set up in the temple (Dan. 9:27; see also Dan. 7:25; 12:7, 11; Rev. 11:2-3; 12:14; 13:5).

In those days, however, most people will be careless and indifferent, just as they were in the days of Noah. Although the days before the flood were days of terrible wickedness, that is not the feature that is emphasized here. The people ate and drank, married and gave in marriage; in other words, they were going through the usual routines of life as if they were going to live forever. Though they had been warned that a flood was coming, they lived as if they were flood-proof. When it came they were completely unprepared. They were outside the only place of safety. And that is just the way it will be when Christ comes again. Only those who are in Christ, the ark of safety, will be delivered.

—————— ❧ ——————

The Son of Man will come when least expected by the mass of the people.

—————— ❧ ——————

Two men will be working in the field; one will be taken away in judgment; the other will be left to enter the millennium. Two women will be grinding at the mill; they will be instantly separated. One will be swept away by the flood of judgment; the other will be left to enjoy the blessings of Christ's reign. (Verses 40 and 41 are often used in reference to the rapture, the first phase of Christ's coming when He takes all believers to heaven and leaves all unbelievers behind for judgment. The verses are thus used as a warning to the unsaved. While that might be a valid *application* of the passage, the context makes it clear that the *interpretation* has to do with Christ's coming to reign.)

In view of the uncertainty as to the day and the hour, men ought to be watchful. If a man knows his house is going to be broken into, he will be ready, even if he doesn't know the exact time. The Son of Man will come when least expected by the mass of the people. Therefore His people should be on the tiptoes of expectancy.

Wise and Wicked Servants (24:45-51)

In the closing section of this chapter, the Lord Jesus shows that a servant manifests his true character by how he behaves in view of his Master's return. Not all who profess to be Christ's servants are genuine.

> ❧
>
> **The wise servant is the one who is found caring for God's people.**
>
> ❧

The wise servant is the one who is found caring for God's people. Such a one will be given the honor of vast responsibility in the kingdom (v. 47). The evil slave represents a nominal believer whose service is not affected by the prospect of his Master's soon return. He "begins to beat his fellow servants, and to eat and drink with the drunkards" (v. 49). By such behavior he demonstrates that he is not ready for the kingdom. When the King comes, He will punish him and make him "share the fate of the impostors" (v. 51, TEV) where men weep and gnash their teeth.

In its context this parable refers to Christ's visible return to the earth as Messiah-King. But the principle applies equally as well to the rapture. Many who profess to be Christians today show by their hostility toward God's people and by their friendliness with the ungodly that they are not looking for Christ's return. For them it will mean judgment and not blessing.

The Parable of the Wise and Foolish Virgins (25:1-13)

The first word, "Then," referring back to the previous chapter, clearly places this parable in the time preceding and during the King's return to earth. Jesus likens the kingdom of heaven at that time to ten virgins who took their lamps and went out to meet the bridegroom. The five who were wise had oil for their lamps; the others had no oil. During the waiting period they all fell asleep. When it was finally announced that the bridegroom was coming, they all woke up and trimmed their lamps. Then the foolish virgins asked the others for oil, but they were sent to the store to buy some. During their absence the bridegroom arrived. The wise ones went in with him to the wedding feast and the door was closed. Eventually the foolish virgins showed up and asked to be let in, but the bridegroom said he didn't know them. The lesson, Jesus said, was to watch, because the day and hour of His coming are unknown.

As to the interpretation, the five wise virgins represent true disciples of Christ in the tribulation period. The lamps speak of testimony or profession, and the oil is generally acknowledged to be a type of the Holy Spirit. The foolish virgins picture those who profess to hold the messianic hope but who have never been converted; they have a profession but they do not have the Holy Spirit. The bridegroom is Christ, the King; His delay symbolizes the period between His two advents. The fact that both wise and foolish virgins slept tells us that outwardly there was not much to differentiate them.

At midnight the announcement rang out that the King was coming. In chapter 24 we learned that His arrival will be announced by awesome signs. The maidens rose and trimmed their lamps—they all wanted to appear ready. But the foolish ones lacked oil. The wise ones seem selfish in their refusal, but in the spiritual realm, no one can dispense the Spirit to another. So the oil-less virgins were sent to the dealers to buy some. We understand that the Holy Spirit cannot be bought, but the Bible does use the literary figure of buying salvation without money and without price (Isa. 55:1).

While they were gone, the bridegroom came. The Syriac and Vulgate versions say that he came with his bride. This fits the prophetic picture perfectly. The Lord Jesus will return from the wedding with His bride, the church (1 Thess. 3:13). (The wedding takes place in heaven (Eph. 5:27) after the rapture.) The faithful remnant of tribulation saints will go in with Him to the marriage feast. The marriage feast is a fitting designation of the joy and blessing of Christ's earthly kingdom. Then the door was shut; it was too late for anyone else to get into the kingdom. When the foolish virgins returned, the bridegroom denied knowing them—a clear proof that they were not genuine disciples.

The cardinal lesson for believers of every age is to live as if the Lord might come at any moment. The day and hour of His coming are unknown; are our lamps trimmed and filled with oil?

The Parable of the Talents (25:14-30)

This parable also teaches that when the King returns, there will be true and false servants. The faithful service of the true will be rewarded; the wickedness of the false will be punished.

The story revolves around a man who was going on a long journey. First he assembled his servants and gave them varying amounts of money, according to their ability. One got five talents, another got two, and the last got one. They were supposed to use this money in such a way as to earn income for the master. The man with five earned five more. The man with two doubled his also. But the man with one dug a hole in the ground and buried it.

After a long time the master returned to settle accounts with them. The first two received exactly the same commendation: "Well done, good and faithful servant; you were faithful over a little, I will make you ruler over many things. Enter into the joy of your lord" (vv. 21, 23).

The third one had nothing but insults and excuses for his master. He accused him of being hard and unreasonable. He excused himself that, being paralyzed with fear, he buried the talent. The master rebuked him as wicked and lazy. If he had such thoughts of his master, why hadn't he turned the talent over to the bankers, so there would have been interest on the money? The talent was taken from him and given to the ten-talent man. And he himself was cast out into darkness to weep and gnash his teeth.

It is not difficult to see that Christ is the master, and the long journey pictures the period between His two advents. The three servants are Israelites living during the tribulation; they are responsible to represent the interests of the absent King. Not all have the same ability, so they are given responsibility according to their individual ability. The test of their service is not how much they earn but how hard they try. The return of the master depicts the second advent of Christ. The one who earned two talents received the same commendation as the man who earned five—in each case they used their ability to the full and earned one hundred percent. These two represent true believers whose reward is to enjoy the blessings of the messianic kingdom.

We know that the one-talent man was an unbeliever; no genuine servant would entertain such unworthy thoughts of his Master. Incidentally, in verse 26, the master does not admit that the charges against him are true. Rather he is saying, "If that's the kind of a master you thought I am, all the more reason you should have put the talent to work. Your words condemn you instead of excusing you." If this man had earned one talent with his one talent, he would have received the same commendation as the others. Instead, all he had to show for his life, as someone has said, was a hole in the ground.

The mention of the bankers in verse 27 suggests that if for any reason we cannot use our possessions for the Lord, we should turn them over to others who can. The bankers in this case may be missionaries, Bible societies, Christian publishing houses, gospel radio programs, etc. In a world like ours, there is no excuse for leaving money idle.

The talent was taken from him and given to the man with ten talents. This follows a fixed law in the spiritual realm: ". . . to everyone who has, more will be given, and he will have abundance; but from him who does not have, even what he has will be taken away" (v. 29). Those who desire to be used for God's glory are given the means to do it. The more they do, the more they are enabled to do for Him. On the other hand, we lose what we don't use. Atrophy is the reward of laziness.

> There is no
> excuse for leaving
> money idle.

The unprofitable servant was cast out; that is, excluded from the kingdom. He shared the anguished, remorseful fate of the wicked. It was not his failure to invest the talent that condemned him; rather, his lack of good works showed that he did not have saving faith.

Judgment of the Nations (25:31-46)

In this section we have a description of the judgment of the nations. This judgment is to be distinguished from the judgment seat of Christ and the judgment of the great white throne. The judgment seat of Christ takes place in heaven after the rapture. It is a time of review and reward for believers only (Rom. 14:10; 1 Cor. 3:11-15; 2 Cor. 5:9-10).

The judgment of the nations takes place on earth after Christ comes to reign. The nations will be judged according to their treatment of Christ's Jewish brethren during the tribulation (Joel 3:1, 2, 12-14; Matt. 25:31-46). The judgment of the great white throne takes place in eternity, after the millennium. The wicked dead will be judged and consigned to the lake of fire (Rev. 20:11-15).

The judgment of the nations could also be called the judgment of the Gentiles. Its time is clearly stated in verse 31: "When the Son of Man comes in His glory, and all the holy angels with Him. . . ." If we are right in identifying it with Joel 3, then we can pinpoint the location as the Valley of Jehoshaphat, outside Jerusalem (Joel 3:2).

It is important to notice that three classes are mentioned: sheep, goats, and Christ's brethren. The first two classes are Gentiles living during the tribulation; these are the ones over whom Christ sits in judgment. The third class is Christ's faithful Jewish brethren who refuse to deny His name during the tribulation in spite of great persecution.

The King separates the sheep from the goats, placing the sheep at His right hand and the goats at the left. He then invites the sheep to enter His glorious kingdom, prepared for them from the foundation of the world. The reasons are given in verses 35-36. The righteous sheep profess ignorance of ever showing such kindnesses to the King; He had not even been on earth in their generation. He explains that in befriending one of the least of His brethren, they befriended Him. Whatever is done for one of His disciples is rewarded as being done to Himself.

> Whatever is done for one of His disciples is rewarded as being done to Himself.

The unrighteous goats are told to depart into the eternal fire prepared for the devil and his angels. The reason in this case is that they failed to care for Him during the terrible time of Jacob's trouble. When they excuse themselves by saying they had never seen Him before, He reminds them that their neglect of His followers constituted neglect of Himself. And so we are told that the goats go away into eternal punishment, and the sheep into eternal life. But this immediately raises two problems.

First of all, the passage seems to teach that nations are saved or lost *en masse*. And second, the narrative creates the impression that the sheep are saved by good works, and the goats are condemned through failure to do good.

With regard to the first difficulty, it must be remembered that God *does* deal with nations as such. Old Testament history abounds with instances where nations were punished because of their sin (Isa. 10:12-19; 47:5-15; Ezek. 25:6,7; Amos 1:3, 6, 9, 11, 13; 2:1, 4, 6; Obad. 10; Zech. 14:1-5). It is not unreasonable to believe that the nations of the world will continue to experience divine retribution. This does not mean that every single individual in the nation will be involved in the final outcome, but it does mean that the principles of divine justice will be applied on a national basis as well as on an individual basis.

The word translated "nations" in this passage could also be translated "Gentiles." Some understand the passage to describe the judgment of individual Gentiles. Whether we think of nations or individuals, there is the problem of how such a vast horde could be gathered before the Lord in Palestine. Perhaps it is best to think of representatives of the nations or individual classes assembled for judgment.

As to the second problem, the passage cannot be used to teach salvation by works. The uniform testimony of the Bible is that salvation is by faith and not by works (e.g. Eph. 2:8-9). But the Bible is just as emphatic in teaching that where there is true faith, there will be good works. And if there are no good works, it is an indication that the person was never saved. So here we must understand that the Gentiles are not saved by befriending the Jewish remnant, but that this kindness is a reflection of their love for the Lord.

Three other points should be mentioned in passing. The first is this: the kingdom is said to have been prepared for the righteous from the foundation of the world (v. 34), whereas hell is said to have been prepared for the devil and his angels (v. 41). God's desire is that people should be blessed; hell was never intended for the human race. But if man willfully refuses life, he necessarily chooses death.

> If man willfully refuses life, he necessarily chooses death.

The second point is that the Lord Jesus spoke of eternal fire (v. 41), eternal punishment (v. 46), and eternal life (v. 46). The same One who taught eternal life taught eternal punishment. Since the same word for *eternal* is used to describe the one as the other, it is inconsistent to accept one without the other. And if the word translated *eternal* does not mean everlasting, there is no word in the Greek language to convey this meaning. But we know that it does mean everlasting because it is used to describe the eternality of God (1 Tim. 1:17).

Finally, the judgment of the Gentiles reminds us forcefully that Christ and His people are one, that what affects them affects Him. We have vast potential for showing kindness to Him by showing kindness to those who love Him.

CHAPTER

12

MATTHEW 26–28

The Approaching Passover (26:1-2)

For the fourth and final time in this gospel record our Lord forewarns His disciples that He must die (16:21; 17:22; 20:18). His announcement implies a close time relationship between the Passover and His crucifixion: "You know that after two days is the Passover, and the Son of Man will be delivered up to be crucified." This year the Passover would find its true meaning. The Passover Lamb had at last arrived and would soon be slain.

> — ☙ —
>
> The Passover would find its true meaning in the death of the Lord Jesus.
>
> — ☙ —

The Palace Plot (26:3-5)

Even as He was uttering the words, the chief priests and elders were gathering in the palace of Caiaphas, the high priest, to map out their strategy. They wanted to arrest Him secretly and have Him killed. But they did not think it would be wise to do it during the feast; the people might react violently against His execution. It is almost incredible that Israel's religious leaders should have taken the lead in plotting the death of their Messiah. They should have been the first to recognize Him and to enthrone Him. As it was, they formed the front line of His enemies.

Jesus Is Anointed at Bethany (26:6-13)

This next incident provides a welcome relief, coming as it does between the plotting of the priests, the pettiness of the disciples, and the treachery of Judas. While Jesus was in the home of Simon the leper in Bethany, a woman came in and poured out a vial of very expensive perfume on His head. John tells us that she was Mary, the sister of Martha (John 12:2-3); she should not be confused with the sinful woman who also anointed Christ (Luke 7:37). The costliness of her sacrifice expressed the deep measure of her devotion for the Lord Jesus. She was saying, in effect, that there was nothing too good for Him. The disciples in general, and Judas in particular (John 12:4-5), viewed the act as an enormous waste. They thought the money might better have been given to the poor.

Jesus corrected their distorted thinking. Her act was not wasteful; it was beautiful. Not only so, it was perfectly timed. There will always be poor people, and they can be helped at any time. But only once in the world's history could the Savior be anointed for burial. That moment had struck, and one lone woman with spiritual discernment had seized it. She had believed the Lord's predictions concerning His death. She must have realized that it was now or never. As it turned out, she was right. The women who planned to anoint His body after His burial were thwarted by the resurrection (Mark 16:1-6).

> There was nothing too good for Jesus.

The Lord Jesus immortalized Mary's simple act of love (v. 13). Any act of true worship fills the courts of heaven with fragrance and is indelibly recorded in the Lord's grateful memory.

Thirty Pieces of Silver (26:14-16)

"Then one of the twelve . . ." One of the disciples who had lived with the Lord Jesus, who had traveled with Him, who had seen His miracles, who had heard His incomparable teaching, and who had witnessed the miracle of a sinless life—one whom Jesus could call "my own familiar friend in whom I trusted, who ate of my bread" (Ps. 41:9)—it was now that one who lifted up his heel against the Son of God. Judas Iscariot went to the chief priests and agreed to sell his Master for thirty pieces of silver—the price of a slave. The priests paid him on the spot. And so the one who had received nothing but kindness from Jesus went out to arrange his part of the dreadful bargain.

The contrast between Mary and Judas is striking:

Mary	Judas
Very costly	Thirty pieces of silver
To prepare Him for burial	To deliver Him to be murdered
A good work	A betrayal of innocent blood
Love	Greed
Perpetual memorial	Perpetual shame

(Source unknown)

The Last Passover (26:17-25)

There are problems connected with the chronology of the Passover. Here the Lord is seen eating the meal with the Twelve. Yet to fulfill prophecy was it not necessary that He be killed at the Passover time? George Williams gives the following explanation: "The Passover was eaten between the evenings, that is, between 6 p.m. of one day and 6 p.m. of the next. So the Lord ate His last Passover after six o'clock on the evening prior to His crucifixion. Thus He commemorated the Passover and He became the Passover on the self-same day."

It was the first day of the Feast of Unleavened Bread—a time when all leaven was removed from Jewish homes. What thoughts must have flooded the mind of the Lord as He sent His disciples into Jerusalem to prepare for the feast! Every detail of the meal would have special significance to His sensitive soul.

> Jesus faced His approaching death with poise.

Jesus sent the disciples to look for an unnamed man who would lead them to the appointed house. What a privilege it was for this anonymous man to lend his house for this final Passover! Perhaps the vagueness of the instructions was designed to foil the conspirators. At any rate, we note Jesus' full knowledge of individuals, their whereabouts, and their willingness to cooperate. Note His message to the man: "The Teacher says, 'My time is at hand; I will keep the Passover at your house with My disciples.'" He faced His approaching death with poise. He arranged the meal with perfect grace.

As the Passover meal progressed, Jesus announced that one of the Twelve would betray Him. Shocked and bewildered, one by one they asked,

"Is it I, Lord?" When all but Judas had inquired, Jesus told them that it was the one who dipped with Him in the dish. The Lord then took a piece of bread, dipped it in the meat juice, and handed it to Judas (John 13:26)—a token of special affection and friendship. As He did this, He reminded them that what was going to happen to Him was inevitable. But that did not leave the traitor free from responsibility; it would be better for him if he had never been born. Judas was not foreordained to betray the Lord. It was prophesied that someone would do it, but Iscariot did not have to be the one. He deliberately chose to sell Jesus and was thus held personally responsible.

When Judas finally asked point-blank if he was the one, Jesus answered, yes.

The Lord's Supper (26:26-29)

In John 13:30 we learn that as soon as Judas received the sop he left. We therefore conclude that he was not present when the Lord's Supper was instituted.

The essential elements of the Lord's Supper—the bread and the wine—were already on the table as part of the Passover meal; Jesus took them and clothed them with new meaning. First He took bread, blessed and broke it. As He gave it to the disciples He said, "Take, eat; this is My body." We pass over the ancient dispute as to whether the bread actually became His body in some mystical, mysterious way. Since His body had not yet been given on the cross, it seems clear to us that He was speaking figuratively, that is, He was using the bread as a symbol of His body.

─────── ❧ ───────

Jesus' blood was sufficient to provide forgiveness for all.

─────── ❧ ───────

The same is true of the cup; the container is used to express the thing contained. The cup contained the fruit of the vine, which in turn was a symbol of the blood of the covenant. The new, unconditional covenant of grace would be confirmed by His precious blood shed for many for the forgiveness of sins. In one sense His blood was shed for all mankind; it was sufficient to provide forgiveness for all. But here it was shed for many in the sense that it was only effective in removing the sins of those who believe.

Jesus then reminded His disciples that He would not drink wine with them again until He returned to earth to reign. Then the wine would have a new significance; it would speak of the joy and blessedness of His glorious kingdom. The question is often raised whether we should use leavened or unleavened bread, fermented or unfermented wine. There can be little doubt that the Lord used unleavened bread and fermented wine (all the wine in those days was fermented). Those who argue that leavened bread spoils the type, since leaven is a picture of sin, should realize that the same is true of fermentation. It is a tragedy when we become so occupied with the elements that we fail to see the Lord Himself. The apostle Paul emphasized that it is the spiritual meaning of the bread rather than the bread itself that counts. "For Christ, our Passover, was sacrificed for us. Therefore let us keep the feast, not with the leaven of malice and wickedness, but with the unleavened bread of sincerity and truth" (1 Cor. 5:7-8). So it is not the leaven in the bread that matters, but the leaven (sin) in our lives.

The Self-Confident Disciples (26:30-35)

Following the Lord's Supper, the little band sang a hymn, generally believed to be taken from Psalms 113-118—"the Great Hallel." After this they left Jerusalem, crossed the Brook Kidron, and climbed part way up the western slope of Olivet to the garden of Gethsemane.

Throughout His earthly ministry the Lord Jesus had faithfully warned His disciples concerning the pathway ahead. Now He told them that they would all abandon Him that night. Fear would overwhelm them when they saw the fury of the storm beginning to break. To save their own skins, they would forsake their Master. The prophecy of Zechariah would be fulfilled: "Strike the Shepherd, and the sheep will be scattered" (13:7). But He did not leave them without hope. Although they would be ashamed of their association with Him, He would never forsake them. After rising from the dead, He would meet them in Galilee. Wonderful, never-failing Friend!

At this point Peter rashly interrupted to assure Jesus that although all the others might desert Him, he never would. Jesus corrected the "never" to "this night . . . three times." Before the cock crowed, the impulsive disciple would deny his Master three times. Still protesting his loyalty, Peter insisted that he would die with Christ rather than deny Him. The other disciples chimed in their agreement. And of course they were sincere; they meant what they said. It was just that they didn't know their own hearts.

Gethsemane (26:36-46)

No one can approach the account of Jesus in the garden of Gethsemane without a realization that he is walking on holy ground. Anyone who attempts to comment on it can be excused for feeling a tremendous sense of awe and reticence. As Guy King once wrote, "The supernal character of the event causes one to fear lest one should in any way spoil it by touching it."

When Jesus entered Gethsemane (the word means "olive vat" or "olive press"), the eleven disciples were with Him. Once inside, He told eight of them to sit and wait, then took Peter, James, and John deeper into the garden. Is there a suggestion here that different disciples have different capacities for empathizing with the Savior in His agony?

As He was there with Peter and the two sons of Zebedee, He began to be sorrowful and troubled. He told them frankly that His soul was very sorrowful, even to death. Calvary was looming before Him. He was going to bear our sins in His body on the cross. The anticipation of contact with sin caused His holy soul the keenest suffering. We cannot understand what it meant to Him. We are sinful; He is holy. It pains us to resist sin; it pained Him to anticipate being made sin for our sake (2 Cor. 5:21). Who could He turn to in His anguish but His Father? No one else could share His suffering or pray His prayer: "O My Father, if it be possible, let this cup pass from Me; nevertheless, not as I will, but as You will" (v. 39). In case we think that this prayer expressed reluctance or a desire to turn back, we should remind ourselves of His words in John 12:27-28: "Now My soul is troubled, and what shall I say? 'Father, save Me from this hour'? But for this purpose came I to this hour. Father, glorify Your name."

Therefore, in praying that the cup might pass from Him, He was not asking to be delivered from going to the cross. That was the purpose of His coming into the world. The prayer was rhetorical, that is, it was not intended to elicit an answer but to teach us a lesson. Jesus was saying, in effect, "My Father, if there is any other way by which ungodly sinners can be saved than by My going to the cross, reveal that way now! But in all of this, I want it to be known that I do not want anything that is contrary to Your will."

What was the answer? There was no answer; the heavens were silent. By this eloquent silence we know that there was no other way by which God could justify guilty sinners than by the sinless Christ dying as our Substitute.

Returning to His disciples, He found them asleep. Their spirits were willing; their flesh was weak. We dare not condemn them when we think of our own prayer lives; we sleep better than we pray, and our minds wander when they should be watching. How often the Lord has to say to us as He said to Peter, "Could you not watch with me one hour? Watch and pray, lest [in case] you enter into temptation" (vv. 40-41).

Jesus went away and prayed a second time, expressing submission to the Father's will. He would drink the cup of suffering and death to the dregs. He was necessarily alone in His prayer life. While He taught the disciples to pray, and while He prayed in their presence, He never prayed with them. The uniqueness of His Person and work precluded others from sharing in His prayer life. When He came back to the disciples the second time, they were sleeping again. And so it was the third time: He prayed, they slept. It was then He said to them, "Are you still sleeping and resting? Behold, the hour is at hand, and the Son of Man is being betrayed into the hands of sinners" (v. 45). The opportunity of watching with Him in His vigil was gone. It was too late. The footsteps of the traitor were already audible. Jesus said, "Rise, let us be going. . ."—not in retreat, but to face the foe.

Before we leave the garden, let us pause once more to hear His sobs, to ponder His sorrow, and to thank Him with all our hearts.

Jesus Is Betrayed and Arrested (26:47-56)

The betrayal of the sinless Savior by one of His own creatures presents one of the most amazing anomalies of history. Apart from the fact of human depravity we would be at a loss to explain the base, inexcusable treachery of Judas.

While Jesus was still talking to the eleven, Judas arrived with an armed gang. Surely the weapons were not Judas's idea; he had never seen Jesus resist or fight back. Perhaps they were a symbol of the determination of the Jewish leaders to capture Him without any possibility of escape. Judas had given an advance sign to the mob to help them identify Jesus from His disciples; the sign was a kiss. The universal symbol of love was to be debased to its lowest use. As he approached the Lord, Judas greeted Him, then kissed Him profusely. Matthew used two different words for "kiss" here. The first, in verse 48, is the normal word for kiss. But in verse 49, a stronger word is used, expressing repeated, affectionate kissing.

With poise and yet with convicting penetration Jesus asked, "Friend, why have you come?" The mob surged in and seized the Lord Jesus without delay. From John 18:10 we know that Peter drew his sword and cut off the ear of the high priest's servant. It is quite unlikely that Peter was aiming for the ear; he had probably planned a mortal blow. The fact that his aim was as poor as his judgment must be attributed to the overruling of divine providence.

---
*

The moral glory of the Lord Jesus shines out radiantly here.

---
*

The moral glory of the Lord Jesus shines out radiantly here. First He rebuked Peter for using the sword. In Christ's kingdom, victories are not won by carnal means. Let the enemies of the kingdom use the sword; they will eventually meet defeat. But let the soldier of Christ resort to prayer, the Word of God, and the power of a Spirit-filled life. We learn from Dr. Luke that Jesus then healed the ear of Malchus—for that was the name of the victim (Luke 22:51; John 18:10). Is this not a wonderful display of grace? He loved those who hated Him and showed kindness to those who were after His life.

If Jesus had desired to resist the mob, He would not have been limited to Peter's puny sword. In an instant of prayer, He could have commandeered more than twelve legions of angels (from 36,000 to 72,000). But that would only have frustrated the divine program. The Scriptures which predicted His betrayal, suffering, crucifixion, and resurrection had to be fulfilled.

---
*

Jesus loved those who hated Him and showed kindness to those who were after His life.

---
*

Then Jesus reminded the crowds how illogical it was for them to come after Him with weapons. They could easily have captured Him any day in the temple area. Humanly speaking, their behavior was completely irrational. And yet Jesus realized that man's wickedness was succeeding only in accomplishing the definite plan of God. "All this was done that the Scriptures of the prophets might be fulfilled."

At this point the disciples realized that there would be no deliverance for their Master, so they fled in panic. If their cowardice was inexcusable, ours is more so. They had not yet been indwelt by the Holy Spirit; we have.

Jesus Before Caiaphas (26:57-68)

Actually there were two main trials of the Lord Jesus. There was a religious trial before the Jewish leaders, and there was a civil trial before the Roman authorities. Each of these trials had three stages, as follows:

Jewish Trial —		_Roman Trial —_	
Stage 1	Jesus brought before Annas (John 18:12-14; 19-23)	Stage 1	Jesus brought before Pilate (Matt. 27:12-14)
Stage 2	Predawn trial before Caiaphas & the Sanhedrin (Luke 23:6-12)	Stage 2	Jesus sent to Herod by Pilate (Matt. 27:57-68)
Stage 3	Morning trial before Sanhedrin (Matt. 27:1)	Stage 3	Final appearance before Pilate (Matt. 27:15-26)

Matthew begins with the second stage of the Jewish trial. The mob had brought Jesus to the home of Caiaphas, where the Sanhedrin had already assembled. Criminal cases were not supposed to be tried at night or during the Passover season, but religious leaders conveniently overlooked these regulations on this occasion. Usually, accused men were given an opportunity to prepare their defense. But the leaders were desperate, so they hurried Jesus away from prison and from justice (Isa. 53:8), in every conceivable way denying Him a fair trial.

Caiaphas, the high priest, was the presiding judge. From the record it appears that the Sanhedrin served not only as the jury but also as the prosecution—an irregular combination to say the least. Jesus was the Defendant. And Peter was a spectator; from a safe distance he sat with the guards to see the end.

The chief priests and the whole council had a hard time finding false testimony against Jesus. They would have been more successful if they had looked for evidence of His innocence! Finally two false witnesses came in with a confusing account of something Jesus had once said. What He had actually said was "Destroy this temple [meaning His body], and in three days I will raise it up" (John 2:19-21). According to their perverted account, He had threatened to destroy the temple in Jerusalem and then rebuild it. Jesus had predicted His own death at the hands of the Jews. Now the Jews used a twisted version of that prediction as an excuse for killing Him.

During this period of accusation the Lord Jesus said nothing; "As a sheep before its shearers is silent, so He opened not His mouth" (Isa. 53:7). The high priest, irritated by His silence, pressed Him for a statement; but still He refrained from answering. Then the high priest said, "I put You under oath by the living God: tell us if you are the Christ, the Son of God!" According to the law of Moses, Jesus was required to answer him (Lev. 5:1), and so He replied, "It is as you said" (v. 64). This was an idiomatic expression meaning, "Yes, you have spoken correctly." In other words Jesus was saying, "I am the Messiah and I am the Son of God."

Our Lord's answer, "You have said so," seems rather weak in English. It is too often understood as meaning, "I never said that. It is you that have said it." But we know that Jesus was making the strongest assertion of His Messiahship and deity by His words that follow: "Nevertheless I say to you, hereafter you will see the Son of Man sitting at the right hand of the Power, and coming on the clouds of heaven." What did He mean by this? He was saying to the high priest, in so many words, "I am the Christ, the Son of God, as you have said. But to outward appearances I am just another man. At present My glory is veiled in a human body. You, Caiaphas, are seeing Me in the days of my humiliation. You cannot tell merely by looking at Me that I am the Christ, equal in all respects with God. But the day is coming when you Jews will see Me as the glorified One, sitting at God's right hand and coming on the clouds of heaven."

"The assertion is sometimes made that Jesus never called Himself 'The Son of God.' Here [in v. 64] He swears that He is no less" (Lenski). Caiaphas did not miss the point of the Lord's words. Jesus had referred to a messianic prophecy of Daniel: "I was watching in the night visions, and behold, one like the Son of Man, coming with the clouds of heaven! He came to the Ancient of Days, and they brought Him near before Him" (Daniel 7:13). Christ was saying, "I am the One of whom Daniel prophesied. When I come the second time, the Jewish people will see Me, no longer in humiliation, but in transcendent glory."

In verse 64, when Christ said "It is as you said," the "you" is singular; the second and third uses of the pronoun "you" in the verse, however, are plural. The first refers to Caiaphas; the second and third refer to the Jews as representative of those Israelites who will be living at the time of Christ's glorious appearing. The Jewish people living at the time of the second advent will see clearly that Jesus of Nazareth is indeed the Son of God.

The reaction of the high priest proves that he understood that Jesus was claiming equality with God (see John 5:18). He tore his priestly garments as a sign that the Witness had been guilty of blasphemy. His inflammatory words to the Sanhedrin assumed that Jesus was guilty. So when asked for their verdict, the Council answered, "He is deserving of death." The second stage of the trial ended with the jurists spitting upon the Accused, striking Him, slapping Him, then taunting Him to use His supernatural power as Messiah to identify His assailants. The entire procedure was not only illegal—it was scandalous.

> The entire trial
> was not only
> illegal—it was
> scandalous.

Peter Denies Knowing Christ (26:69-75)

Peter's darkest hour had now arrived. As he sat in the courtyard, a young woman came by and accused him of being an associate of Jesus. His denial was as strong as it was prompt, "I do not know what you are saying." He went out on the porch, perhaps to escape further notice. But there another young woman spotted him and publicly identified him as one who had been with Jesus of Nazareth. This time he swore that he did not know the man. "The man" was his Master.

Shortly afterwards several bystanders came to him, saying, "Surely you also are one of them, for your speech betrays you." A simple denial was no longer enough; this time he confirmed it with oaths and curses. With an extraordinary sense of timing, a rooster in the neighborhood crowed. The familiar sound pierced not only the quiet of the early hours but Peter's heart as well. The deflated disciple, remembering what the Lord had said, went out and wept bitterly.

The Morning Trial Before the Sanhedrin (27:1-2)

The third stage of the religious trial took place before the Sanhedrin in the morning. It has been said that no case was supposed to be completed on the same day it was begun unless the defendant was acquitted. A night was supposed to elapse before the verdict was pronounced to allow time for the judges to "sleep on it," and maybe temper their judgment with mercy. In this case the chief priests and elders seemed intent on stifling any feelings of mercy. However, since night trials were irregular, they convened a morning session to give legal validity to their verdict.

The Jewish leaders did not have the authority to inflict capital punishment since they were under Roman rule. That is why we now see the religious leaders hurrying Jesus to Pontius Pilate, the Roman governor. Though their hatred of everything Roman was intense, they were willing to "use" this power to satisfy a greater hatred. Opposition to Jesus unites the bitterest foes.

Judas's Remorse and Death (27:3-10)

Realizing that he had sinned in betraying innocent blood, Judas tried to persuade the chief priests and elders to take back the money. These arch conspirators who had cooperated so eagerly a few hours ago now refused to have any further part in the matter. This is one of the rewards of treachery.

In verse 3, it says that Judas "was remorseful" about betraying Jesus. There are two kinds of repentance. There is a godly repentance that leads to salvation, but there is also a shallow repentance that produces death (see 2 Cor. 7:10). The repentance of Judas was remorse rather than godly contrition. He was sorry for the effects which his crime brought on himself, but he was not willing to acknowledge Jesus Christ as Lord and Savior.

In desperation the traitor threw the thirty pieces of silver inside the temple where only the priests could go. Then he went out and committed suicide. This narrative and Acts 1:18 record that Judas hanged himself on a tree, the rope (or branch) broke, and his body was hurled over a precipice, causing it to be disemboweled.

The chief priests were too "spiritual" to put the money into the temple treasury because it was the price of blood. Yet they were the guilty ones who had paid that money to have the Messiah turned over to them. This didn't seem to bother them. As the Lord had said, they made the outside of the cup clean, but inside it was full of deceit, treachery, and murder. Their decision was to use the money to buy a potter's field where unclean Gentile strangers might be buried. Little did they realize how many Gentile hordes would invade their land and splatter their streets with blood. Many of these Gentile invaders have been buried there. In purchasing this burial field, the chief priests unwittingly fulfilled a prophecy found in Zechariah 11:12-13 where it was predicted that the betrayal money would be used to make a purchase from a potter. Matthew assigns this prophecy to Jeremiah whereas it obviously comes from the book of Zechariah. In his commentary on Zechariah, Unger suggests that:

> "The most satisfactory explanation is that Matthew actually cites the prophet Zechariah, but labels the citation from Jeremiah because that prophet stood at the head of the prophetic roll he used, according to the ancient order preserved in numerous Hebrew manuscripts and familiar from Talmudic tradition. A similar usage occurs in Luke 24:44 where the book of Psalms gives its name to the entire third section of the Hebrew canon."

Jesus' First Appearance Before Pilate (27:11-14)

The real grievances of the Jews against Jesus were of a religious nature, and they tried Him on that basis. But religious charges would carry no weight in the civil court of Rome. They knew that, and so when they brought Him before Pilate, they pressed three political charges against Him (Luke 23:2):

1. He was a revolutionary, and therefore represented a potential threat to the peace of the empire.

2. He urged people not to pay their taxes, and therefore was undermining the prosperity of the empire.

3. He claimed to be a king, and therefore was a threat to the power and position of the Emperor.

Here in Matthew's gospel we hear Pilate interrogating Him on the third charge. The governor asked Him if He was the King of the Jews, and Jesus naturally answered that He was. This brought forth abuse and slander from the chief priests and elders. What puzzled Pilate was that the Defendant remained silent; He would not dignify even one of their charges with an answer. Probably never before in his experience had the governor seen anyone remain silent under such attack.

Barabbas or Jesus? (27:15-23)

It was customary for the Roman authorities to pacify the Jews by releasing a Jewish prisoner at Passover time. One such eligible convict was Barabbas, a Jew who had been guilty of insurrection and murder (Mark 15:7). As a rebel against Roman rule, he had probably become very popular with his fellow countrymen. So when Pilate gave the people their choice between Jesus and Barabbas, they cried for the latter. The governor was not surprised; he knew that public opinion had been molded in part by the chief priests, who were envious of Jesus.

The proceedings were temporarily interrupted by the arrival of a messenger from Pilate's wife. She was urging her husband to adopt a hands-off policy with regard to Jesus; she had had a very disturbing dream about Him.

Behind the scenes the chief priests and elders were passing the word for the release of Barabbas and the death of Jesus. So when Pilate asked the people again which one they wanted to be freed, they cried for the murderer. Caught in the web of his own indecisiveness, Pilate asked, "What then shall I do with Jesus who is called Christ?" They were unanimous in their demand for His crucifixion. Pilate couldn't comprehend it. Why crucify Him? What crime had He committed? But it was too late to plead for calm logic; mob hysteria had taken over. The cry rang out, "Let Him be crucified!"

> **Mob hysteria had taken over.**

The Fateful Decision (27:24-26)

It was obvious to the governor that a riot was beginning, so he publicly washed his hands in sight of the howling, bloodthirsty mob, declaring his innocence of the blood of the accused. But water will never clear Pilate from guilt of being involved in history's gravest miscarriage of justice.

The crowd was too frenzied to worry about guilt. They were willing to bear the blame. "His blood be on us and on our children" (v. 25). God heard that self-imposed curse, and ratified it in heaven. Ever since then the people of Israel have staggered from ghetto to massacre, from concentration camp to gas chamber, suffering under the awful guilt of the blood of their rejected Messiah. They still face the fearsome "time of Jacob's trouble"—those seven years of tribulation described in Matthew 24 and Revelation 6-19. The curse will not be removed until they acknowledge the rejected Jesus as their Messiah-King.

Pilate released Barabbas to the crowd, and the spirit of Barabbas has dominated the world scene ever since. The murderer is still enthroned, and the righteous King is rejected. Then, as was customary, the condemned One was scourged. A large leather strap with bits of sharp metal embedded in it was brought down across His back, each lash opening up the flesh and releasing streams of blood. Now there was nothing for the spineless governor to do but to turn Jesus over to the soldiers for crucifixion.

"Bearing Shame and Scoffing Rude" (27:27-31)

Pilate's soldiers took Jesus into the governor's palace and gathered the whole battalion before Him—probably several hundred men. What followed is hard to imagine. The Creator and Sustainer of the universe suffered unspeakable indignities from His unworthy, sinful creatures. First they stripped Him and put a scarlet robe on Him—probably an imitation of a king's robe. But that scarlet robe has a message for us. Since scarlet is associated with sin (Isa. 1:18), perhaps that the robe pictures my sins being placed on Jesus so that God's robe of righteousness might be placed on me (2 Cor. 5:21).

Then they wove a crown of thorns and pressed it down firmly on His sacred head. But beyond their crude joke, we perceive that He wore a crown of thorns so that we might wear a crown of glory. They mocked Him as the King of sin; we worship Him as the Savior of sinners. They also gave Him a reed—a mock scepter. What they didn't know was that the hand that held that reed is the hand that rules the world. It now holds the scepter of universal dominion—that nail-scarred hand of Jesus.

—————— ❧ ——————

Jesus wore a crown of thorns so that we might wear a crown of glory.

—————— ❧ ——————

They knelt before Jesus and addressed Him as King of the Jews. Not content with that, they spat on the face of the only perfect Man who ever lived, then took the reed and rapped Him over the head with it. Jesus bore it all patiently; He didn't say a word. "Consider Him who endured such hostility from sinners against Himself" (Heb. 12:3). Finally they put His own clothes back on Him and led Him away to crucify Him.

The Crucifixion (27:32-44)

Our Lord carried His own cross part of the way (John 19:17). Then the soldiers ordered a man named Simon to carry it for Him. Simon was from Cyrene, in northern Africa. Some think he was a Jew; others think he was a black man. It really doesn't matter. The important thing is that he had the wonderful privilege of carrying Jesus' cross. The fact that his name is given and that Mark adds the note that he was "the father of Alexander and Rufus" (Mark 15:21; cf. Rom. 16:13) indicates that he was known to his readers and very likely became a believer in Christ.

Outside the city was the place of execution. Golgotha was its Hebrew name; Calvary, the Latin equivalent. Both words mean "skull" or "place of a skull."

Prior to His being impaled, the soldiers offered Jesus a drink of vinegar and gall. This was given to condemned criminals as a drug. When the Lord tasted it, He would not drink it. For Him it was necessary that He bear the full load of man's sins with no impairment of His senses and with no alleviation of the pain. Matthew's restraint in describing the actual crucifixion is noteworthy. He says simply, "Then they crucified Him . . ." (v. 35). He does not indulge in dramatics, or resort to sensational journalism, or dwell on the sordid details. He simply states the fact—that is all. Yet eternity itself will not exhaust the depths of those tremendous words.

As the Scriptures had predicted (Ps. 22:18), the soldiers divided His garments among themselves and cast lots for the seamless vesture. This was the extent of His earthly estate. "The one perfect life that has been lived in this world is the life of Him who owned nothing, and who left nothing but the clothes He wore" (Denney).

Then they sat down and watched Him, representatives of a world of little men. They did not know that history was being made. If they had known, they would not have sat down and watched—they would have knelt down and worshiped. Over the head of Christ was placed a sign—Matthew terms it an "accusation"—with the words, "THIS IS JESUS THE KING OF THE JEWS." The exact wording of the superscription varies slightly in the four gospel accounts. Mark says, "The King of the Jews" (15:26). Luke says, "This is the King of the Jews" (23:38). John's description is the most complete; "Jesus of Nazareth, the King of the Jews" (19:19). The chief priests protested that the title should not be a statement of fact, but the mere claim of the Accused. However, Pilate overruled them; and the truth was there for all to see—in Hebrew, Latin, and Greek (John 19:19-22).

The sinless Son of God was flanked by two robbers, for had not Isaiah predicted seven hundred years previously that He would be numbered with the transgressors (53:12)? At first, both thieves hurled insults at Him (v. 44).

But then one repented and was saved; within just a few hours he was with Christ in Paradise (Luke 23:42-43).

If the cross reveals God's love, it also reveals man's depravity. The crowd of passers-by jeered at the Shepherd as He was dying for the sheep: "You who destroy the temple and build it in three days, save yourself! If You are the Son of God, come down from the cross" (v. 40). Here we have the language of rationalistic unbelief. "Let us see and we will believe. Prove you are the Son of God by coming down from the cross." It is also the language of modernism and liberalism. "Come down from the cross—in other words, remove the offense of the cross and we will believe." William Booth said, "They claimed they would have believed if He had come down; we believe because He stayed up."

The chief priests, scribes, and elders joined the chorus. With unintentional insight they cried, "He saved others; Himself He cannot save" (v. 42). They meant it as a taunt song; we adapt it as a hymn of praise. They mocked His claim to be Savior. They mocked His claim to be the King of Israel and the Son of God (vv. 42-43).

Three Hours of Darkness (27:45-50)

And yet all the sufferings and indignities which Jesus bore at the hands of men were minor compared to what He now faced. From noon until 3 p.m., there was darkness not only over the land of Palestine but in His holy soul as well. For it was during that time that He bore the indescribable curse of our sins. In those three hours were compressed the hell which we deserved. He endured the wrath of God against all our transgressions. We simply cannot know what it meant for Him to satisfy all God's righteous claims against sin. All we know is that in those three hours He paid the price, He settled the debt, He finished the work that was necessary for man's redemption.

> *Jesus finished the work that was necessary for man's redemption.*

At about 3 p.m., Jesus cried with a loud voice, "My God, My God, why have You forsaken Me?" The answer is found in Psalm 22:3: "But You are holy, enthroned in the praises of Israel." It is because God is holy that He forsook His Son during those three hours of darkness. Because God is holy, He cannot overlook sin. On the contrary, He must punish it. Although the

Lord Jesus had no sin of His own, yet He took the guilt and responsibility of our sins upon Himself. When God, as Judge, looked down and saw our sins placed upon the sinless Substitute, He withdrew from the Son of His love.

When they heard Jesus cry, "Eli, Eli, . . ." some of the bystanders said He was calling for Elijah. Whether they actually confused the names or were simply mocking is not clear. One came to Him with a sponge soaked with vinegar or sour wine. By using a long reed, the sponge was lifted up to His lips. Judging from Psalm 69:21, this was not intended as an act of mercy, but as an added form of suffering.

The general attitude was to wait and see if Elijah would fulfill the role which Jewish tradition assigned to him—that of coming to the aid of the righteous. But it was not the time for Elijah to come (Mal. 4:5); it was time for Jesus to die. When He had cried with a loud voice, He yielded up His spirit. The loud cry demonstrates that He died in strength, not in weakness. The fact that He yielded up His spirit distinguished His death from all others. We die because we have to; He died because He chose to. Had He not said, "I lay down My life that I may take it again. No one takes it from Me, but I lay it down of Myself. I have power to lay it down, and I have power to take it again" (John 10:17-18)?

The Rent Veil (27:51-54)

At the time Jesus expired, a strange event took place in the temple. The heavy woven curtain that separated the two main rooms was torn by an Unseen Hand from the top to the bottom. Up till now that veil had kept everyone in Israel except the high priest from the Most Holy Place where God dwelt. (Only the high priest could enter the inner sanctuary, and on only one day of the year.)

In the book of Hebrews we learn that the veil represented the body of Jesus. The rending of the veil pictured the giving of His body in death. Through His death, we have "boldness to enter the Holiest by the blood of Jesus, by a new and living way which He consecrated for us through the veil, that is, His flesh" (Heb. 10:19-20). Now the humblest believer can enter the presence of God on any day, at any hour, in prayer and praise. But let us never forget that the privilege was purchased for us at tremendous cost—the sacrificial death of Jesus.

The death of God's Son also produced tremendous upheavals in the natural realm—as if there was an empathy between inanimate creation and its Creator. There was an earthquake which split great rocks and opened many tombs. But notice that it was not until after Jesus rose from the dead that the occupants of these tombs were raised and went to Jerusalem, where many saw them. Christ is the first-fruits of those who have died (1 Cor. 15:20); He is the firstborn from the dead (Col. 1:18). Therefore, it was a moral necessity that He be the first to rise in the power of an endless life (Heb. 7:16). The Bible does not say whether these risen saints died again or went to heaven with the Lord Jesus.

—————— ✍ ——————

Christ is the first-fruits of those who have died.

—————— ✍ ——————

The strange convulsions of nature convinced the Roman centurion and his men that Jesus was indeed a son of God (there is no definite article in the Greek before "son of God"). Was he making a full confession that Jesus was the Christ? Or that Jesus was more than man? Or was it simply a profound conviction that the One hanging on the middle cross was innocent? We cannot be sure. It does indicate a profound sense of awe, and a realization that the disturbances of nature were somehow connected with the death of Jesus and not with the death of those who were crucified with Him.

The Faithful Women (27:55-56)

Special mention is made in verses 55 and 56 of the women who had faithfully ministered to the Lord, and who had followed Him all the way from Galilee to Jerusalem. Mary Magdalene was there. Mary, the mother of James and Joseph was there. Salome, the wife of Zebedee was there. The fearless devotion of these women was remarkable. They remained with Christ when the other disciples ran for their lives.

Jesus Is Buried (27:57-61)

Joseph of Arimathea was a rich man and a member of the Jewish Sanhedrin. He had not agreed with the decision of the Council to deliver Jesus to Pilate (Luke 23:51). If he had been a secret disciple up to this point, he now threw caution to the wind. Boldly he went to Pilate and asked permission to bury his Lord. We must try to imagine what a surprise this would be to Pilate, and what a provocation to the Jews—that a member of the Sanhedrin would publicly take his stand for the Crucified. There is a real sense in which Joseph buried himself economically, socially, and religiously when he buried the body of Jesus. This act separated him forever from the world that killed the Lord Jesus.

——————— ❧ ———————

Joseph buried himself economically, religiously, and socially when he buried the body of Jesus.

——————— ❧ ———————

Pilate granted permission. How lovingly Joseph must have embalmed Jesus' body, winding strips of clean linen around it, and placing spices between the windings. Then he lay it in his own new tomb, carved out of solid rock. The mouth of the sepulcher was closed by a great round stone, shaped like a millstone and standing on its edge in a channel that was also carved out of stone. Centuries before, Isaiah predicted, "And they made His grave with the wicked—but with the rich in His death" (53:9). His enemies had no doubt planned to throw His body into the Valley of Hinnom where it would be consumed by dump-fires or eaten by foxes. But God overruled their plans and used Joseph to ensure that Jesus was buried with the rich.

After Joseph had left, Mary Magdalene and the mother of James and Joseph stayed to keep vigil by the tomb.

The Watch on the Tomb (27:62-66)

The first day of the Passover was called the day of Preparation. That was the day of the crucifixion. The next day the chief priests and Pharisees were uneasy. They remembered what Jesus had said about rising again; that must be prevented at all costs. So they went to Pilate and asked for a special guard to be placed at the tomb. This was allegedly to prevent the disciples from stealing the body and thus creating the impression that He had risen. If this should happen, they feared, the last error would be worse than the first; that is, the deception concerning His resurrection would be worse than His claim to be the Messiah and the Son of God.

Pilate answered, "You have a guard; go your way, make it as secure as you know how." Was there irony in Pilate's voice as he said this? They tried hard. They did their best. They sealed the stone and set a watch, but their best security measures were just not good enough. "The precautions His enemies took to make the sepulcher sure, sealing it and stationing a guard, only resulted in God's overruling the plans of the wicked and offering indisputable proof of the King's resurrection" (Unger).

The Empty Tomb and the Risen Lord (28:1-10)

The narrative now moves forward to early Sunday morning. Before dawn the two Marys had come to the tomb. As they arrived there was an earthquake. An angel of the Lord descended from heaven, rolled the stone away from the mouth of the sepulcher and sat on it. The Roman guard, terrified by this radiant being clothed in glistening white, fainted.

The angel spoke reassuringly to the women. There was nothing for them to fear. The One they were looking for had arisen out from among the dead, as He had promised! "Come, see the place where the Lord lay." The stone had been rolled away—not to let the Lord out, but to let the women see that He had already risen.

The angelic messenger then deputized the women to go to the disciples and announce the glorious news. The Lord was alive again and would meet them in Galilee! After delivering the message, they returned to the empty tomb. It was then that Jesus Himself appeared to them. He greeted them with a single word, "Rejoice!" They responded by falling at His feet and worshipping Him. He then personally commissioned them to notify the disciples that they would see Him in Galilee.

> Jesus greeted them with a single word, "Rejoice!"

The Bribery Plot (28:11-15)

As soon as they regained consciousness, some of the humiliated soldiers went to the chief priests to break the news. They had failed in their mission! The tomb was empty! It is not hard to imagine how the religious leaders must have reacted. The priests met with the elders to map strategy. In desperation, they bribed the soldiers to tell a fantastic tale, namely, that while the soldiers slept, the disciples came and stole the body of Jesus. But the alleged "explanation" raises more questions than it answers.

1. Why were the soldiers sleeping when they should have been on guard?

2. How could the disciples have rolled the stone away without waking the soldiers?

3. How could all the soldiers have fallen asleep at the same time?

4. If they were asleep, how did they know that the disciples stole the body?

5. If the story was true, why did the soldiers have to be bribed to tell it?

6. If the disciples had stolen the body, why had they taken time to remove the grave-clothes and fold the napkin? (Luke 24:12; John 20:6-7).

Actually, the soldiers were paid to tell a story that incriminated themselves, as sleeping on duty was punishable by death under Roman law. So the Jewish leaders had to promise to intervene for them if the story ever got back to the governor. The Sanhedrin was learning that while truth is self-verifying, a lie has to be supported by countless other lies. Yet this myth (and others) persists today among many Jews, and among Gentiles as well. Wilbur Smith summarizes two of them as follows:

"First of all it has been suggested that the women went to the wrong tomb.

"Think about this for a moment. Would you miss the tomb of your dearest loved one between Friday afternoon and Sunday morning? Furthermore, this was not a cemetery of Joseph of Arimathea. This was his private garden. No other tombs were there.

"Now, let's say there were other tombs, which there weren't, and suppose the women with their tear-filled eyes stumbled around and got to the wrong tomb. Well, let's grant that for the women. But hard-fisted Simon Peter and John, two fishermen who were not crying, also went to the tomb and found it empty. Do you think they went to the wrong tomb? But more than that, when they got to this tomb and found that it was empty, there was an angel who said, 'He is not here. He is risen. Come, see the place where the Lord lay.' Do you think the angel went to the wrong tomb too? Yet, don't forget, brainy men have advanced these theories. This is a nonsensical one!

> The resurrection of the Lord Jesus is a well-attested fact of history.

"Others have suggested that Jesus did not die, but swooned away, and that he was resuscitated somehow in this damp tomb and then came forth. They had a great big stone rolled against this tomb and this was sealed with seals of the Roman government. No man on the inside of that tomb could ever roll back the stone which came down an incline and fitted into a groove. He did not come out of that tomb as an anemic invalid."

The simple truth is that the resurrection of the Lord Jesus is a well-attested fact of history. He presented Himself alive to His disciples after His death by many infallible proofs. Think of these specific instances when He appeared to His own:

1. To Mary Magdalene (Mark 16:9-11)

2. To the women (Matt. 28:8-10)

3. To Peter (Luke 24:34)

4. To the two disciples on the road to Emmaus (Luke 24:13-32)

5. To the disciples, except Thomas (John 20:19-25)

6. To the disciples, including Thomas (John 20:26-31)

7. To the seven disciples by the Sea of Galilee (John 21)

8. To over 500 believers at one time (1 Cor. 15:6)

9. To James, His half-brother (1 Cor. 15:7)

10. To the disciples on the Mount of Olives (Acts 1:3-12)

"One of the great foundation stones, unshakable and unmovable, of our Christian faith, is the historic evidence for the resurrection of the Lord Jesus Christ. Here you and I can stand and do battle for the faith because we have a situation which cannot be contradicted. It can be denied, but it cannot be disproved." (W. Smith).

— ❧ —

The resurrection can be denied, but it cannot be disproved.

— ❧ —

The Great Commission (28:16-20)

In Galilee the risen Lord Jesus appeared to His disciples at a mountain which is not named. This is the same appearance as recorded in Mark 16:15-18 and 1 Corinthians 15:6. What a wonderful reunion it was! His sufferings were passed forever. Because He lived, they too would live. He stood before them in His glorified body. They worshiped their living, loving Lord—though doubts still lurked in the minds of some.

214 ❖ The Gospel of Matthew

Then the Lord explained to them that all authority had been given to Him in heaven and on earth. In one sense, of course, He always had all authority. But here He was speaking of authority as Head of the new creation. Since His death and resurrection, He had authority to give eternal life to all whom God had given to Him (John 17:2). He had always had power as the firstborn of all creation. But now that He had completed the work of redemption, He had authority as the first-born from the dead—"that in all things He may have the preeminence" (Col. 1:18).

—— ✥ ——

"Go therefore and make disciples of all the nations . . ."

—— ✥ ——

As Head of the new creation, He then issued the Great Commission. This contains the standing orders for all believers during the present phase of the kingdom (the time between the rejection of the King of Israel and His second advent).

Christ's commission contains three commands and an accompanying promise. The commands are:

1. *Go therefore and make disciples of all the nations . . .* This does not presuppose world conversion, but it surely does call for world evangelization. By the preaching of the gospel, the disciples were to see others become learners or followers of the Savior from every nation, tribe, people, and tongue.

2. *baptizing them in the name of the Father and of the Son and of the Holy Spirit . . .* Here the responsibility seems to rest on Christ's messengers to teach baptism and to press it as a command to be obeyed. In believer's baptism, men and women publicly identify themselves with the Triune Godhead. They acknowledge that God is their Father, that Jesus Christ is their Lord and Savior, and that the Holy Spirit is the One who indwells, empowers, and teaches them.

3. *teaching them to observe all things that I have commanded you . . .* The Great Commission goes beyond evangelism; it is not enough to make converts and let them fend for themselves. They must be taught to obey the commandments of Christ as found within the covers of the New Testament.

Then the Savior added a promise of His presence with His disciples until the consummation of the age. They would not go forth alone or unaided.

In all their service and travel, they would know the companionship of the Son of God (in the Person of His Spirit).

Thus Matthew's gospel closes with commission and comfort from our glorious Lord. Twenty centuries later His words have the same force, the same relevance, and the same application.

The task is still uncompleted. What are we doing to carry out Christ's last command?

Appendix

DIVORCE AND REMARRIAGE

Of one thing we can be absolutely sure; namely, that divorce was never God's intention for man. He hates divorce (Mal. 2:16). His ideal is that a man and woman should remain married until the union is broken by death (Rom. 7:1-3).

The Lord Jesus taught this clearly. When the Pharisees asked him if it was legal to divorce one's wife for any reason at all, He replied:

"Have you not read that he who made them from the beginning made them male and female, and said, 'For this reason a man shall leave his father and mother and be joined to his wife, and the two shall become one flesh'? So, then, they are no longer two but one flesh. Therefore what God has joined together, let not man separate" (Matt. 19:4-6; see also Mark 10:2-9).

To further emphasize that divorce is contrary to God's will, as a general rule, the Lord said: "Whoever divorces his wife and marries another commits adultery; and whoever marries her who is divorced from her husband commits adultery" (Luke 16:18).

This is repeated in Mark 10:11-12; but here it is broadened to include not only a man putting away his wife, but also a woman putting away her husband.

If these verses in Luke 16 and Mark 10 were the only verses in the New Testament on the subject, then there would be no further need of discussion. It would be clear that the Lord does not permit divorce under any circumstances. But we must not base our conclusions on one or two verses; we must study *all* the passages that are relevant.

In Matthew 5:31 and 32 we have already seen that the Savior Himself made an exception to the general rule against divorce. He said that a man could not divorce his wife *except on the ground of sexual immorality.* The same exception is repeated in Matthew 19:9.

Our conclusion thus far, then, is that although divorce is not the Lord's ideal, He does allow it in the case where one's partner has been unfaithful. Even here divorce is not commanded; it is permitted. The offended person may show grace and forgiveness, and the original marriage relationship may be resumed (Matt. 18:21-22).

Is unfaithfulness the only scriptural ground on which a divorce may be obtained? Some Bible students suggest that another ground is given in 1 Corinthians 7:12-16; namely, the desertion of a believer by an unbeliever. The Scripture says that in such a case the believer is "not under bondage." This may mean separation or divorce. The writer's opinion is that the passage assumes that the unbeliever departs, not in order to live a life of immorality, but in order to live with someone else. This, of course, would give the believer a valid ground for divorce.

The question also arises, "What about people who were divorced before they were saved?" There should be no question that unlawful divorces and remarriages contracted before conversion are sins which have been fully and freely forgiven. Some of the Corinthian believers had formerly been adulterers, homosexuals, thieves, and drunkards; but they had been washed, sanctified, and justified in the name of the Lord Jesus Christ and in the Spirit of our God (1 Cor. 6:11). Their pre-conversion record did not bar them from full participation in the privileges of the local church.

A more difficult question concerns Christians who are divorced for reasons not allowed in the New Testament and then remarried. Can they ever be received back into the fellowship of the local church? The answer depends on whether adultery is the initial act of physical union or a continued state. If these people are living in a state of adultery, then they would not only have to confess their sin but also forsake their present partner. But God's solution for a problem is never one that creates worse problems. If, in order to untangle a marital snarl, men or women are driven into sin, or women and children are left homeless and penniless, the cure is worse than the disease.

In the writer's opinion, Christians who have been divorced without scriptural grounds and then remarried can truly repent of their sin—though it rarely happens—and be restored to the Lord and to the fellowship of the church.

In the matter of divorce, it seems that almost every case is different. The elders of the local church must investigate and deliberate in the fear of God and in obedience to His Word. When they take disciplinary action in a godly manner, the other Christians should submit to the decision and not seek to defend the disciplined parties.

It is often contended that although divorce is permitted in the New Testament, remarriage is never contemplated. Such a position is pointless:

1. In Matthew 19:9 remarriage is not condemned in the one case where the partner has been unfaithful.

2. One of the main purposes of a scriptural divorce is to permit remarriage; otherwise, separation would serve the purpose just as well.

The innocent party in a scriptural divorce is free to remarry. In many cases of divorce neither party is entirely guiltless, but that is beside the question. It *is* possible for one partner to be completely innocent and for the other to be wholly to blame.

THE SABBATH

The Sabbath day is the seventh day of the week (Saturday); it always was and always will be.

God rested on the seventh day, after the six days of creation (Gen. 2:2). He did not command man to keep the Sabbath day at that time, although He may have intended the principle—one day of rest in every seven—to be followed. The nation of Israel was commanded to keep the Sabbath when the Ten Commandments were given (Exod. 20:8-11). The law was given to Israel, the nation that God had brought out of Egypt (Exod. 20:2).

The law of the Sabbath was different from the other nine commandments; it was a ceremonial law while the others were moral. The only reason it was wrong to work on the Sabbath was because God said so. The other commandments had to do with sins that were intrinsically wrong.

The prohibition against work on the Sabbath day was never intended to apply to:

1. the service of God (Matt. 12:5).

2. deeds of necessity (Matt. 12:3-4).

3. deeds of mercy (Matt. 12:11-12).

Nine of the Ten Commandments are repeated in the New Testament, not as law but as instructions for Christians living under grace. The only commandment that is not repeated is that of the Sabbath. Christians are never told to keep the Sabbath. Rather, Paul teaches that the Christian cannot be condemned for failing to keep it (Col. 2:16).

The distinctive day of Christianity is the first day of the week (Sunday). The Lord Jesus rose from the dead on that day (John 20:1), a proof that the work of redemption had been completed and divinely approved.

The Holy Spirit was given on the first day of the week (Acts 2:1; cf. Lev. 23:15-16).

The early disciples met on that day to break bread, showing forth the Lord's death (Acts 20:7).

It is the day appointed by God on which Christians should set aside funds for the work of the Lord (1 Cor. 16:1-2).

The Sabbath or seventh day came at the end of a week of labor; the Lord's Day, or Sunday, begins a week with the restful knowledge that the work of redemption has been completed. The Sabbath commemorated the first creation; the Lord's Day is linked with the new creation. The Sabbath day was a day of responsibility; the Lord's Day is a day of privilege.

Christians do not "keep" the Lord's Day as a means of earning salvation or achieving holiness, nor from fear of punishment. They set it apart because of loving devotion to the One who gave Himself for them. Because we are released from the routine, secular affairs of life on this day, we can set it apart in a special way for the worship and service of Christ.

It is not right to say that the Sabbath was changed to the Lord's Day. The Sabbath is Saturday and the Lord's Day is Sunday. But the Sabbath was a shadow; the substance is Christ (Col. 2:16-17). The resurrection of Christ marked a new beginning, and the Lord's Day signifies that new beginning.

As a faithful Jew living under the law, Jesus kept the Sabbath (in spite of the accusations of the Pharisees to the contrary). As the Lord of the Sabbath, He freed it from the false rules and regulations with which it had become encrusted.

Rom 14:5

THE LAW AND
OUR RELATION TO IT

The law is the system of legislation given by God through Moses in Exodus 20:1-31:18, and also in Leviticus and Deuteronomy. The core or essence of the law is found in the Ten Commandments. When Jesus spoke of the law and the prophets, He took in the entire Old Testament.

The law was never given as a means of salvation (Acts 13:39; Rom. 3:20a; Gal. 2:16, 21; 3:11). It was designed to show man his exceeding sinfulness and then send him to God for salvation by grace through faith (Rom. 3:20b; 5:20; 7:7; 1 Cor. 15:56; Gal. 3:19).

It was given to the nation of Israel (Ex. 20:2; 31:13) although there are moral principles in it which are valid for all people in every age (Rom. 2:14-15). God tested Israel under the law as a sample of the human race, and Israel's guilt proved the world's guilt (Rom. 3:19).

That the legal system was never intended to be permanent is clearly stated in Gal. 3:19: "It was added because of transgressions, *till the Seed should come* to whom the promise was made" (italics added). In other words, it was preparatory to the coming of Christ.

The law had penalty attached to it—death (Gal. 3:10). To break one commandment was to be guilty of all (James 2:10). Now since man had broken the law, he was under the curse of death. The righteousness and holiness of God demanded that the penalty must be paid. Of course, if man paid the penalty he would perish eternally.

And so the Lord Jesus came into the world, not only to uphold the law in His life, but to pay its dread penalty by His death. He died as a Substitute for guilty law-breakers, bearing the curse for them. He did not wave the